UP FROM

THE

PEDESTAL

UP FROM THE PEDESTAL

SELECTED WRITINGS IN THE HISTORY OF AMERICAN FEMINISM

Edited with an Introduction by

Aileen S. Kraditor

Quadrangle/The New York Times Book Co.

Fifth Printing

Copyright © 1968 by Aileen S. Kraditor.

All rights reserved, including the right to reproduce this book or portions thereof in any form. For information, address: Quadrangle/The New York Times Book Co., 10 East 53 Street, New York, N.Y. 10022

Manufactured in the United States of America.
Published simultaneously in Canada by Fitzhenry & Whiteside, Ltd., Toronto.

Library of Congress Catalog Card Number: 68-26443
ISBN: 0-8129-6127-7

Designed by Vincent Torre

Grateful acknowledgment is made to the following for permission to reprint copyright material: American Council on Education and the *Educational Record* for "The Radcliffe Institute for Independent Study" by Mary I. Bunting; *American Mercury* (Torrance, California) for "Women Are Household Slaves" by Edith M. Stern; Denning Miller for excerpts from *Are Women People?* by Alice Duer Miller; and The New York Public Library, Manuscript Division, the Astor, Lenox, and Tilden Foundations, for Elizabeth Smith Miller's writing on the bloomer costume.

PREFACE

THE EDITOR of an anthology of documents in an area of history at once so rich and so little explored as American feminism has a difficult choice, if the volume is to be of manageable size. Rather than try to include an item from each variety and offshoot and aspect of feminism, I have chosen to concentrate on documents representing the principal emphases of the feminist movement in each period, opting for unity over comprehensiveness. This accounts for the absence of excerpts from Margaret Sanger's writings on birth control and of documents from organizations of trade-union women or others secondarily concerned with feminism. Moreover, with some exceptions I omitted other relevant items that have recently been published or republished, in favor of documents not as easily available. That accounts for the omission of relevant excerpts from such important works as Charlotte Perkins Gilman's *Women and Economics*, Walter Lippmann's *Drift and Mastery*, Betty Friedan's *Feminine Mystique*, Max Lerner's *America as a Civilization*, and various essays by Jane Addams. This anthology represents, in short, one editor's rather personal choices among many.

I wish to thank Dr. Edward T. James, editor of *Notable American Women, 1607–1950*, for generously providing me with biographical information on certain individuals not listed in the standard reference works from which I obtained most of the data preceding the various documents; Doris W. Dashew, for reading the introductory essay, which is much the better for her criticisms and suggestions; Carl N. Degler, for his many helpful comments regarding my selection of documents; and Mr. Dennis Costa, who helped me sharpen some of the ideas that are to be found in the last section of the introductory essay.

EDITOR'S NOTE

A number of the documents in this volume are taken from the first five volumes of the *History of Woman Suffrage*, a six-volume collection of speeches, writings, and other documents that is of first-rate importance in the literature of American feminism. For the sake of brevity these volumes will be referred to as *HWS* I, *HWS* II, and so on. The full bibliographic information on each is as follows:

Vol. I: Edited by Elizabeth Cady Stanton, Susan B. Anthony, and Matilda Joslyn Gage. New York, 1881.

Vols. II and III: Edited by Elizabeth Cady Stanton, Susan B. Anthony, and Matilda Joslyn Gage. Rochester, N.Y., 1887.

Vol. IV: Edited by Susan B. Anthony and Ida Husted Harper. Rochester, N.Y., 1902.

CONTENTS

PREFACE   V

INTRODUCTION   3

I
THE QUESTION OF "SPHERES"

1. EARLY MISGIVINGS   29
   Anne Bradstreet, The Prologue (1642)
   John Winthrop, Journal (1645)
   Constantia, On the Equality of the Sexes (1790)
   Hannah Mather Crocker, Observations on the Real
     Rights of Women (1818)

2. THE OPPOSITION   45
   Thomas R. Dew, Dissertation on the Characteristic
     Differences Between the Sexes (1835)
   Jonathan F. Stearns, Discourse on Female Influence
     (1837)
   Pastoral Letter of the Massachusetts Congregationalist
     Clergy (1837)

3. THE BEGINNING OF AGITATION   53
   Sarah Moore Grimké, Two Essays (1837 and 1838)
   Angelina Emily Grimké, Letters to Catherine E. Beecher
     (1838)
   Margaret Fuller, The Great Lawsuit (1843)
   Lucy Stone, Speech (1855)

II
THE ARGUMENT BECOMES SPECIFIC

1. INTELLECT AND EDUCATION   79
   Emma Hart Willard, Address to the Public (1819)
   Catherine E. Beecher, Suggestions Respecting
     Improvements in Education (1829)
   Sarah Moore Grimké, Intellect of Woman (1838)
   Matilda Joslyn Gage, Woman as Inventor (1870)
   M. Carey Thomas, Present Tendencies in Women's
     College and University Education (1908)
   Anna Garlin Spencer, Woman's Share in Social Culture
     (1912)

2. RELIGION AND WOMAN'S STATUS   108
   Debate at Woman's Rights Convention (1854)—
     Rev. Henry Grew, Hannah Tracy Cutler, Lucretia
     Mott, William Lloyd Garrison, and Emma R. Coe
   Elizabeth Cady Stanton, The Woman's Bible (1895)
   Elizabeth Cady Stanton, Letter to the Editor, *The Critic*
     (1896)
   Catharine Waugh McCulloch, The Bible on Women
     Voting

3. THE RELATION OF WOMEN'S FASHIONS TO WOMAN'S STATUS   122
   Sarah Moore Grimké, Dress of Women (1838)
   Elizabeth Smith Miller on the Bloomer Costume
   Correspondence Between Gerrit Smith and Elizabeth Cady
     Stanton (1855)
   Tennie C. Claflin, Constitutional Equality a Right of
     Woman (1871)
   Thorstein Veblen, Theory of the Leisure Class (1899)

4. SCIENCE ENLISTED IN THE CAUSE OF FEMINISM   137
   Matilda Joslyn Gage, Address at a Convention (1884)
   Elizabeth Cady Stanton, The Matriarchate (1891)

5. MARRIAGE, DIVORCE, AND THE HOME   148
   Marriage Documents: Robert Dale Owen and Mary
     Robinson (1832); Henry B. Blackwell and Lucy Stone
     (1855)
   Antoinette Brown Blackwell, Relation of Woman's Work
     in the Household to the Work Outside (1873)
   Susan B. Anthony, Social Purity (1875)
   Harriot Stanton Blatch, Voluntary Motherhood (1891)
   Charlotte Perkins Gilman, Economic Basis of the Woman
     Question (1898)

III
WOMAN AND GOVERNMENT

1. DECLARATION OF SENTIMENTS AND RESOLUTIONS, SENECA
   FALLS CONVENTION (1848)   183

2. THE ANTISUFFRAGISTS: WOMAN'S SPHERE IS HOME, NOT
   GOVERNMENT   189
   Editorial, New York *Herald* (1852)
   New York State Legislative Report (1856)
   Orestes A. Brownson, The Woman Question (1869 and
      1873)
   Remarks of Senator George G. Vest in Congress (1887)
   Remarks of Abraham L. Kellogg in New York State
      Constitutional Convention (1894)
   Grover Cleveland, Would Woman Suffrage Be Unwise?
      (1905)

3. GENERAL DEFENSES OF WOMAN SUFFRAGE   204
   Alice Stone Blackwell, Losing Her Privilege (1890)
   Carrie Chapman Catt, President's Annual Address (1902)
   Finley Peter Dunne, Mr. Dooley on Woman's Suffrage
      (1909)
   Alice Duer Miller, Are Women People? (1915)

4. THE "JUSTICE" ARGUMENT   220
   Resolutions Passed at a Woman's Rights Convention
      (1851)
   Ernestine Rose on Legal Discrimination (1851)
   Harriot K. Hunt, Tax Protest (1852)
   Plaintiffs' Brief and Argument, *Minor vs. Happersett*
      (1872)
   Susan B. Anthony's Constitutional Argument (1873)

5. THE "EXPEDIENCY" ARGUMENT. I: RACISM AND
      XENOPHOBIA ENLISTED IN THE CAUSE OF WOMAN
      SUFFRAGE   253
   Henry B. Blackwell, What the South Can Do (1867)
   Olympia Brown on the Foreign Menace (1889)
   Resolutions Adopted at a Convention (1893)
   Carrie Chapman Catt, Danger to Our Government (1894)
   Belle Kearney, The South and Woman Suffrage (1903)

6. THE "EXPEDIENCY" ARGUMENT. II: OTHER FORMS   266
   Anna Garlin Spencer, Duty to the Women of Our New
      Possessions (1899)—and discussion by Helen Philleo
      Jenkins, Octavia W. Bates, Henry B. Blackwell, and
      Susan B. Anthony

Florence Kelley, Three Addresses (1898, 1903, and 1905)
Jessie Ashley, Relation of Suffragism to Working-Class
    Women (1911)
Jane Addams on Woman Suffrage (1915 and 1906)
Six Predictions of the Results of Women's Enfranchisement
    (1852, 1891, 1898, 1903, and 1914)

IV
UNFINISHED BUSINESS

1. PUBLIC POLICY   293
    The Equal-Rights Amendment: Senate Hearing (1931)—
    Burnita Shelton Matthews, Anita Pollitzer, Rose
    Schneiderman, Frieda Miller, and Mrs. William J. Carson
American Women: Report of the President's Commission
    (1965)

2. GLANCES TOWARD THE FUTURE   315
    Frances E. Willard, How to Win: A Book for Girls
    (1888)
    Thorstein Veblen, Theory of the Leisure Class (1899)
    Charlotte Perkins Gilman, Are Women Human Beings?
    (1912)
    Sylvia Kopald, Where Are the Female Geniuses? (1924)
    Emily Newell Blair, Discouraged Feminists (1931)
    Edith M. Stern, Women Are Household Slaves (1949)
    Mary I. Bunting, The Radcliffe Institute for Independent
    Study (1961)
    National Organization for Women, Statement of Purpose
    (1966)

SELECTED BIBLIOGRAPHY   371

UP FROM

THE

PEDESTAL

INTRODUCTION

Women in History and Historiography

UNTIL TOWARD the end of the nineteenth century, most history was written in terms of kings' reigns and presidents' administrations, of wars and revolutions; in these, women took little or no part. And, since women wrote as little history as they made, it is not surprising that historiography faithfully reflected their exclusion from those events historians considered important enough to record. That their exclusion was itself a datum of history never entered the historians' minds, for was not the domestic sphere—ahistorical by definition—"naturally" ordained to be woman's? "Natural" phenomena—geographical, meteorological, astronomical, ecological, and so on—are noticed by the historian only when they intrude in a positive—i.e., unnatural—way in the human drama; ordinarily they are simply "there," negative, the stage on which the drama takes place. Hence the older histories sometimes opened with a chapter setting the geographical stage and often included narrative-breaking chapters on social life, family patterns, dress styles, and other such entertaining topics that changed either too slowly or too fast to be part of the main stream of "real" history. It is hardly coincidental that such chapters, which of course mentioned women, performed a function in these tomes parallel to that of comic interludes in Shakespeare's tragedies. Until a few years ago this situation had continued with little noticeable change.

In 1946 Mary Beard noted that twenty-two years earlier Arthur M. Schlesinger had called for a rewriting of American history to give proper credit to the role women had played in it. She complained that his suggestion had gone unheeded, and observed that Ralph Gabriel, in his *Course of American Democratic Thought*, published in 1940, had completely ignored even the woman's-rights movement.[1] The seventy-year struggle for woman suffrage had evidently contributed nothing to the course of American democratic thought. In 1968 Schlesinger's complaint of 1922 and Mrs. Beard's of 1946 are still timely: the index of a widely used college text in United States history lists only forty-nine women, and their segregation into special sections is made more invidious by the fact that these individuals or women in general are mentioned on only 4.1 per cent of the work's 1,600 pages.[2] But there are signs that no historian in 1990 will have occasion to quote three such complaints, each a generation later than the one before, and add a fourth. Two major facts provide grounds for optimism: first, the entrance of women into those areas of American life that traditionally furnished the data of history, and, second, the rise to popularity of social history and the growing tendency of even the political, constitutional, diplomatic, and economic historians to incorporate data of social history in their studies. The history of women's role and women's status may follow the pattern of Negro history: before World War II it was largely ignored except by Negro scholars; since then it has become an important area of specialization and will continue to be until the enormous gaps in our knowledge begin to narrow. A third stage, heralded by a recent article,[3] will begin when Negro history is incorporated into all

[1] Mary R. Beard, *Woman as Force in History: A Study in Traditions and Realities* (New York, 1946), pp. 58–59; Arthur M. Schlesinger, *New Viewpoints in American History* (New York, 1922); Ralph H. Gabriel, *The Course of American Democratic Thought: An Intellectual History since 1815* (New York, 1940).

[2] Harry J. Carman, Harold C. Syrett, and Bernard W. Wishy, *A History of the American People*, 2 vols., paperback (3rd ed., New York, 1967). The title is ironic.

[3] Robert Starobin, "The Negro: A Central Theme in American History," *Journal of Contemporary History*, III (April 1968), 37–53.

other aspects of American history, as scholars both recognize the integral role of Negroes in American life from the beginning and possess sufficient specialized studies to perform the synthesis. The history of women is at the beginning of the second stage of this process.

Until a few years ago, scholarly works on the role and status of women in American history fell into two categories. The first consisted of only two books—Eleanor Flexner's *Century of Struggle* (Cambridge, Mass., 1959) and Andrew Sinclair's *The Better Half* (New York, 1965)—both broad surveys and both about as good as the paucity of the specialized knowledge at their disposal allowed. By far the majority of works in this field fell into the second category: biographies of important women and minute accounts of activities of suffragists in various states.

The biographical approach is not by accident the most popular; nor is it accidental that almost all these works are by women. Most men, even today, when women are legally almost their equal, think of the woman's-rights movement as the demand by neurotic females to be like men, and they assume that a significant proportion of its members were hawk-faced spinsters who wore blue stockings and marched in parades for lack of more feminine employments to occupy them. (It may be more than a coincidence that most male historians, when they do mention the suffragists, call them "suffragettes," the epithet that during the life of the movement was used only by their enemies.) With a few exceptions, only women have seen fit to write about the lives of women leaders, and these biographies, while they give the lie to the stereotype, are rarely accorded by male historians a respectable place in historical literature and are hardly ever mentioned in bibliographies appended to books that deal with the times in which these women affected history. Hence women scholars who can be expected to harbor a better opinion of their sex have had the field to themselves. But even they have not been fully immune to the dominant ideological assumptions. This accounts in part for their biographical approach, which manifests a concentration of attention on and interest in the personal motivations of leading participants in the movement and a corresponding slighting of the objective historical significance of the movement in the main stream of American history. Moreover, the biographical approach results partly from their desire to demonstrate the normality of their subjects; this laudable aim unfortunately has resulted in some portrayals that are larger than lifesize and hence smaller than reality.

The articles on suffragist activity hardly deserve the name of history. They are, rather, the raw material for history, meticulously gathered from private papers, newspapers, state legislative documents, and the like. They list names and dates in bewildering profusion. They tell which lady gave a tea party for suffragists on which afternoon in which town, how much money was raised, and which local paper recorded the event. They tell little about why these women wanted the vote or why the movement arose where and when it did.

This genre recalls a penetrating observation by the anthropologist Claude Lévi-Strauss:

Biographical and anecdotal history . . . is low-powered history, which is not intelligible in itself and only becomes so when it is transferred *en bloc* to a form of history of a higher power than itself; and the latter stands in the same relation to a class above it. It would, however, be a mistake to think that we progressively reconstitute a total history by dint of these dove-tailings. For any gain on one side is offset by a loss on the other. Biographical and anecdotal history is the least explanatory; but it is the richest in point of information, for it considers individuals in their particularity and details for each of them the shades of character, the twists and turns of their motives, the phases of their deliberations. . . . [T]he historian loses in information what he gains in comprehension or vice versa. . . . The historian's relative choice, with respect to each domain of history he gives up, is always confined to the choice between history which teaches us more and explains less, and history which explains more and teaches less.[4]

The informative studies of women continue to be needed, but they do not themselves suggest how they will be integrated into larger explanatory patterns. This depends on a new attitude, on

[4] *The Savage Mind* (Chicago, 1966), pp. 261–62.

the part of historians, toward women and toward the relation of social history to other aspects of history. Already young male scholars are devoting serious attention to this field, and a few scholars, such as William R. Taylor,[5] are considering women's roles and status as part of the necessary data for intellectual history. The requisite shift in attitude can be described by means of a phrase that American feminists repeatedly used in their propaganda: a change from regarding women as females who happen to be human, to regarding them as humans who happen to be female. For, as long as the first attitude prevailed, it was logical to omit women from accounts of the lives and activities of human beings—that is, from history—and to mention them for the same reason that other nonhistorical phenomena were mentioned, as part of the "natural" setting against which the human drama was enacted. In view of the primitive state of historiography in this field, the larger explanatory patterns suggested in the following pages can be no more than tentative.

Feminism and Antifeminism: The Real Issues

Feminism is customarily thought of as the theory that women should have political, economic, and social rights equal to those of men. As a definition of a theory, this is satisfactory, but a theory has a way of changing when it is translated into practice over a long period of time. At times some of the feminists whose writings are sampled in this book demanded social rights superior to those of men; at other times, political, economic, and social rights inferior to those of men but superior to those that women had; and at still other times, rights different from but "equal" to those of men. In one period the most commonly demanded right was higher education; in another, access to professions; in a third, the vote. Clearly, the history of American feminism implies far more than the practical application of the theory stated above—

[5]*Cavalier and Yankee: The Old South and the National Character* (London, 1963).

that women should have rights equal to men's. What the feminists have wanted has added up to something more fundamental than any specific set of rights or the sum total of all the rights that men have had.

This fundamental something can perhaps be designated by the term "autonomy." Whether a feminist's demand has been for all the rights men have had, or for some but not all of the rights men have had, or for certain rights that men have not had, the grievance behind the demand has always seemed to be that women have been regarded not as people but as female relatives of people. And the feminists' desire has, consequently, been for women to be recognized, in the economic, political, and/or social realms, as individuals in their own right. Such a recognition could be consistent with a distinction between men's and women's "spheres," even with a continued subordination of the feminine "sphere," as well as with a merging of men's and women's "spheres." The essential change demanded has always been that women's "sphere" must be defined by women. The questions have always been: What is women's proper sphere? and, even more, Who should decide what that sphere is?

Two documents illustrate both the fundamental nature of the insistence on self-determination and its persistence in time. The first was written in 1838 and the second in 1891, but the theme of autonomy may also be discerned in documents written long before the first and long after the second. The first is a letter from a feminist to her fiancé describing a lyceum debate on the proposition: "Would the condition of woman and of society be improved by placing the two sexes on an equality in respect to civil rights and duties?" The feminist's comment, significantly, was not on what was said at the debate but on the fact that all the participants were men:

There our lords & masters undertook to discuss *our* rights & settle what was most for *our* benefit, but we were not permitted to plead our own cause, nor were *we* called upon to give our votes[.] As well might the Slaveholders of the So[uth] hold a meeting to discuss whether the condition of Society & the slaves would be improved by emancipation, whilst they sat gagged before them & the question decided by acclamation by the masters without the voice of the slaves.[6]

Fifty-three years later a woman minister voiced essentially the same complaint:

It has always seemed to me remarkable how clear the definitions of men are in regard to women, their duties, their privileges, their responsibilities, their relations to each other, to men, to government, and . . . to God. . . .

The great divine who suggested . . . [the subject of this speech] to me was lecturing before an Institute of Sacred Theology in the city of New York. Before him was a class of students, male and female, and he was defining to the male students what they, the males, might permit the females to do. He says, "There are some things which the women may be permitted to do." Now we like that, don't we? Some things that we may be permitted to do! "They may be permitted to dispense certain charities; they may be permitted to speak in prayer and class-meetings; they may be permitted to do certain lines of church work. There are other things which women may not be permitted to do. Among the things which they may not be permitted to do, is to hold high official relation to the church, to become its ministers, and to dispense its sacraments. These things women may not be permitted to do." [7]

The suggestion that autonomy, rather than the redefinition of women's proper sphere, should be considered the objective toward which the feminists, consciously or unconsciously, worked is not meant to deny the importance of the question of "spheres." Rather, it is meant to show that that question has broader implications than commonly thought. The feminists seemed to sense that the distance between the spheres of men and women encouraged people to lose sight of the differences among individual women. Strictly speaking, men have never had a "proper sphere," since their sphere has been the world and all its activities. They have always been, accordingly, human beings who happened to be male. Women, on the contrary, have occupied sharply circum-

[6] Angelina E. Grimké to [Theodore D. Weld], [January 7, 1838], Weld Papers, Clements Library, University of Michigan, Ann Arbor.

[7] Anna Howard Shaw, "God's Women," speech at Woman's National Council meeting, reported in *Woman's Journal*, March 7, 1891.

scribed spheres—the home, the church, the philanthropic society or sewing circle—regardless of differences among individuals in talents and tastes, and have, accordingly, been thought of as females who happened to be human. It has been taken for granted that men's activities should vary according to their potentialities, but it has been assumed that women's activities should be defined by their sex. Thus, it was proper for men to live for themselves— to achieve self-fulfillment by developing their individual talents— whereas women should live for others—to achieve self-fulfillment by caring for their husbands and children. Church and charity work was a logical extension of that role outside the home and hence was socially acceptable.

Women have been the only subordinated group that has belonged to the same families as its rulers. The ambiguous status of well-to-do women, as both ruler and ruled, generated contradictions and ambiguities in both feminists' and antifeminists' attitudes toward women. On the one hand, the middle-class women who in the nineteenth century comprised the feminist movement shared the economic and social status of their men, but, on the other, they were excluded from the economic functions that maintained that status. While they shared the middle-class ideology, on all issues besides feminism, that rationalized their status, their desire for individual autonomy seemed to conflict with that ideology's understanding of the nature of the family and its relation to society. The feminist movement began in the middle of the nineteenth century, when both individualism and the cult of domesticity occupied extremely important places in American popular thought. Two such contrary doctrines could coexist only if individualism was marked "For Men Only." The glorification of the Jacksonian go-getter businessman, the intrepid pioneer, the log-cabin-born President, coincided with the decline in women's status and the increasing restriction of middle-class women to domestic and ornamental functions.

One of the commonly expressed grievances of feminists was that a man was considered a member of both his family and society, while a woman was thought of as a member only of her family. Feminists tirelessly quoted the Declaration of Independence, arguing that "men" in "all men are created equal, and have certain unalienable rights" was a generic term that included women, and that exclusion of women was as inconsistent as exclusion of Negroes. "The consent of the governed," the Protestant glorification of the individual soul, the proud boast that Americans had discarded European distinctions of status in favor of open opportunities for talent—if we are people, they asked their men, how can you without contradiction accept these ideas for yourselves alone? They were right, of course, but they too were guilty of inconsistencies. Most of the time they accepted the cult of domesticity and the doctrine of inherent sexual differences in temperament and talents, while they demanded freedom to work outside the domestic sphere and to be recognized as individuals with temperaments and talents as varied as men's.

They developed several ingenious theories to reconcile the acceptance of inherent sexual differences in temperament with the demand to be treated as individuals. Some feminists took the cult of chivalry, scorned by others as a mask for oppression, at face value. Chivalry claimed that woman, superior to man in the spiritual realm, was too good, too pure to be permitted contact with the sordid world of politics and business. Yes, they cheerfully agreed, they *were* superior. In fact (finding implications in female superiority that chivalry never intended), *they* were the originators of civilization, having developed, through their love for and care of offspring, the values of altruism and peace that made social evolution possible, and having taught them to the warlike, predatory, selfish men, who unfortunately had not learned the lessons thoroughly. The first women who argued along these lines—Elizabeth Cady Stanton, for one—insisted that the superior sex should have the vote in order to impose on society at large the values they had imposed on the individual family; but they accepted fully the cult of domesticity and never dreamed of altering the conventional division of functions within the family.

Other women tried to reconcile the cult of domesticity with sex *equality*—by redefining the economic relation of husband and wife to show that woman was not dependent upon man. It is not true, they said, that a husband supports his wife. They cannot eat the money he earns; she must transform it into food, clothing, and shelter. Hence she supports him just as he supports her. This argument never died out during the life of the feminist movement—or, at least, as long as housekeeping required long hours of labor. Significantly, those feminists who rejected the cult of domesticity rejected the theory invented to justify it. Charlotte Perkins Gilman, in particular, repeatedly declared that a husband did support his wife, and that it was precisely her economic dependence that underlay her inferiority.

When women who wanted equal rights and opportunities accepted the traditional conception of the family, and its concomitant premise that woman's place was in the home, some of them thus adopted a sort of "separate but equal" doctrine surprisingly parallel to that of antifeminists who reiterated that women were not inferior, only "different." There is no doubt that most of the feminists who used such arguments believed them, but probably some were hoping to allay the fears of certain conservatives that votes, education, and careers for women would rend the social fabric. The question then arises: What did these demands represent to the antifeminist majority of American men and women?

Just as the specific content of the feminists' demands expressed a deeper and broader urge for self-determination in general, the specific content of their opponents' conservatism on the woman question reflected their attitude toward American society in general. Certain recurrent themes in antifeminist literature portray the business and political world as one of strife, and the home as a peaceful refuge, where the higher values are nourished. The ugly features of the outside world are accepted as necessary for progress, but progress would be futile unless balanced and ennobled by the conservative influence of the home. Destruction of the home means destruction of the delicate balance between progress and stability, between warfare and peace, between a certain necessary brutality and an equally necessary refinement. How might the home be destroyed? By eradicating the distinction between the spheres of men and women. If women enter the political and business world, they will become like men—or rather, owing to their inherently emotional nature, become even more brutal and coarse than men. Thus, not all antifeminists contended that women were inferior to men; in fact, a few conceded that women could vote as intelligently, conduct businesses as shrewdly, or engage in scholarly pursuits as creatively as men. But what price would society pay for these additional voters, merchants, and scholars? Social disorder. The home was the bulwark against social disorder, and woman was the creator of the home. Not all nineteenth-century antifeminists were insincere when they sang poetic praises to the Queen of the Household, who was superior to the man even though she was excluded from the polls and professions. In their curiously ambiguous conception of American society—a conception that glorified its quick change and yet feared the consequences of that change—she occupied a desperately necessary place as symbol and center of the one institution that prevented society from flying apart. Hence the apparent contradiction of a society increasingly seen as a conglomerate of separate individuals which nevertheless insisted on assigning a "sphere" to half its population according not to their individual but to their common characteristics, and insisting that the unit of representation in the state was not the individual but the family. And hence the apparent anomaly of antifeminist tracts antedating the rise of the feminist movement. If antifeminism is understood as largely representing fear of social disorder, the contradiction and the anomaly disappear. It was not that social order required the subordination of women; rather, to the conservatives it required *a family structure* that involved the subordination of women.

Aspects of the History of American Feminism

Why did the feminist movement appear in the United States when it did, in the second third of the nineteenth century? The immediate cause was the experience of a few women in the abolitionist movement in the 1830's, who found their religiously inspired work for the slave impeded by prejudices against public activity by women. They and many others began to ponder the parallels between women's status and the Negro's status, and to notice that white men usually applied the principles of natural rights and the ideology of individualism only to themselves. The feminist movement was founded by abolitionists and grew directly out of their experiences within the abolitionist movement.

A deeper look at the antebellum generation, however, suggests that the Industrial Revolution was the soil in which feminism grew. The influence was indirect, for the women exploited in the new factories were not those who became feminists; in fact, feminist propaganda rarely mentioned women's wages and conditions in industrial enterprises until about the turn of the century, when the woman's-rights movement was half a century old. And it is difficult to attribute a direct influence to the congestion of population in cities and the tendency of families to become smaller, both consequences of industrialism; many of the early feminists were small-town residents with large broods. In any case, these processes might make a feminist movement possible; they would not cause its development. On the other hand, the growth of industry made the United States a magnet for Irish immigration in the forties, providing middle-class women with abundant domestic help, which in turn gave them leisure for self-education and reform activities. (The reform movements themselves can be seen as reactions to the social problems created by rapid economic development.) Women whose horizons had been thus broadened and who wished to enlarge their sphere of activity then encountered the prejudice against such activity that lit the first spark of feminism. The growth of industry also broadened the distinctions between men's and women's occupations and certainly provoked new thinking about the significance and permanence of their respective "spheres." [8] The rise in the urban population resulted in the enfranchisement of all white men and

[8] For a full discussion of the impact of the Industrial Revolution on women's status and the rise of feminism, see Keith E. Melder, "The Beginnings of the Women's Rights Movement in the United States, 1800–1840," Ph.D. dissertation, Yale, 1964. Some of the points mentioned above are in Melder, Preface and chap. 1.

consequently in the belief that a man earned the vote by his membership in the human race rather than by his ownership of property; a woman who considered herself a member of the human race might question the justice of her disfranchisement. Most important of all, perhaps, was the rapid social change caused ultimately by the rise of industry. The feminist movement may, then, be best characterized as an effect of various effects of the Industrial Revolution.

Throughout its history American feminism has been overwhelmingly a white, middle-class movement. This does not mean that Negro and working-class women have not wanted equality of the sexes. They have formed their own organizations (demanding, among other things, woman suffrage), and have in small numbers belonged to various feminist organizations. One reason for the minor part they have played in them has been the obvious prejudice against them within the woman's-rights movement. Far more important has been their own sense of priorities. Whereas middle-class women wanted the same freedom to develop individual talents as their men apparently had, black and working-class women knew that these things were denied *them* not primarily because they were women but because they belonged to groups whose male members were denied them as well. The demand for woman suffrage necessarily seemed less important than the demand for security of person or for a living wage, and the request for admission to colleges had to appear irrelevant to a mother whose children left school to work in factory or field. Hence Negro and working-class women have always put their needs and grievances as Negroes and workers first and as women second. Primary emphasis on feminism seems to have been a luxury that only white, middle-class women have been able to afford.

In the face of the nineteenth-century assumption that men and women differed innately in mental, moral, and personality traits, the feminists undertook a formidable task when they challenged the notion of separate "spheres" and demanded autonomy for women as individuals. Even those who agreed that woman's place was in the home had to demonstrate that homemakers could also be professionals, voters, and businesswomen. But until the late nineteenth century there were few such women they could point to as living proofs of their contention, and they had to admit that a much larger proportion of women than of men were politically naïve, emotional, uncreative mechanically and artistically, slavish followers of fashion, and interested in little beyond their homes and families. Since the feminists' demand for autonomy could not be justified by much empirical evidence and indeed seemed to contradict the evidence, they at first adopted two main tactics that permitted them to ignore or even admit unpleasant facts: they appealed to abstract justice and they insisted that these "feminine" traits were not innate but the results of training.

In the appeal to abstract justice, the Declaration of Independence was so perfectly tailored to their needs that in 1848 the first woman's-rights convention in history adopted a manifesto that *was* the Declaration, with a few appropriate changes in wording. The New Testament was also useful in the antebellum generation, when religion played a far larger role in American life than at any later time, especially among participants in the reform crusades out of which the first feminist movement emerged. But antifeminists could reply that the Declaration was never intended to apply to women any more than to Negroes: it had, after all, been written by a slaveholder. And the Bible was a dubious support for feminism, for antifeminists also could find in it what they wanted.

The thesis that typically feminine traits were the results of training led to the first effort to translate the abstract demand for autonomy into concrete demands for rights. This first effort was the campaign for better education for girls. Those women, like Mary Lyon, Emma Willard, and Catherine Beecher, who worked primarily in the education field used rather conservative arguments; they sincerely disclaimed any intention of training their pupils to be dissatisfied with their assigned sphere, and argued that broader education would make them better wives and mothers. But other women who were interested in education, having no connection with school-founding and thus no need to solicit subsidies from legislatures or reassure parents of prospective pupils, argued that women's proper sphere had yet to be revealed, since they had been denied the opportunity and education to discover all their potentialities, and that whatever that sphere turned out to be, women themselves must find it. Clearly, then, it was not enough simply to train girls to be homemakers and teachers or even doctors and journalists; education must also be an instrument for self-discovery and self-development, to turn females who happened to be human into humans who happened to be female.

The contention that only when women had the opportunity to discover all their aptitudes could their proper sphere be defined appeared regularly in feminist propaganda from its first appearance to our own day. Feminists have at the same time been eager to show that this or that particular career was appropriate for women, and so the demand for education was only the first of many demands for specific rights. They included the right to become physicians, to go to college, to practice law, to be the legal guardians of their children, and so on. Propaganda along these lines had a double function: first, it was a plea for a wider range of opportunities; second, it exploited every bit of evidence it could uncover to prove that women had already demonstrated the qualifications for fulfilling these roles, perhaps as much to instill self-confidence in women as to show that women's talents were as varied as men's. Thus, feminist newspapers, tracts, and speeches often mention Mistress Margaret Brent, the seventeenth-century Maryland lady who was executrix of Lord Baltimore's estate; widows who successfully ran their late husbands' businesses; and women who in other ways distinguished themselves in "masculine" occupations.

From 1848 until 1920 the specific right most often demanded was the right to vote. The other campaigns did not die out, but many of them were incorporated into the suffrage campaign. For one thing, several of the other specific rights seemed to be contingent on political equality—for example, the right of women to practice law, to make wills and contracts without their husbands' consent, and to serve on juries. Second, one of the major grievances was the existence of laws that discriminated against women—for example, the husband's legal ownership of all the property a couple acquired after their marriage, his sole right to choose their domicile and to bequeath to others than the mother the guardianship of their children upon his death, and bias in favor of the husband in legal grounds for divorce. The chance to change these laws was a powerful incentive for suffragism. A third reason for concentration on the vote was that the "consent of the governed" and "no taxation without representation" slogans, so popular in feminist literature, made the right to vote an obvious and indispensable symbol of equality. And fourth, as time went on, most feminists began to demand the ballot as a means to effect certain reforms in American society—such as prohibition of liquor and, from about the turn of the century on, other legislation desired by Progressive men (it was then that the suffrage movement increasingly attracted the support of working-class women).

When the link between the vote and reform began to dominate suffragist propaganda, the "justice" argument took second place to what may be called the "expediency" argument. That is, the suffragists said less often: Give us the vote because we are taxed and therefore should be represented, because as human beings it is just that we should help rule ourselves; *share your political power with us*—and more often said: Give us the vote so that we can help you pass Progressive laws; *double your political power* by enfranchising us. This argument proved most effective in the Progressive period; outside the South there is a correlation between congressmen's Progressive leanings and their support for woman suffrage.

It appears, however, that the expediency argument of itself was insufficient to convert an antisuffragist lawmaker, for there was another variety of that argument, which, although used at least as often, failed decisively. In the North this variation went: Give us the vote because there are more native-born women than "new immigrant" men and women combined; woman suffrage will therefore help maintain the political supremacy of the "fit" portion of the population. In the South the argument went: There are more white women in our section than blacks of both sexes; give us the vote and we will help you maintain white supremacy. Neither of these propositions impressed those legislators who feared that woman suffrage would double the voting strength of the "unfit" portions of the population. Southerners, especially, remained overwhelmingly antisuffragist to the end, probably owing to their general conservatism concerning woman's proper sphere. Just as feminists' demands for specific rights were expressions of their general discontent with restrictions on women's autonomy, the reception given their arguments for those rights appears to have been determined not by the logic of those appeals but by their audience's general attitude toward woman's "sphere."

Why did most feminists focus their campaign for equality so sharply on the vote between the Civil War and the passage of the Nineteenth Amendment to the Constitution in 1920? An obvious reason, besides those suggested above, was that most of the other rights they had agitated for either had been won or were clearly on the way to being won. Part of the answer, however, probably lies in the thoroughly main-stream character of the feminist movement. As noted earlier, the feminists were for the most part middle-class women who on every other subject shared their men's opinions. In that period, politics was the great national pastime; especially during the Progressive period, the feminists shared the widespread conviction that many social evils could be cured and sweeping social reforms effected by legislation. To the suffragists, the ballot was an instrument of actual power. Significantly, the socialists, who believed that power resided in ownership of the means of production, were seldom active suffragists, although they naturally supported the demand for the vote. True, Jessie Ashley, a wealthy New York lawyer who was a socialist, was for a time an officer of the National American Woman Suffrage Association, and other socialists participated in the movement. But they were exceptional. More typical of socialist thinking was the thesis that woman's place in a society depended ultimately on its economic arrangements, and that after private property, and the family relations it produced and perpetuated, had been abolished, sex equality would come about as a natural consequence.[9]

One of the common antisuffragist arguments reveals an insight that many suffragists and socialists in that day seem to have lacked—recognition of the importance of ideology. Socialists, in foreseeing the automatic equalization of the sexes after the overthrow of capitalist property relations, underestimated the persistence of old attitudes; the suffragists overestimated the influence on American life that the vote would give to "feminine" traits. The "anti's" argued that an election registers public opinion and that anyone, including a disfranchised woman, who helps mold public opinion is exercising power. But the suffragists realized an important truth that the "anti's" failed to grasp: that in a society as fascinated by politics as American society was, a group's prestige is affected by its political status. While some suffragists overestimated what women would accomplish with the vote, others saw political equality merely as a symbol of a more inclusive equality. Here again the theme of autonomy appeared: the point was not only *how* a group exercised its right to vote but also *that* it possessed that right.

Very likely many of the suffragists who expected sweeping changes to result from women's enfranchisement were merely reflecting the tendency, common to reform groups, of exaggerating the significance of their crusade. The error has a certain practical value, for it encourages optimism and commitment. In the case of the feminists, it helped to focus the movement's work on a specific goal that was attainable and that could be agitated for in specific ways. The abolitionist movement of the 1830–60 generation is analogous; abolitionists too had a double objective: the wider goal of race equality, and the specific and more limited step toward that goal represented by abolition of chattel slavery. They too sometimes had unrealistic expectations of the degree to which Negroes would be accepted into American society after

[9] See, for example, Olive M. Johnson, *Woman and the Socialist Movement* (New York, 1918; written in 1907), a Socialist Labor Party tract: "In a Socialist society the question solves itself" (p. 36).

emancipation. Another possible parallel may be found in the modern black-freedom movement, which agitated for specific rights—to be served at lunch counters, to vote, to attend integrated schools, and so on—which really were aspects of the wider goal of full manhood. The abolitionist movement lived to see slavery abolished, the feminist movement saw almost all its specific demands met, and the civil-rights movement of the early 1960's won certain of its demands. All three then awoke to the fact that legal and formal reforms did not bring the wider goal in their train.

The Family vs. Autonomy

The years since the enactment of the Nineteenth Amendment have seen the publication of countless essays explaining modern American woman's discontent with the results of suffrage and of the large measure of freedom she has won. Many of these bear a remarkable resemblance to very early antifeminist tracts in their contention that woman is after all destined to be fulltime wife, mother, and homemaker. Betty Friedan's *Feminine Mystique* documents the fact that these ideas are winning increasing acceptance among young women themselves.

If the "autonomy" thesis is correct, perhaps the discontent is due not to disappointment with the results of the attainment of equality, but to the discovery that the array of specific, formal rights has not added up to substantive equality and autonomy. Although many discriminatory laws still exist in many states, they are minor and hardly touch the lives of most women. Yet the old grievance remains: women are still, in popular thought and custom, females first and human beings second. Is this merely an instance of "cultural lag"? Or is it that the persistence of the old attitude reflects the persistence of the institution of the family in essentially the same form it had when the feminist movement first arose?

Many tracts written between the Civil War and World War I

either called for or predicted the mechanization and profession-
alization of homemaking chores. They noted that all other vari-
eties of necessary labor had become social, had been made efficient
through division of labor, had become the work of paid experts.
Yet housework remained the job of untrained isolated women.
They assumed that once middle-class women had won the right
to work beyond the domestic sphere they would automatically do
so, if only they could be freed from household drudgery. Co-
operative kitchens and other such improvements would give them
the freedom and enable them to find remunerative careers suited
to their individual tastes, while those women (and men) with
talent and liking for housework would become skilled, well-paid
professionals doing jobs hitherto done inefficiently by housewives
who in many cases had neither talent nor liking for the work.

The frequency of such predictions cannot be a coincidence.
Obviously the inferior position of women was somehow associated
with the isolation of each family from every other family and with
the sex-determined division of labor within the family. Yet the
predictions have not been fulfilled. A century ago the sexual division of labor within the middle-class family could be justified by
the fact that housekeeping (even with the help of a maid) was a
time-consuming job. But in our day cause and effect seem to have
been reversed: the conviction that the sexual division of labor
within the home is "right" has now become an incentive to *make*
housekeeping a fulltime job when technology has rendered it no
longer necessary. And so we find women baking their own bread,
making their children's clothes, and in other ways multiplying
their household chores—enacting a sort of Parkinson's Law of
housewifery.[10]

It is no longer possible for a middle-class feminist to argue that
women are relegated to the domestic sphere by either law or the
need of a wife to keep house while her husband works to support
the family. In a period when there is no longer a rational basis for
allocating either remunerative work or homemaking tasks according to sex, the institution of the family itself, as popularly con-

---

[10] See Betty Friedan, *The Feminine Mystique* (New York, 1963), chap. x,
"Housewifery Expands to Fill the Time Available."

ceived, stands revealed as the obstacle to full sex equality. As long as the man engages more in the work of the world and the woman spends a large proportion of her time and energies in the isolated family circle, men will continue to lead in government, the professions, and all the other fields that provide us with our criteria of human achievement. Some contend that women can use their education and talents (innately equal to men's) in training their children. But it may be argued that the training of children requires less than the highest level of specialization and provides no incentive and opportunity to push back the frontiers of knowledge. These must remain the province of men so long as women, regardless of their individual aptitudes, retain the principal responsibility of child care. And the current entrance of many men into the elementary-school teaching profession will help to discredit the assumption that child care is innately woman's work. It is also sometimes argued that women need not lament their lack of opportunity to specialize in given fields of knowledge; they can be the "generalists," reading in many more subjects than their specialist husbands have time to do. But such generalization ordinarily precludes that depth of mastery of one field that permits original and creative contributions to it; again, the pioneers and geniuses must be the men. A third common argument is that the difference in familial roles need not be synonymous with inequality: women will continue to be the nurturers and conservers, men the explorers and innovators, each's contribution to society equally necessary. It can be argued that this separate-but-equal doctrine disguises the fact that the roles of men and women, thus defined, perpetuate the ancient source of the feeling that women are inferior. Men's role as explorers and innovators places a premium on their individual talents, whereas women's role as nurturers and conservers actually places such talents at a discount.[11] This third argument, then, is a new way of stating an old myth:

[11] For a perceptive discussion of this problem, see Alice S. Rossi, "Barriers to the Career Choice of Engineering, Medicine, or Science among American Women," in Jacquelyn A. Mattfeld and Carol G. Van Aken, eds., *Women and the Scientific Professions: The M.I.T. Symposium on American Women in Science and Engineering* (Cambridge, Mass., 1965), pp. 51–127, esp. pp. 116–24. The article is of more generalized interest than its title suggests.

that men are male *humans* whereas women are human *females*.

Just as antifeminists in the past considered as innate female characteristics the traits that grew inevitably out of women's isolation and work patterns, the persistence of the sexual division of labor accounts for the continuance of the same assumptions, now abetted by advertising and the mass media. The old maid is regarded with contempt and pity for her obviously involuntary failure to play the role most appropriate for her as a woman; the old bachelor is envied for his exemption from the necessity of role-playing, his freedom to be an individual. A standard plot of TV dramas portrays the "suffragette" or career woman who finds love and a masterful man and promptly abandons her suffragism or career for demure domesticity.

In short, inequality of the sexes still exists because the family structure has remained basically unchanged. Unless a middle-class feminist is prepared to challenge that family structure head-on, contemporary feminism will perhaps revert to the form of the earliest feminism—the generalized urge toward individual autonomy—before feminists concentrated their efforts on winning a long list of specific rights which they assumed would add up to autonomy.

I

THE QUESTION
OF "SPHERES"

ONE WAY OF dividing the chronological history of American feminism is to enumerate three periods. Characterizing the earliest and the most recent is the question: What is woman's proper sphere? In the first period, feminism largely represented a general feeling among educated, middle-class women that the domestic sphere was too confining. Only later, between about the middle of the nineteenth century and the enactment of the Nineteenth Amendment, did the vague urge for more freedom receive specific definition in terms of access to professions, legal equality, and so on. That the general question of spheres was not forgotten in the second period is evidenced by the date of the last document in this section. But the Seneca Falls Declaration of 1848 (see pp. 183–88) marks a break between the period in which most feminist tracts expressed a general grievance against artificial limitations on women's activities and that in which they demanded one or more specific changes in law and custom. At the present time the question of spheres is again receiving attention, because although most of the specific demands have been met, women have still to achieve full equality. It has become apparent that the specific changes did not, separately or all together, obliterate those differences between men's and women's spheres that are not biologically determined.

I

EARLY MISGIVINGS

Anne Bradstreet, The Prologue (1642)

Long before the emergence of a feminist "movement," there had always been some women who felt the need for greater intellectual activity than was required by their domestic tasks. Anne Bradstreet (1612–72), who came with her husband in the Great Migration to New England in 1630, here asks the reader to accept the propriety of a woman's attempt to write poetry. ["The Prologue" (1642), *The Tenth Muse Lately Sprung Up in America* (London, 1650), p. 4.]

> . . . *I am obnoxious to each carping tongue,*
> *Who says, my hand a needle better fits,*
> *A Poets Pen, all scorne, I should thus wrong;*
> *For such despight they cast on female wits:*
> *If what I doe prove well, it wo'nt advance,*
> *They'l say its stolne, or else, it was by chance.*
>
> *But sure the antick* Greeks *were far more milde,*
> *Else of our Sex, why feigned they those nine,*
> *And poesy made,* Calliope's *owne childe,*
> *So 'mongst the rest, they plac'd the Arts divine:*
> *But this weake knot they will full soone untye,*
> *The* Greeks *did nought, but play the foole and lye.*
>
> *Let* Greeks *be* Greeks, *and* Women *what they are,*
> *Men have precedency, and still excell,*

It is but vaine, unjustly to wage war,
Men can doe best, and Women know it well:
Preheminence in each, and all is yours,
Yet grant some small acknowledgement of ours. . . .

John Winthrop, Journal (1645)

Another member of the Great Migration to New England explains the awful consequences that befall a woman who forgets her proper sphere and vocation. John Winthrop (1588–1649) had been a justice of the peace in England and became the first governor of Massachusetts Bay Colony. [James Kendall Hosmer, ed., *Winthrop's Journal: "History of New England," 1630–1649* (2 vols.; New York, 1908), II, 225.]

(*April*) 13.] Mr. Hopkins, the governor of Hartford upon Connecticut, came to Boston, and brought his wife with him, (a godly young woman, and of special parts,) who was fallen into a sad infirmity, the loss of her understanding and reason, which had been growing upon her divers years, by occasion of her giving herself wholly to reading and writing, and had written many books. Her husband, being very loving and tender of her, was loath to grieve her; but he saw his error, when it was too late. For if she had attended her household affairs, and such things as belong to women, and not gone out of her way and calling to meddle in such things as are proper for men, whose minds are stronger, etc., she had kept her wits, and might have improved them usefully and honorably in the place God had set her. He brought her to Boston, and left her with her brother, one Mr. Yale, a merchant, to try what means might be had here for her. But no help could be had.

Constantia, On the Equality of the Sexes (1790)

"Constantia" was the penname of Judith Sargent Stevens Murray (1751–1820), of Gloucester, Massachusetts, the daughter of a sea captain and merchant. These articles, written in 1779, anticipate many of the themes that later feminists stressed. [Constantia, "On the Equality of the Sexes," *Massachusetts Magazine*, II (March 1790), 132–35, and II (April 1790), 223–26.]

. . . May not the intellectual powers be ranged under these four heads—imagination, reason, memory, and judgment. The province of imagination hath long since been surrendered up to us, and we have been crowned undoubted sovereigns of the regions of fancy. Invention is perhaps the most arduous effort of the mind; this branch of imagination hath been particularly ceded to us, and we have been time out of mind invested with that creative faculty. Observe the variety of fashions (here I bar the contemptuous smile) which distinguish and adorn the female world; how continually they are changing, insomuch that they almost render the wise man's assertion problematical, and we are ready to say, *there is something new under the sun.* Now what a playfulness, what an exuberance of fancy, what strength of inventive imagination, doth this continual variation discover? Again, it hath been observed, that if the turpitude of the conduct of our sex, hath been ever so enormous, so extremely ready are we, that the very first thought presents with an apology, so plausible, as to produce our actions even in an amiable light. Another instance of our creative powers, is our talent for slander; how ingenious are we at inventive scandal? what a formidable story can we in a moment fabricate merely from the force of a prolifick imagination? how many reputations, in the fertile brain of a female, have been utterly despoiled? how industrious are we at improving a hint? suspicion how easily do we convert into conviction, and conviction, embellished by the power of eloquence, stalks abroad to the surprise and confusion of unsuspecting innocence. Perhaps it will be asked if I furnish these facts as instances of excellency in our sex. Certainly not; but as proofs of a creative faculty, of a lively imagination. Assuredly great activity of mind is thereby discovered, and was this activity properly directed, what beneficial effects would follow. Is the needle and kitchen sufficient to employ the operations of a soul thus organized? I should conceive not. Nay, it is a truth that those very departments leave the intelligent principle vacant, and at liberty for speculation. Are we deficient in reason? we can only reason from what we know, and if an opportunity of acquiring knowledge hath been denied us, the inferiority of our sex cannot fairly be deduced from thence. Memory, I believe, will be allowed us in common, since every one's experience must testify, that a loquacious old woman is as frequently met with, as a communicative old man; their subjects are alike drawn from the fund of other times, and the transactions of their youth, or of maturer life, entertain, or perhaps fatigue you, in the evening of their lives. "But our judgment is not so strong—we do not distinguish so well."—Yet it may be questioned, from what doth this superiority, in this determining faculty of the soul, proceed. May we not trace its source in the difference of education, and continued advantages? Will it be said that the judgment of a male of two years old, is more sage than that of a female of the same age? I believe the reverse is generally observed to be true. But from that period what partiality! how is the one exalted, and the other depressed, by the contrary modes of education which are adopted! the one is taught to aspire, and the other is early confined and limited. As their years increase, the sister must be wholly domesticated, while the brother is led by the hand through all the flowery paths of science. Grant that their minds are by nature equal, yet who shall wonder at the *apparent* superiority, if indeed custom becomes *second nature;* nay if it taketh the place of nature, and that it doth the experience of each day will evince. At length arrived at womanhood, the uncultivated fair one feels a void, which the employments allotted her are by no means capable of filling. What can she do? to books she may not apply; or if she doth, *to those only of the novel kind,* lest she merit the appellation of a *learned lady;* and what ideas have been affixed to this term, the observation of many can testify. Fashion, scandal, and sometimes what is still more reprehensible, are then called in to her relief; and who can say to what lengths the liberties she takes may proceed. Meantime she herself is most unhappy; she feels the want of a cultivated mind. Is she single, she in vain seeks to fill up time from sexual employments or amusements. Is she united to a person whose soul nature made equal to her own, education hath set him so far above her, that in those entertainments which are productive of such rational felicity, she is not qualified to accompany him. She experiences a mortifying consciousness of inferiority, which embitters every enjoyment. Doth the person to whom her adverse fate hath consigned her, possess a mind incapable of improvement, she is equally wretched, in being so closely connected with an individual whom she cannot but despise. Now, was she permitted the same instructors as her brother (with an eye however to their particular departments) for the employment of a rational mind an ample field would be opened. In astronomy she might catch a glimpse of the immensity of the Deity, and thence she would form amazing conceptions of the august and supreme Intelligence. In geography she would admire Jehovah in the midst of his benevolence; thus adapting this globe to the various wants and amusements of its inhabitants. In natural philosophy she would adore the infinite majesty of heaven, clothed in condescension; and as she traversed the reptile world, she would hail the goodness of a creating God. A mind, thus filled, would have little room for the trifles with which our sex are, with too much justice, accused of amusing themselves, and they would thus be rendered fit companions for those, who should one day wear them as their crown. Fashions, in their variety, would then give place to conjectures, which might perhaps conduce to the improvement of the literary world; and there would be no leisure for slander or detraction. Reputation would not then be blasted, but serious speculations would occupy the lively imaginations of the sex. Unnecessary visits would be precluded, and that custom would only be indulged by way of relaxation, or to answer the demands of consanguinity and friendship. Females would become discreet, their judgments would be invigorated, and their partners for life being circumspectly chosen, an unhappy Hymen would then be as rare, as is now the reverse.

Will it be urged that those acquirements would supersede our domestick duties. I answer that every requisite in female economy is easily attained; and, with truth I can add, that when once attained, they require no further *mental attention*. Nay, while we are pursuing the needle, or the superintendency of the family, I

repeat, that our minds are at full liberty for reflection; that imagination may exert itself in full vigor; and that if a just foundation
is early laid, our ideas will then be worthy of rational beings. If
we were industrious we might easily find time to arrange them
upon paper, or should avocations press too hard for such an indulgence, the hours allotted for conversation would at least become more refined and rational. Should it still be vociferated,
"Your domestick employments are sufficient"—I would calmly
ask, is it reasonable, that a candidate for immortality, for the joys
of heaven, an intelligent being, who is to spend an eternity in
contemplating the works of Deity, should at present be so degraded, as to be allowed no other ideas, than those which are
suggested by the mechanism of a pudding, or the sewing the
seams of a garment? Pity that all such censurers of female improvement do not go one step further, and deny their future
existence; to be consistent they surely ought.

Yes, ye lordly, ye haughty sex, our souls are by nature *equal* to
yours; the same breath of God animates, enlivens, and invigorates
us; and that we are not fallen lower than yourselves, let those
witness who have greatly towered above the various discouragements by which they have been so heavily oppressed; and though
I am unacquainted with the list of celebrated characters on either
side, yet from the observations I have made in the contracted
circle in which I have moved, I dare confidently believe, that from
the commencement of time to the present day, there hath been
as many females, as males, who, by the *mere force of natural
powers*, have merited the crown of applause; who, *thus unassisted*,
have seized the wreath of fame. I know there are those who assert,
that as the animal powers of the one sex are superiour, of course
their mental faculties also must be stronger; thus attributing
strength of mind to the transient organization of this earth born
tenement. But if this reasoning is just, man must be content to
yield the palm to many of the brute creation, since by not a few of
his brethren of the field, he is far surpassed in bodily strength.
Moreover, was this argument admitted, it would prove too much,
for occular demonstration evinceth, that there are many robust
masculine ladies, and effeminate gentlemen. Yet I fancy that Mr.

Pope, though clogged with an enervated body, and distinguished by a diminutive statnre, could nevertheless lay claim to greatness of soul; and perhaps there are many other instances which might be adduced to combat so unphilosophical an opinion. Do we not often see, that when the clay built tabernacle is well nigh dissolved, when it is just ready to mingle with the parent soil, the immortal inhabitant aspires to, and even attaineth heights the most sublime, and which were before wholly unexplored. Besides, were we to grant that animal strength proved any thing, taking into consideration the accustomed impartiality of nature, we should be induced to imagine, that she had invested the female mind with superiour strength as an equivalent for the bodily powers of man. But wa[i]ving this however palpable advantage, for *equality only*, we wish to contend.

I am aware that there are many passages in the sacred oracles which seem to give the advantage to the other sex; but I consider all these as wholly metaphorical. Thus David was a man after God's own heart, yet see him enervated by his licentious passions! behold him following Uriah to the death, and shew me wherein could consist the immaculate Being's complacency. Listen to the curses which Job bestoweth upon the day of his nativity, and tell me where is his perfection, where his patience—*literally* it existed not. David and Job were types of him who was to come; and the superiority of man, as exhibited in scripture, being also emblematical, all arguments deduced from thence, of course fall to the ground. The exquisite delicacy of the female mind proclaimeth the exactness of its texture, while its nice sense of honour announceth its innate, its native grandeur. And indeed, in one respect, the preeminence seems to be tacitly allowed us, for after an education which limits and confines, and employments and recreations which naturally tend to enervate the body, and debilitate the mind; after we have from early youth been adorned with ribbons, and other gewgaws, dressed out like the ancient victims previous to a sacrifice, being taught by the care of our parents in collecting the most showy materials that the ornamenting our exteriour ought to be the principal object of our attention; after, I say, fifteen years thus spent, we are introduced into the world, amid the united adulation of every beholder. Praise is sweet to the soul; we are immediately intoxicated by large draughts of flattery, which being plentifully administered, is to the pride of our hearts the most acceptable incense. It is expected that with the other sex we should commence immediate war, and that we should triumph over the machinations of the most artful. We must be constantly upon our guard; prudence and discretion must be our characteristicks; and we must rise superiour to, and obtain a complete victory over those who have been long adding to the native strength of their minds, by an unremitted study of men and books, and who have, moreover, conceived from the loose characters which they have seen portrayed in the extensive variety of their reading, a most contemptible opinion of the sex. Thus unequal, we are, notwithstanding forced to the combat, and the infamy which is consequent upon the smallest deviation in our conduct, proclaims the high idea which was formed of our native strength; and thus, indirectly at least, is the preference acknowledged to be our due. And if we are allowed an equality of acquirements, let serious studies equally employ our minds, and we will bid our souls arise to equal strength. We will meet upon even ground, the despot man; we will rush with alacrity to the combat, and, crowned by success, we shall then answer the exalted expectations which are formed. Though sensibility, soft compassion, and gentle commiseration, are inmates in the female bosom, yet against every deep laid art, altogether fearless of the event, we will set them in array; for assuredly the wreath of victory will encircle the spotless brow. If we meet an equal, a sensible friend, we will reward him with the hand of amity, and through life we will be assiduous to promote his happiness; but from every deep laid scheme for our rule, retiring into ourselves, amid the flowery paths of science, we will indulge in all the refined and sentimental pleasures of contemplation. And should it still be urged, that the studies thus insisted upon would interfere with our more peculiar department, I must further reply, that *early hours,* and close application, will do wonders; and to her who is from the first dawn of reason taught to fill up time rationally, both the requisites will be easy. I grant that niggard fortune is too generally unfriendly to the mind, and that much of that valuable treasure, time, is necessarily expended upon the wants of the body; but it should be remembered, that in embarrassed circumstances our companions have as little leisure for literary improvement, as is afforded to us; for most certainly their provident care is at least as requisite as our exertions. Nay, we have even more leisure for sedentary pleasures, as our avocations are more retired, much less laborious, and, as hath been observed, by no means require that avidity of attention which is proper to the employments of the other sex. In high life, or, in other words, where the parties are in possession of affluence, the objection respecting time is wholly obviated, and of course falls to the ground; and it may also be repeated, that many of those hours which are at present swallowed up in fashion and scandal, might be redeemed, were we habituated to useful reflections. But in one respect, O ye arbiters of our fate! we confess that the superiority is indubitably yours; you are by nature formed for our protectors; we pretend not to vie with you in bodily strength; upon this point we will never contend for victory. Shield us then, we beseech you, from external evils, and in return *we* will transact *your* domestick affairs. Yes, *your*, for are you not equally interested in those matters with ourselves? Is not the elegancy of neatness as agreeable to your sight as to ours; is not the well favoured viand equally delightful to your taste; and doth not your sense of hearing suffer as much, from the discordant sounds prevalent in an ill regulated family, produced by the voices of children and many *et ceteras?*

CONSTANTIA.

By way of Supplement to the foregoing pages, I subjoin the following extract from a letter, wrote to a friend in the December of 1780.

. . . The superiority of your sex hath, I grant, been time out of mind esteemed a truth incontrovertible; in consequence of which persuasion, every plan of education hath been calculated to establish this favourite tenet. Not long since, weak and presuming as I was, I amused myself with selecting some arguments from nature, reason, and experience, against this so generally received idea.

I confess that to sacred testimonies I had not recourse. I held them to be merely metaphorical, and thus regarding them, I could not persuade myself that there was any propriety in bringing them to decide in this *very important debate*. However, as you, sir, confine yourself entirely to the sacred oracles, I mean to bend the whole of my artillery against those supposed proofs, which you have from thence provided, and from which you have formed an intrenchment *apparently* so invulnerable. And first, to begin with our great progenitors; but here, suffer me to premise, that it is for mental strength I mean to contend, for with respect to animal powers, I yield them undisputed to that sex, which enjoys them in common with the lion, the tyger, and many other beasts of prey; therefore your observations respecting the *rib, under the arm, at a distance from the head*, &c. &c. in no sort militate against my view. Well, but the woman was first in the transgression. Strange how blind *self love* renders you men; were you not wholly absorbed in a partial admiration of your own abilities, you would long since have acknowledged the force of what I am now going to say. It is true some ignoramuses have absurdly enough informed us, that the beauteous fair of paradise, was seduced from her obedience, by a malignant demon, *in the guise of a baleful serpent*; but we, who are better informed, know that the fallen spirit presented himself to her view, *a shining angel still*; for thus, saith the criticks in the Hebrew tongue, ought the word to be rendered. Let us examine her motive—Hark! the seraph declares that she shall attain a perfection of knowledge; for is there aught which is not comprehended under one or other of the terms *good* and *evil*. It doth not appear that she was governed by any sensual appetite; but merely by a desire of adorning her mind; a laudable ambition fired her soul, and a thirst for knowledge impelled the predilection so fatal in its consequences. Adam could not plead the same deception; assuredly he was not deceived; nor ought we to admire his superiour strength, or wonder at his sagacity, when we so often confess that example is much more influential than precept. His gentle partner stood before him, a melancholy instance of the direful effects of disobedience; he saw her not possessed of that wisdom which she had fondly hoped to obtain, but he beheld the once blooming female, disrobed of that innocence, which had heretofore rendered her so lovely. To him then deception became impossible, as he had proof positive of the fallacy of the argument, which the deceiver had suggested. What then could be his inducement to burst the barriers, and to fly directly in the face of that command, which *immediately* from the mouth of deity *he* had received, since, I say, he could not plead that fascinating stimulous, the accumulation of knowledge, as indisputable conviction was so visibly portrayed before him. What mighty cause impelled him to sacrifice myriads of beings yet unborn, and by one impious act, which *he saw* would be productive of such fatal effects, entail undistinguished ruin upon a race of beings, which he was yet to produce. Blush, ye vaunters of fortitude; ye boasters of resolution; ye haughty lords of the creation; blush when ye remember, that he was influenced by no other motive than a bare pusillanimous attachment to a woman! by sentiments so exquisitely soft, that all his sons have, from that period, when they have designed to degrade them, described as highly feminine. Thus it should seem, that all the arts of the grand deceiver (since means adequate to the purpose are, I conceive, invariably pursued) were requisite to mislead our general mother, while the father of mankind forfeited his own, and relinquished the happiness of posterity, merely in compliance with the blandishments of a female. . . .

Hannah Mather Crocker, Observations on the Real Rights of Women (1818)

Hannah Mather Crocker (1752–1829) was the granddaughter of Cotton Mather and the mother of ten children. Her essay represents a step backward from Constantia's forthright assertion of potential equality. The difference between the two is the difference between a period in which rationalism and free thought were "in the air" and one in which women's status declined, domesticity was glorified, and the distinctions between men's and women's spheres widened. [*Observations on the Real Rights of Women, with Their Appropriate Duties, Agreeable to Scripture, Reason and Common Sense* (Boston, 1818), pp. 5–6, 15–21, 41, 49–50, 54–55, 72.]

This little work is not written with a design of promoting any altercation or dispute respecting superiority or inferiority, of the sexes; but the aim will be to prove, in a pleasant manner, and, we hope, to even demonstration, that though there are appropriate duties peculiar to each sex, yet the wise Author of nature has endowed the female mind with equal powers and faculties, and given them the same right of judging and acting for themselves, as he gave to the male sex; although it is plain, from scripture account, that the woman was the first in the transgression, she justly forfeited her original right of equality for a certain space of time, and a heavy and humiliating sentence was past [*sic*] upon her, that her sorrow should be multiplied, and that under the Jewish dispensation, the man should rule over her; and she was under the yoke of bondage, till the birth of our blessed Saviour, which, according to the promise given, was the seed of the woman, that should bruise the serpent's head.

We shall consider woman restored to her original right and dignity at the commencement of the christian dispensation, although there must be allowed some moral and physical distinction of the sexes agreeably to the order of nature, and the organization of the human frame, still the sentiment must predominate, that the powers of mind are equal in the sexes. . . . For the interest of their country, or in the cause of humanity, we shall strictly adhere to the principle and the impropriety of females ever trespassing on masculine ground; as it is morally incorrect and physically improper. . . .

It must be the appropriate duty and privilege of females, to convince by reason and persuasion. It must be their peculiar province to sooth[e] the turbulent passions of men, when almost sinking in the sea of care, without even an anchor of hope to support them. Under such circumstances women should display their talents by taking the helm, and steer them safe to the haven of rest and peace, and that should be their own happy mansion, where they may always retire and find a safe asylum from the rigid cares of business. It is a woman's peculiar right to keep calm and serene under every circumstance in life, as it is undoubtedly her appropriate duty, to sooth[e] and alleviate the anxious cares of man, and her friendly and sympathetic breast should be found the best solace for him, as she has an equal right to partake with him the cares, as well as the pleasure of life.

It was evidently the design of heaven, by the mode of our first formation, that they should walk side by side, as mutual supports in all times of trial. There can be no doubt, that, in most cases, their judgment may be equal with the other sex; perhaps even on the subject of law, politics, or religion, they may form good judgment, but it would be morally improper, and physically very incorrect, for the female character to claim the statesman's birth [*sic*], or ascend the rostrum to gain the loud applause of men, although their powers of mind may be equal to the task. . . .

. . . There may be a few groveling minds who think woman should not aspire to any further knowledge than to obtain enough of the cymical art to enable them [*sic*] to compound a good pudding, pie, or cake, for her lord and master to discompound. Others, of a still weaker class, may say, it is enough for woman scientifically to arrange the spinning-wheel and distaff, and exercise her extensive capacity in knitting and sewing, for since the fall and restoration of woman these employments have been the appropriate duties of the female sex. The art of dress, which in some measure produced the art of industry, did not commence till sin, folly, and shame, introduced the first invention of dress, which ought to check the modest female from every species of wantonness and extravagance in dress; cultivate the mind, and trifling in dress will soon appear in its true colours.

To those who appear unfriendly to female literature let me say, in behalf of the sex, they claim no right to infringe on any domestic economy; but those ladies, who continue in a state of celibacy, and find pleasure in literary researches, have a right to indulge the propensity, and solace themselves with the feast of reason and knowledge; also those ladies who in youth have laid up a treasure of literary and scientific information, have a right to improve in further literary researches, after they have faithfully discharged their domestic duties. With maternal affections, when her olive branches have spread forth to form new circles in society, the maternal mind has become satiated with the common concerns of life, and the real christian wishes for peace and retirement, for contemplation; and this is the most convenient season for to take a retrospect of past scenes, and this is a fully ripe season to read, write, meditate, and compose, if the body and mind are not enfeebled by infirmities. The well informed mind, if still in full vigour, is now fully ripe for composing; and females of that class must have a right to unbend their minds in well digested thought for the improvement of the rising generation; and if they can by well digested sentiments, implant in the youthful breast, by precept and their example, the seeds of virtue and religion, it will fully compensate, for a long life of toil and study. . . .

Women have an equal right, with the other sex, to form societies for promoting religious, charitable and benevolent purposes. Every association formed for benevolence, must have a tendency to make man mild, and sociable to man; an institution formed for historical and literary researches, would have a happy effect on the mind and manners of the youth of both sexes. As the circulating libraries are often resorted to after novels by both sexes for want of judgment to select works of more merit, the study of history would strengthen their memory, and improve the mind, whereas novels have a tendency to vitiate the mind and morals of the youth of each sex before they are ripe for more valuable acquisitions. Much abstruse study or metaphysical reasoning seldom agrees with the natural vivacity or the slender frame of many females, therefore the moral and physical distinction of the sex must be allowed; if the powers of the mind are fully equal, they must still estimate the rights of men, and own it their prerogative exclusively to contend for public honours and preferment, either in church or state, and females may console themselves and feel happy, that by the moral distinction of the sexes they are called to move in a sphere of life remote from those masculine contentions, although they hold equal right with them of studying every branch of science, even jurisprudence.

But it would be morally wrong, and physically imprudent, for any woman to attempt pleading at the bar of justice, as no law can give her the right of deviating from the strictest rules of rectitude and decorum. . . .

It must be woman's prerogative to shine in the domestic circle, and her appropriate duty to teach and regulate the opening mind of her little flock, and teach their juvenile ideas how to shoot forth into well improved sentiments. It is most undoubtedly the duty and privilege of woman to regulate her garrison with such good order and propriety, that the generalissimo of her affection, shall never have reason to seek other quarters for well disciplined and regulated troops. . . .

Mary Wol[l]stonecraft was a woman of great energy and a very independent mind; her Rights of Women are replete with fine sentiments, though we do not coincide with her opinion respecting the total independence of the female sex. We must be allowed to say, her theory is unfit for practice, though some of her sentiments and distinctions would do honour to the pen, even of a man. . . .

But of all studies most necessary and most natural to women is the study of men, as their government must be that of persuasion; it is necessary for them to know the main springs by which men are actuated. If any thing can add to the pleasure derived from a selected society, it is the charms of friendship. The injustice they have done women by excluding them the privilege of being friends, they cannot account for on any principle, as women are born with more sensibility than men, and are as capable of being friends. . . .

The surest foundation to secure the female's right, must be in family government, as without that, women can have no established right. This must be the touchstone of the matrimonial faith; and on this depends very much the safety and happiness of a free republic. Family government should, in some measure, resemble a well regulated garrison; there should be sentinels continually on the watch-tower, and general orders should be given for the day, and these should be attended with the morning and evening orisons, that should ascend like holy incense, with gratitude of soul, for the divine care and protection. Women have a right to join in the family prayer and praise. Family worship must be mutual, as any jar or animosity will disorder the whole garrison, and a mutiny may ensue and throw the whole into confusion, and thus frustrate the cause of religion and virtue, and the demon of discord may enter, with all the accumulated miseries of Pandora's box, and perhaps storm and carry the garrison. For want of mutual skill and judgment to defend the fortress, there must be a fixed principle in the mind, that no real happiness can be attained, but in a religious course of life, and that will give a calm serenity, and peace of mind, that will afford us real satisfaction in every situation of life. . . .

As there is no spiritual distinction of sexes, the twin souls shall there [in the realms of bliss] join the general choir of all those who are equally redeemed by the precious blood of Jesus Christ, the Lamb of God. Such will be the advantage of forming sacred love and friendship here, that it shall be the foretaste of our future bliss, and the temporal death will not dissolve the sacred tie, and there the sexual rights will be mutual; our God is no respecter of persons or sexes.

From what has been here offered on behalf of female rights, it appears plainly, virtue, hamony, love and friendship, religiously improved, will be the surest passport to the realms of bliss and happiness. And may the voice of philanthropy unite to embrace in the arms of her affection the whole human race, which the sexes have equal right to extend to every individual person throughout the whole order of society.

2

THE OPPOSITION

Thomas R. Dew, Dissertation on the Characteristic Differences
Between the Sexes (1835)

Thomas R. Dew (1802–46) taught at William and Mary College
and is remembered chiefly as a proslavery pamphleteer. The early
date of this essay indicates that opposition to feminism antedated
the feminist movement and represented that concern for social
stability which motivated much conservatism on the woman question. ["Dissertation on the Characteristic Differences between the
Sexes, and on the Position and Influence of Woman in Society,"
Southern Literary Messenger (Richmond, Va.), I (May 1835),
493–512.]

The relative position of the sexes in the social and political
world, may certainly be looked upon as the result of organization.
The greater physical strength of man, enables him to occupy the
foreground in the picture. He leaves the domestic scenes; he
plunges into the turmoil and bustle of an active, selfish world;
in his journey through life, he has to encounter innumerable
difficulties, hardships and labors which constantly beset him. His
mind must be nerved against them. Hence courage and boldness
are his attributes. It is his province, undismayed, to stand against
the rude shocks of the world; to meet with a lion's heart, the

dangers which threaten him. He is the shield of woman, destined by nature to guard and protect her. Her inferior strength and sedentary habits confine her within the domestic circle; she is kept aloof from the bustle and storm of active life; she is not familiarized to the out of door dangers and hardships of a cold and scuffling world: timidity and modesty are her attributes. In the great strife which is constantly going forward around her, there are powers engaged which her inferior physical strength prevents her from encountering. She must rely upon the strength of others; man must be engaged in her cause. How is he to be drawn over to her side? Not by menace—not by force; for weakness cannot, by such means, be expected to triumph over might. No! It must be by conformity to that character which circumstances demand for the sphere in which she moves; by the exhibition of those qualities which delight and fascinate—which are calculated to win over to her side the proud lord of creation, and to make him an humble suppliant at her shrine. Grace, modesty and loveliness are the charms which constitute her power. By these, she creates the magic spell that subdues to her will the more mighty physical powers by which she is surrounded. Her attributes are rather of a passive than active character. Her power is more emblematical of that of divinity: it subdues without an effort, and almost creates by mere volition; whilst man must wind his way through the difficult and intricate mazes of philosophy; with pain and toil, tracing effects to their causes, and unraveling the deep mysteries of nature—storing his mind with useful knowledge, and exercising, training and perfecting his intellectual powers, whilst he cultivates his strength and hardens and matures his courage; all with a view of enabling him to assert his rights, and exercise a greater sway over those around him. Woman we behold dependant [sic] and weak; but out of that very weakness and dependance [sic] springs an irresistible power. She may pursue her studies too—not however with a view of triumphing in the senate chamber—not with a view to forensic display—not with a view of leading armies to combat, or of enabling her to bring into more formidable action the physical power which nature has conferred on her. No! It is but the better to perfect all those feminine graces, all those fascinating attributes, which render her the centre of attraction, and which delight and charm all who breathe the atmosphere in which she moves. . . .

Jonathan F. Stearns, Discourse on Female Influence (1837)

Jonathan F. Stearns (1808–89) was a clergyman in Newburyport, Massachusetts. This sermon delivered to his own congregation was reprinted in pamphlet form. [*Female Influence, and the True Christian Mode of Its Exercise: A Discourse Delivered in the First Presbyterian Church in Newburyport, July 30, 1837* (Newburyport, 1837), excerpts from pp. 8–24.]

The influence of woman in forming the character of her relatives, gentle and unobserved as it is, is one which can never be adequately appreciated, till the great day of revelation shall disclose the secret springs of human action and feeling. We all know, by experience, what a charm there is in the word HOME, and how powerful are the influences of domestic life upon the character. It is the province of woman to make home, *whatever it is*. If she makes that delightful and salutary—the abode of order and purity, though she may never herself step beyond the threshold, she may yet send forth from her humble dwelling, a power that will be felt round the globe. She may at least save some souls that are dear to her from disgrace and punishment, present some precious ornaments to her country and the church, and polish some jewels, to shine brightly in the Saviour's crown. . . .

But the influence of woman is not limited to the domestic circle. *Society* is her empire, which she governs almost at will. . . . It is her province to *adorn* social life, to throw a *charm* over the intercourse of the world, by making it lovely and attractive, pure and improving. . . .

The cause of benevolence is peculiarly indebted to the agency of woman. She is fitted by nature to cheer the afflicted, elevate the depressed, minister to the wants of the feeble and diseased,

and lighten the burden of human misery, in all its varied and trying forms. God has endowed her with qualities peculiarly adapted
to these offices; and the history of benevolence will testify how
well she has fulfilled her trust. The friendless orphan blesses her.
The homeless sailor, the wandering exile, the child of affliction,
and even the penitent outcast, find in her a patroness and friend.

But the highest merit of all is yet to be mentioned. *Religion*
seems almost to have been entrusted by its author to her particular
custody. . . . It is the standing sneer of the infidel, and his last
resort when arguments fail, that the religion of Christ is chiefly
prevalent among women, and chiefly indebted to them for its
spread. . . .

Nor is it strange that such should be the fact. In thus devoting
her heart to the cause of christianity, she does but attempt to
requite, in some humble measure, the peculiar benefits she herself
has received from this religion. . . . When we consider what
woman was in classic Greece, and what she still is, in barbarous
and savage lands, darkened and degraded, without knowledge,
without influence, without honor, the mere drudge of society, or
still worse, the miserable slave of sensual passion; and contrast
with this dark picture, the happier scenes which christianity presents, where she stands forth in her true dignity, as the *companion*
and *equal* of man, his helper on earth, and co-heir of immortal
felicity, we cannot wonder that *she* should exhibit peculiar attachment to a faith which has bestowed upon her such
blessings. . . .

Much dispute has arisen in modern times in regard to the comparative intellectual ability of the sexes. . . . Now the whole debate, as it seems to me, proceeds from a mistake. The truth is,
there is a natural *difference*, in the mental as well as physical
constitution of the two classes—a difference which implies not
inferiority on the one part, but only *adaptation to a different
sphere.* Cultivate as highly as you will the mind of a female, and
you do not deprive it of its distinguishing peculiarities. On the
other hand, deprive man of his advantages, keep him in ignorance
and intellectual depression, and you make him a kind of *brute
beast*, but you do not approximate his character to the character
of a woman. . . .

Let us turn to the Bible for a moment, and see what we can gather from the teachings of inspiration. . . . [Stearns here quotes and discusses passages from the New Testament, such as those commanding women to be silent in church and to be in subjection to their husbands.] I am confident no virtuous and delicate female, who rightly appreciates the design of her being, and desires to sustain her own influence and that of her sex, and fulfil the high destiny for which she is formed, would desire to abate one jot or tittle from the seeming restrictions imposed upon her conduct in these and the like passages. They are designed, not to *degrade*, but to *elevate* her character,—not to cramp, but to afford a *salutary* freedom, and give a useful direction to the energies of the feminine mind. . . . Let her lay aside delicacy, and her influence over our sex is gone.

And for what object should she make such sacrifices? That she may do good more extensively? Then she sadly mistakes her vocation. But why then? That she may see her name blazoned on the rolls of fame, and hear the shouts of delighted assemblies, applauding her eloquence? That she may place her own sex on a fancied equality with men, obtain the satisfaction of calling herself *independent*, and occupy a station in life which she can never adorn? For this would she sacrifice the almost magic power, which, in her own proper sphere, she now wields over the destinies of the world? Surely *such privileges*, obtained at *such cost*, are unworthy of a wise and virtuous woman's ambition. . . .

That there are ladies who are capable of public debate, who could make their voice heard from end to end of the church and the senate house, that there are those who might bear a favorable comparison with others as eloquent orators, and who might speak to better edification than most of those on whom the office has hitherto devolved, I am not disposed to deny. The question is not in regard to *ability*, but to *decency*, to order, to christian *propriety*. . . .

My hearers must pardon me for speaking thus explicitly. The advocates of such principles and measures have, in times past, been confined principally to the ranks of unbelievers, whom no pious and respectable female would desire to encourage. But when popular female writers, and women professing godliness, begin to take the same ground, it is time for the pulpit as well as the press to speak plainly. I verily believe, that should the practice I have censured become *prevalent*, and the consequent change in the treatment of females, already anticipated by some of its advocates, take place in the community, the influence of ladies, now so important to the cause of philanthropy and piety, would very speedily be crushed, and religion, morality and good order, suffer a wound from which they would not soon nor easily recover. . . .

On you, ladies, depends, in a most important degree, the destiny of our country. In this day of disorder and turmoil, when the foundations of the great deep seem fast breaking up, and the flood of desolation threatening to roll over the whole face of society, it peculiarly devolves upon you to say what shall be the result. Yours it is to determine, whether the beautiful order of society . . . shall continue as it has been, to be a source of blessings to the world; or whether, despising all forms and distinctions, all boundaries and rules, society shall break up and become a chaos of disjointed and unsightly elements. Yours it is to decide, under God, whether we shall be a nation of refined and high minded Christians, or whether, rejecting the civilities of life, and throwing off the restraints of morality and piety, we shall become a fierce race of semi-barbarians, before whom neither order, nor honor, nor chastity can stand.

And be assured, ladies, if the hedges and borders of the social garden be broken up, the lovely vine, which now twines itself so gracefully upon the trellis, and bears such rich clusters, will be the first to fall and be trodden under foot. . . .

Pastoral Letter of the Massachusetts Congregationalist Clergy
(1837)

The following document was the Congregationalist clergy's shocked reaction to Sarah and Angelina Grimké's speeches on abolitionism. ["Pastoral Letter of the General Association of Massachusetts (Orthodox) to the Churches under Their Care," The *Liberator* (Boston), August 11, 1837.]

. . . We invite your attention to the dangers which at present seem to threaten the female character with wide-spread and permanent injury.

The appropriate duties and influence of woman are clearly stated in the New Testament. Those duties and that influence are unobtrusive and private, but the source of mighty power. When the mild, dependent, softening influence of woman upon the sternness of man's opinions is fully exercised, society feels the effects of it in a thousand forms. The power of woman is in her dependence, flowing from the consciousness of that weakness which God has given her for her protection, and which keeps her in those departments of life that form the character of individuals and of the nation. There are social influences which females use in promoting piety and the great objects of Christian benevolence which we cannot too highly commend. We appreciate the unostentatious prayers and efforts of woman in advancing the cause of religion at home and abroad; in Sabbath-schools; in leading religious inquirers to the pastors for instruction; and in all such associated effort as becomes the modesty of her sex; and earnestly hope that she may abound more and more in these labors of piety and love.

But when she assumes the place and tone of man as a public reformer, our care and protection of her seem unnecessary; we put ourselves in self-defence against her; she yields the power which God has given her for protection, and her character becomes unnatural. If the vine, whose strength and beauty is to lean upon the trellis-work and half conceal its clusters, thinks to assume the independence and the overshadowing nature of the elm, it will not only cease to bear fruit, but fall in shame and dishonor into the dust. We cannot, therefore, but regret the mistaken conduct of those who encourage females to bear an obtrusive and ostentatious part in measures of reform, and countenance any of that sex who so far forget themselves as to itinerate in the character of public lecturers and teachers.—We especially deplore the intimate acquaintance and promiscuous conversation of females with regard to things "which ought not to be named"; [1] by which that modesty

[1] The reference is to the fact that the Grimké sisters included, in the list of

and delicacy which is the charm of domestic life, and which constitutes the true influence of woman in society, is consumed, and the way opened, as we apprehend, for degeneracy and ruin. We say these things, not to discourage proper influences against sin, but to secure such reformation as we believe is Scriptural, and will be permanent.

---

outrages common in the South, the facts that slaves were forbidden to marry and that slave women were powerless to protect themselves against the lusts of overseers and masters.—*Ed.*

3

THE BEGINNING OF AGITATION

Sarah Moore Grimké, Two Essays (1837 and 1838)

Sarah Moore Grimké (1792–1873) was a Charleston-born member of a famous slaveholding family. She became a Quaker and then an abolitionist and, with her sister Angelina, toured New England in 1837, lecturing against slavery. They were the first American women to speak publicly to mixed audiences. The first selection is her reply to the "Pastoral Letter," and the second is the fourth of a series of *Letters on the Condition of Woman and the Equality of the Sexes*, later published as a pamphlet in Boston in 1838. ["Province of Woman. The Pastoral Letter," reprinted from the *New-England Spectator* in the *Liberator*, October 6, 1837; and Letter IV: "Social Intercourse of the Sexes," *ibid.*, January 12, 1838.]

. . . [The Pastoral Letter] says, "We invite your attention to the dangers which at present seem to threaten the FEMALE CHARACTER with wide-spread and permanent injury." I rejoice that they have called the attention of my sex to this subject, because I believe if woman investigates it, she will soon discover that danger is impending, though from a totally different source from that which the Association apprehends,—danger from those who, having long held the reins of *usurped* authority, are unwilling to permit us to fill that sphere which God created us to move in, and who have entered into league to crush the immortal mind of woman. I rejoice, because I am persuaded that the rights of woman, like the rights of slaves, need only be examined, to be understood and asserted, even by some of those who are now endeavoring to smother the irrepressible desire for mental and spiritual freedom which glows in the breast of many who hardly dare to speak their sentiments.

"The appropriate duties and influence of woman are clearly stated in the New Testament. Those duties are unobtrusive and private, but the sources of *mighty power*. When the mild, *dependent*, softening influence of woman upon the sternness of man's opinions, is fully exercised, society feels the effects of it in a thousand ways." No one can desire more earnestly than I do, that woman may move exactly in the sphere which her Creator has assigned her; and I believe her having been displaced from that sphere, has introduced confusion into the world. It is therefore of vast importance to herself, and to all the rational creation, that she should ascertain what are her duties and privileges as a responsible and immortal being. The New Testament has been referred to, and I am willing to abide by its decision, and must enter my protest against the false translations of some passages by the MEN who did that work, and against the perverted interpretations by the MEN who undertook to write commentaries thereon. I am inclined to think, when we are admitted to the honor of studying Greek and Hebrew, we shall produce some various readings of the Bible, a little different from those we now have.

I find the Lord Jesus defining the duties of his followers in his sermon on the Mount, laying down grand principles by which they should be governed, without any preference to sect or condition:—"Ye are the light of the world. A city that is set on a hill cannot be hid. Neither do men light a candle and put it under a bushel, but on a candlestick, and it giveth light unto all that are in the house. Let your light so shine before men, that they may see your good works, and glorify your Father which is in heaven." I follow him through all his precepts, and find him giving the same directions to women as to men, never even referring to the distinction now so strenuously insisted upon between masculine and feminine virtues: this is one of the anti-christian "traditions of men" which are taught instead of the "commandments of God." Men and women were CREATED EQUAL; they are both moral and accountable beings, and whatever is right for man to do, is right for woman to do.

But the influence of woman, says the Association, is to be private and unobtrusive; her light is not to shine before man like that of her brethren; but she is passively to let the lords of the creation, as they call themselves, put the bushel over it, lest peradventure it might appear that the world has been benefitted by the rays of her candle. Then her quenched light is of more use than if it were set on the candlestick:—"Her influence is the source of mighty power." This has ever been the language of man since he laid aside the whip as a means to keep woman in subjection. He spares her body, but the war he has waged against her mind, her heart, and her soul, has been no less destructive to her as a moral being. How monstrous is the doctrine that woman is to be dependent on man! Where in all the sacred scriptures is this taught? But, alas, she has too well learned the lesson which he has labored to teach her. She has surrendered her dearest RIGHTS, and been satisfied with the privileges which man has assumed to grant her, whilst he has amused her with the show of power, and absorbed all the reality into himself. He has adorned the creature, whom God gave him as a companion, with baubles and gewgaws, turned her attention to personal attractions, offered incense to her vanity, and made her the instrument of his selfish gratification, a plaything to please his eye, and amuse his hours of leisure.—"Rule by obedience, and by submission sway," or in other words, study to be a hypocrite, pretend to submit, but gain your point, has been the code of household morality which woman has been taught. The poet has sung in sickly strains the loveliness of woman's dependence upon man, and now we find it re-echoed by those who profess to teach the religion of the Bible. God says, "Cease ye from man whose breath is in his nostrils, for wherein is he to be accounted of?" Man says, depend upon me. God says, "He will teach us of his ways." Man says, believe it not; I am to be your teacher. This doctrine of dependence upon man is utterly at variance with the doctrine of the Bible. In that book I find nothing like the softness of woman, nor the sternness of man; both are equally commanded to bring forth the fruits of the Spirit—Love, meekness, gentleness.

But we are told, "the power of woman is in her dependence, flowing from a consciousness of that weakness which God has given her for her protection." If physical weakness is alluded to, I cheerfully concede the superiority; if brute force is what my brethren are claiming, I am willing to let them have all the honor they desire: but if they mean to intimate that mental or moral weakness belongs to woman more than to man, I utterly disclaim the charge; our powers of mind have been crushed, as far as man could do it, our sense of morality has been impaired by his interpretation of our duties, but no where does God say that he made any distinction between us as moral and intelligent beings. . . .

MY DEAR FRIEND,—Before I proceed with the account of that oppression which woman has suffered in every age and country from her *protector*, man, permit me to offer for your consideration, some views relative to the social intercourse of the sexes. Nearly the whole of this intercourse is, in my apprehension, derogatory to man and woman, as moral and intellectual beings. We approach each other, and mingle with each other, under the constant pressure of a feeling that we are of different sexes; and, instead of regarding each other only in the light of immortal creatures, the mind is fettered by the idea which is early and industriously infused into it, that we must never forget the distinction between male and female. Hence our intercourse, instead of being elevated and refined, is generally calculated to excite and keep alive the lowest propensities of our nature. Nothing, I believe, has tended more to destroy the true dignity of woman, than the fact that she is approached by man in the character of a female. The idea that she is sought as an intelligent and heaven-born creature, whose society will cheer, refine and elevate her companion, and that she will receive the same blessings she confers, is rarely held up to her view. On the contrary, man almost always addresses himself to the weakness of woman. By flattery, by an appeal to her passions, he seeks access to her heart; and when he has gained her affections, he uses her as the instrument of his pleasure,—the minister of his temporal comfort. He furnishes himself with a housekeeper, whose chief business is in the kitchen, or the nursery. And whilst he goes abroad and enjoys the means of improvement afforded by collision of intellect with cultivated minds, his wife is condemned to draw nearly all her instruction from books, if she has time to peruse them; and if not, from her meditations, whilst engaged in those domestic duties, which are necessary for the comfort of her lord and master.

Surely no one who contemplates, with the eye of a Christian philosopher, the design of God in the creation of woman, can believe that she is now fulfilling that design. The literal translation of the word "help-meet" is a helper like unto himself; it is so rendered in the Septuagint, and manifestly signifies a companion. Now I believe it will be impossible for woman to fill the station assigned her by God, until her brethren mingle with her as an equal, as a moral being; and lose, in the dignity of her immortal nature, and in the fact of her bearing like himself the image and superscription of her God, the idea of her being a female. . . . Man has inflicted an unspeakable injury upon woman, by holding up to her view her animal nature, and placing in the back ground her moral and intellectual being. Woman has inflicted an injury upon herself by submitting to be thus regarded; and she is now called upon to rise from the station where *man*, not God, has placed her, and claim those sacred and inalienable rights, as a moral and responsible being, with which her Creator has invested her. . . .

Angelina Emily Grimké, Letters to Catherine E. Beecher (1838)

Angelina Emily Grimké (1805–79) shared her sister Sarah's reaction to the attacks on their "unfeminine" behavior in lecturing in public. One of the attackers was Catherine E. Beecher, a pioneer in women's education, and Angelina addressed a series of open letters to her which were printed in the *Liberator* and later published as a pamphlet. [*Letters to Catherine E. Beecher, in Reply to an Essay on Slavery and Abolitionism, Addressed to A. E. Grimké* (Boston, 1838), excerpts from Letters XI and XII, pp. 103–9, 114–21.]

LETTER XI
The Sphere of Woman and Man As Moral Beings the Same.
BROOKLINE, Mass. 8*th month*, 28*th*, 1837.
DEAR FRIEND: I come now to that part of thy book, which is, of all others, the most important to the women of this country; thy "general views in relation to the place woman is appointed to fill by the dispensations of heaven." I shall quote paragraphs from thy book, offer my objections to them, and then throw before thee my own views.

Thou sayest, "Heaven has appointed to one sex the *superior*, and to the other the *subordinate* station, and this without any reference to the character or conduct of either." This is an assertion without proof. Thou further sayest, that "it was designed that the mode of gaining influence and exercising power should be *altogether different and peculiar*." Does the Bible teach this? "Peace on earth, and good will to men, is the character of all the rights and privileges, the influence and the power of *woman*." Indeed! Did our Holy Redeemer preach the doctrines of *peace to our sex* only? "A *man* may act on Society by the collision of intellect, in public debate; *he* may urge his measures by a sense of shame, by fear and by personal interest; *he* may coerce by the combination of public sentiment; *he* may drive by physical force, and *he* does *not* overstep the boundaries of his sphere." Did Jesus,

then, give a different rule of action to men and women? Did he
tell his disciples, when he sent them out to preach the gospel, that
man might appeal to the fear, and shame, and interest of those
he addressed, and coerce by public sentiment, and drive by physical force? "But (that) all the power and all the conquests that
are lawful to *woman* are those only which appeal to the kindly,
generous, peaceful and benevolent principles?" [*sic*] If so, I should
come to a very different conclusion from the one at which thou
hast arrived: I should suppose that *woman was the superior*, and
man the subordinate being, inasmuch as moral power is immeasurably superior to "physical force."

"Woman is to win every thing by peace and love; by making
herself so much respected, &c. that to yield to *her* opinions, and
to gratify *her* wishes, will be the free-will offering of the heart."
This principle may do as the rule of action to the fashionable
belle, whose idol is *herself*; whose every attitude and smile are
designed to win the admiration of others to *herself*; and who
enjoys, with exquisite delight, the double-refined incense of flattery
which is offered to *her* vanity, by yielding to *her* opinions, and
gratifying *her* wishes, because they are *hers*. But to the humble
Christian, who feels that it is *truth* which she seeks to recommend
to others, *truth* which she wants them to esteem and love, and
not herself, this subtle principle must be rejected with holy indignation. Suppose she could win thousands to her opinions, and
govern them by her wishes, how much nearer would they be to
Jesus Christ, if she presents no higher motive, and points to no
higher leader?

"But this is all to be accomplished in the domestic circle." Indeed! "Who made thee a ruler and a judge over all?" I read in
the Bible, that Miriam, and Deborah, and Huldah, were called
to fill *public stations* in Church and State. I find Anna, the
prophetess, speaking in the temple "unto all them that looked
for redemption in Jerusalem." During his ministry on earth, I see
women following him from town to town, in the most public
manner; I hear the woman of Samaria, on her return to the city,
telling the *men* to come and see a man who had told her all the
things that ever she did. I see them even standing on Mount

Calvary, around his cross, in the most exposed situation; but He never *rebuked* them; He never told them it was unbecoming *their sphere in life* to mingle in the crowds which followed his footsteps. Then, again, I see the cloven tongues of fire resting on each of the heads of the one hundred and twenty disciples, some of whom were *women*; yea, I hear *them preaching* on the day of Pentecost to the multitudes who witnessed the outpouring of the spirit on that glorious occasion; for, unless *women* as well as men received the Holy Ghost, and *prophesied*, what did Peter mean by telling them, "This is *that* which was spoken by the prophet Joel: And it shall come to pass in the last days, said God, I will pour out my spirit upon *all* flesh: and your sons and your *daughters shall prophesy*. . . . And on my servants and on my *handmaidens*, I will pour out in those days of my spirit; and *they shall prophesy*." . . .

I find, too, that Philip had four daughters which did *prophesy*; and what is still more convincing, I read in the xi. of 1. Corinthians, some particular directions from the Apostle Paul, as to *how* women were to pray and prophesy in the assemblies of the people—*not* in the domestic circle. On examination, too, it appears that the very same word, *Diakonos*, which, when applied to Phoebe, Romans xvi. 1, is translated *servant*, when applied to Tychicus, Ephesians vi. 21, is rendered *minister*. Ecclesiastical History informs us, that this same Phoebe was pre-eminently useful, as a minister in the Church, and that female ministers suffered martyrdom in the first ages of Christianity. And what, I ask, does the Apostle mean when he says in Phillipians [*sic*] iv. 3.— "Help those women who labored with me in the gospel"? Did these holy women of old perform all their gospel labors in "the domestic and social circle"? I trow not.

Thou sayest, "the moment woman begins to feel the promptings of ambition, or the thirst for power, her aegis of defence is gone." Can man, then, retain his aegis when he indulges these guilty passions? Is it woman only who suffers this loss?

"All the generous promptings of chivalry, all the poetry of romantic gallantry, depend upon woman's retaining her place as *dependent* and *defenceless*, and making no claims, and maintaining no rights, but what are the gifts of honor, rectitude and love."

I cannot refrain from pronouncing this sentiment as beneath the dignity of any woman who names the name of Christ. No woman, who understands her dignity as a moral, intellectual and accountable being, cares aught for any attention or any protection, vouchsafed by "the promptings of chivalry, and the poetry of romantic gallantry." Such a one loathes such littleness, and turns with disgust from all such silly insipidities. Her noble nature is insulted by such paltry, sickening adulation, and she will not stoop to drink the foul waters of so turbid a stream. If all this sinful foolery is to be withdrawn from our sex, with all my heart I say, *the sooner the better.* Yea, I say more, no woman who lives up to the true glory of her womanhood, will ever be treated with such *practical contempt.* Every man, when in the presence of true moral greatness, "will find an influence thrown around him," which will utterly forbid the exercise of "the poetry of romantic gallantry.". . .

"A woman may seek the aid of co-operation and combination among her own sex, to assist her in her appropriate offices of piety, charity," &c. *Appropriate* offices! Ah! here is the great difficulty. What are they? Who can point them out? Who has ever attempted to draw a line of separation between the duties of men and women, as *moral* beings, without committing the grossest inconsistencies on the one hand, or running into the most arrant absurdities on the other?

"Whatever, in any measure, throws a woman into the attitude of a combatant, either for herself or others—whatever binds her in a party conflict—whatever obliges her in any way to exert coercive influences, throws her out of her appropriate sphere." If, by a *combatant*, thou meanest one who "drives by *physical force*," then I say, *man* has no more right to appear as *such* a combatant than woman; for all the pacific precepts of the gospel were given to *him*, as well as to her. If, by a *party conflict*, thou meanest a struggle for power, either civil or ecclesiastical, a thirst for the praise and the honor of man, why, then I would ask, is this the proper sphere of *any* moral, accountable being, man or woman? If, by *coercive influences*, thou meanest the use of force or of fear, such as slaveholders and warriors employ, then, I repeat, that *man* has no more right to exert these than *woman*. All such influences are repudiated by the precepts and examples of Christ, and his apostles; so that, after all, this appropriate sphere of woman is *just as appropriate to man*. These "general principles are correct," if thou wilt only permit them to be of *general application*. . . .

LETTER XII

Human Rights Not Founded on Sex.

EAST BOYLSTON, Mass. 10*th mo*. 2d, 1837.

DEAR FRIEND: . . . The investigation of the rights of the slave has led me to a better understanding of my own. I have found the Anti-Slavery cause to be the high school of morals in our land —the school in which *human rights* are more fully investigated, and better understood and taught, than in any other. Here a great fundamental principle is uplifted and illuminated, and from this central light, rays innumerable stream all around. Human beings have *rights*, because they are *moral* beings: the rights of *all* men grow out of their moral nature; and as all men have the same moral nature, they have essentially the same rights. These rights may be wrested from the slave, but they cannot be alienated: his title to himself is as perfect *now*, as is that of Lyman Beecher: it is stamped on his moral being, and is, like it, imperishable. Now if rights are founded in the nature of our moral being, then the *mere circumstance of sex* does not give to man higher rights and responsibilities, than to woman. To suppose that it does, would be to deny the self-evident truth, that the "physical constitution is the mere instrument of the moral nature." To suppose that it does, would be to break up utterly the relations, of the two natures, and to reverse their functions, exalting the animal nature into a monarch, and humbling the moral into a slave; making the former a proprietor, and the latter its property. When human beings are regarded as *moral* beings, *sex*, instead of being enthroned upon the summit, administering upon rights and responsibilities, sinks into insignificance and nothingness. My doctrine then is, that whatever it is morally right for man to do, it is morally right for woman to do. Our duties originate, not from difference of sex, but from the diversity of our relations in life, the various gifts and talents committed to our care, and the different eras in which we live.

This regulation of duty by the mere circumstance of sex, rather than by the fundamental principle of moral being, has led to all that multifarious train of evils flowing out of the anti-christian doctrine of masculine and feminine virtues. By this doctrine, man has been converted into the warrior, and clothed with sternness, and those other kindred qualities, which in common estimation belong to his character as a *man;* whilst woman has been taught to lean upon an arm of flesh, to sit as a doll arrayed in "gold, and pearls, and costly array," to be admired for her personal charms, and caressed and humored like a spoiled child, or converted into a mere drudge to suit the convenience of her lord and master. . . . This principle has given to man a charter for the exercise of tyranny and selfishness, pride and arrogance, lust and brutal violence. It has robbed woman of essential rights, the right to think and speak and act; the right to share their responsibilities, perils, and toils; the right to fulfil the great end of her being, as a moral, intellectual and immortal creature, and of glorifying God in her body and her spirit which are His. Hitherto, instead of being a helpmeet to man, as a companion, a co-worker, an equal; she has been a mere appendage of his being, an instrument of his convenience and pleasure, the pretty toy with which he w[h]iled away his leisure moments, or the pet animal whom he humored into playfulness and submission. Woman, instead of being regarded as the equal of man, has uniformly been looked down upon as his inferior, a mere gift to fill up the measure of his happiness. In "the poetry of romantic gallantry," it is true, she has been called "the last *best* gift of God to man;" but I believe I speak forth the words of truth and soberness when I affirm, that woman never was given to man. She was created, like him, in the image of God, and crowned with glory and honor; created only a little lower than the angels,—not, as is almost universally assumed, a little lower than man; on her brow, as well as on his, was placed the "diadem of beauty," and in her hand the sceptre of universal

dominion. Gen: i. 27, 28. "The last *best gift* of God to Man!"
Where is the scripture warrant for this "rhetorical flourish, this
splendid absurdity?" Let us examine the account of her creation.
"And the rib which the Lord God had taken from man, made he
a woman, and brought her unto the man." Not as a gift—for
Adam immediately recognized her *as a part of himself*—("this is
now bone of my bone, and flesh of my flesh")—a companion and
equal, not one hair's breadth beneath him in the majesty and
glory of her moral being; not placed under his authority as a *subject*, but by his side, on the same platform of human rights, under
the government of God only. This idea of woman's being "the last
best gift of God to man," however pretty it may sound to the
ears of those who love to discourse upon "the poetry of romantic
chivalry," has nevertheless been the means of sinking her from
an *end* into a mere *means*—of turning her into an *appendage* to
man, instead of recognizing her as *a part of man*—of destroying
her individuality, and rights, and responsibilities, and merging her
moral being in that of man. Instead of *Jehovah* being *her* king,
her lawgiver, and *her* judge, she has been taken out of the exalted
scale of existence in which He placed her, and subjected to the
despotic control of man.

I have often been amused at the vain efforts made to define
the rights and responsibilities of immortal beings as *men* and
women. No one has yet found out just where the line of separation between them should be drawn, and for this simple reason,
that no one knows just how far below man woman is, whether she
be a head shorter in her moral responsibilities, or head and
shoulders, or the full length of his noble stature, below him, i.e.
under his feet. Confusion, uncertainty, and great inconsistencies,
must exist on this point, so long as woman is regarded in the
least degree inferior to man; but place her where her Maker
placed her, on the same high level of human rights with man,
side by side with him, and difficulties vanish, the mountains of
perplexity flow down at the presence of this grand equalizing principle. Measure her rights and duties by the unerring standard of
moral being, not by the false weights and measures of a mere
circumstance of her human existence, and then the truth will be

self-evident, that whatever it is *morally* right for a man to do, it is *morally* right for a woman to do. I recognize no rights but *human* rights—I know nothing of men's rights and women's rights; for in Christ Jesus, there is neither male nor female. It is my solemn conviction, that, until this principle of equality is recognised and embodied in practice, the Church can do nothing effectual for the permanent reformation of the world. Woman was the first transgressor, and the first victim of power. In all heathen nations, she has been the slave of man, and Christian nations have never acknowledged her rights. Nay more, no Christian denomination or Society has ever acknowledged them on the broad basis of humanity. I know that in some denominations, she is permitted to preach the gospel; not from the conviction of her rights, nor upon the ground of her equality as a *human being*, but of her equality in spiritual gifts—for we find that woman, even in these Societies, is allowed no voice in framing the Discipline by which she is to be governed. Now, I believe it is woman's right to have a voice in all the laws and regulations by which she is to be *governed*, whether in Church or State; and that the present arrangements of society, on these points, are *a violation of human rights, a rank usurpation of power*, a violent seizure and confiscation of what is sacredly and inalienably hers—thus inflicting upon woman outrageous wrongs, working mischief incalculable in the social circle, and in its influence on the world producing only evil, and that continually. *If* Ecclesiastical and Civil governments are ordained of God, *then* I contend that woman has just as much right to sit in solemn counsel in Conventions, Conferences, Associations and General Assemblies, as man—just as much right to sit upon the throne of England, or in the Presidential chair of the United States.

Dost thou ask me, if I would wish to see woman engaged in the contention and strife of sectarian controversy, or in the intrigues of political partizans? I say no! never—never. I rejoice that she does not stand on the same platform which man now occupies in these respects; but I mourn, also, that he should thus prostitute his higher nature, and vilely cast away his birthright. I prize the purity of *his* character as highly as I do that of hers. As a moral being, *whatever it is morally wrong for her to do, it is morally wrong for him to do.* The fallacious doctrine of male and female virtues has well nigh ruined all that is morally great and lovely in his character: he has been quite as deep a sufferer by it as woman, though mostly in different respects and by other processes. . . .

Thou sayest, "an ignorant, a narrow-minded, or a stupid woman, cannot feel nor understand the rationality, the propriety, of the beauty of this relation"—i.e. subordination to man. Now, verily, it does appear to me, that nothing but a narrow-minded view of the subject of human rights and responsibilities can induce any one to believe in *this subordination to a fallible* being. Sure I am, that the signs of the times clearly indicate a vast and rapid change in public sentiment, on this subject. Sure I am that she is not to be, as she has been, *"a mere second-hand agent"* in the regeneration of a fallen world. Not that "she will carry her measures by tormenting when she cannot please, or by petulant complaints or obtrusive interference, in matters which are out of her sphere, and which she cannot comprehend." But just in proportion as her moral and intellectual capacities become enlarged, she will rise higher and higher in the scale of creation, until she reaches that elevation prepared for her by her Maker, and upon whose summit she was originally stationed, only "a little lower than the angels." Then will it be seen that nothing which concerns the well-being of mankind is either beyond her sphere, or above her comprehension: *Then* will it be seen "that America will be distinguished above all other nations for well educated women, and for the influence they will exert on the general interests of society." . . .

Margaret Fuller, The Great Lawsuit (1843)

Margaret Fuller (1810–50), member of the Transcendentalist circle that included Emerson, first attained notoriety with her philosophical "conversations" among Boston women starting in

1839. In 1840 she became editor of *The Dial*. She died in a shipwreck off Fire Island on her return from Europe with her husband, Marquis Giovanni Ossoli, and their infant son. Her most famous work, *Woman in the Nineteenth Century* (1845), was based on the following essay. ["The Great Lawsuit. Man *versus* Men. Woman *versus* Women," *The Dial*, IV (July 1843), 1–47. The excerpts are from pp. 10–11, 23–24, 27–28, 35, 44–45, and begin with an imaginary dialogue; Miss Fuller has just said that the abolitionists are the warmest champions of woman.]

"Is it not enough," cries the sorrowful trader, "that you have done all you could to break up the national Union, and thus destroy the prosperity of our country, but now you must be trying to break up family union, to take my wife away from the cradle, and the kitchen hearth, to vote at polls, and preach from a pulpit? Of course, if she does such things, she cannot attend to those of her own sphere. She is happy enough as she is. She has more leisure than I have, every means of improvement, every indulgence."

"Have you asked her whether she was satisfied with these indulgences?"

"No, but I know she is. She is too amiable to wish what would make me unhappy, and too judicious to wish to step beyond the sphere of her sex. I will never consent to have our peace disturbed by any such discussions."

" 'Consent'—You? it is not consent from you that is in question, it is assent from your wife."

"Am I not the head of my house?"

"You are not the head of your wife. God has given her a mind of her own."

"I am the head and she the heart."

"God grant you play true to one another then. If the head represses no natural pulse of the heart, there can be no question as to your giving your consent. Both will be of one accord, and there needs but to present any question to get a full and true answer. There is no need of precaution, of indulgence, or consent. But our doubt is whether the heart consents with the head, or only acquiesces in its decree; and it is to ascertain the truth of this point, that we propose some liberating measures."

Thus vaguely are these questions proposed and discussed at present. But their being proposed at all implies much thought, and suggests more. Many women are considering within themselves what they need that they have not, and what they can have, if they find they need it. Many men are considering whether women are capable of being and having more than they are and have, and whether, if they are, it will be best to consent to improvement in their condition.

The numerous party, whose opinions are already labelled and adjusted too much to their mind to admit of any new light, strive, by lectures on some model-woman of bridal-like beauty and gentleness, by writing or lending little treatises, to mark out with due precision the limits of woman's sphere, and woman's mission, and to prevent other than the rightful shepherd from climbing the wall, or the flock from using any chance gap to run astray. . . .

It is not the transient breath of poetic incense, that women want; each can receive that from a lover. It is not life-long sway; it needs but to become a coquette, a shrew, or a good cook to be sure of that. It is not money, nor notoriety, nor the badges of authority, that men have appropriated to themselves. If demands made in their behalf lay stress on any of these particulars, those who make them have not searched deeply into the need. It is for that which at once includes all these and precludes them; which would not be forbidden power, lest there be temptation to steal and misuse it; which would not have the mind perverted by flattery from a worthiness of esteem. It is for that which is the birthright of every being capable to receive it,—the freedom, the religious, the intelligent freedom of the universe, to use its means, to learn its secret as far as nature has enabled them, with God alone for their guide and their judge.

Ye cannot believe it, men; but the only reason why women ever assume what is more appropriate to you, is because you prevent them from finding out what is fit for themselves. Were they free, were they wise fully to develop the strength and beauty of woman, they would never wish to be men, or manlike. The well-instructed moon flies not from her orbit to seize on the glories of her partner. No; for she knows that one law rules, one heaven contains, one universe replies to them alike. . . .

. . . A great majority of societies and individuals are still doubtful whether earthly marriage is to be a union of souls, or merely a contract of convenience and utility. Were woman established in the rights of an immortal being, this could not be. She would not in some countries be given away by her father, with scarcely more respect for her own feelings than is shown by the Indian chief, who sells his daughter for a horse, and beats her if she runs away from her new home. Nor, in societies where her choice is left free, would she be perverted, by the current of opinion that seizes her, into the belief that she must marry, if it be only to find a protector, and a home of her own.

Neither would man, if he thought that the connection was of permanent importance, enter upon it so lightly. He would not deem it a trifle, that he was to enter into the closest relations with another soul, which, if not eternal in themselves, must eternally affect his growth.

Neither, did he believe woman capable of friendship, would he, by rash haste, lose the chance of finding a friend in the person who might, probably, live half a century by his side. Did love to his mind partake of infinity, he would not miss his chance of its revelations, that he might the sooner rest from his weariness by a bright fireside, and have a sweet and graceful attendant, "devoted to him alone." Were he a step higher, he would not carelessly enter into a relation, where he might not be able to do the duty of a friend, as well as a protector from external ill, to the other party, and have a being in his power pining for sympathy, intelligence, and aid, that he could not give. . . .

. . . So much is said of women being better educated that they may be better companions and mothers *of men!* They should be fit for such companionship. . . . Earth knows no fairer, holier relation than that of a mother. But a being of infinite scope must not be treated with an exclusive view to any one relation. Give the soul free course, let the organization be freely developed, and the being will be fit for any and every relation to which it may be called. The intellect, no more than the sense of hearing, is to be cultivated, that she may be a more valuable companion to man, but because the Power who gave a power by its mere existence signifies that it must be brought out towards perfection.

In this regard, of self-dependence and a greater simplicity and fulness of being, we must hail as a preliminary the increase of the class contemptuously designated as old maids. . . .

Every relation, every gradation of nature, is incalculably precious, but only to the soul which is poised upon itself, and to whom no loss, no change, can bring dull discord, for it is in harmony with the central soul.

If any individual live too much in relations, so that he becomes a stranger to the resources of his own nature, he falls after a while into a distraction, or imbecility, from which he can only be cured by a time of isolation, which gives the renovating fountains time to rise up. With a society it is the same. Many minds, deprived of the traditionary or instinctive means of passing a cheerful existence, must find help in self-impulse or perish. It is therefore that while any elevation, in the view of union, is to be hailed with joy, we shall not decline celibacy as the great fact of the time. It is one from which no vow, no arrangement, can at present save a thinking mind. For now the rowers are pausing on their oars, they wait a change before they can pull together. All tends to illustrate the thought of a wise contemporary. Union is only possible to those who are units. To be fit for relations in time, souls, whether of man or woman, must be able to do without them in the spirit.

It is therefore that I would have woman lay aside all thought, such as she habitually cherishes, of being taught and led by men. . . . I would have her free from compromise, from complaisance, from helplessness, because I would have her good enough and strong enough to love one and all beings, from the fulness, not the poverty of being. . . .

Lucy Stone, Speech (1855)

Lucy Stone (1818–93), born in Massachusetts, was graduated from Oberlin in 1847. She lectured for abolition, temperance, and feminism and with her husband founded *The Woman's Journal* in 1870; it was the principal suffragist paper until 1917. She refused to be known by her husband's name and was called "Mrs. Stone"; ever since, women who keep their maiden names have been called Lucy Stoners. She delivered the following extemporaneous speech at a national woman's-rights convention in Cincinnati in October 1855. [*HWS* I, 165–66.]

The last speaker alluded to this movement as being that of a few disappointed women. From the first years to which my memory stretches, I have been a disappointed woman. When, with my brothers, I reached forth after the sources of knowledge, I was reproved with "It isn't fit for you; it doesn't belong to women." Then there was but one college in the world where women were admitted, and that was in Brazil. I would have found my way there, but by the time I was prepared to go, one was opened in the young State of Ohio—the first in the United States where women and Negroes could enjoy opportunities with white men. I was disappointed when I came to seek a profession worthy an immortal being—every employment was closed to me, except those of the teacher, the seamstress, and the housekeeper. In education, in marriage, in religion, in everything, disappointment is the lot of woman. It shall be the business of my life to deepen this disappointment in every woman's heart until she bows down to it no longer. I wish that women, instead of being walking show-cases, instead of begging of their fathers and brothers the latest and gayest new bonnet, would ask of them their rights.

The question of Woman's Rights is a practical one. The notion has prevailed that it was only an ephemeral idea; that it was but women claiming the right to smoke cigars in the streets, and to frequent bar-rooms. Others have supposed it a question of comparative intellect; others still, of sphere. Too much has already been said and written about woman's sphere. Trace all the doctrines to their source and they will be found to have no basis except in the usages and prejudices of the age. This is seen in the fact that what is tolerated in woman in one country is not tolerated in another. In this country women may hold prayer-meetings, etc., but in Mohammedan countries it is written upon their mosques, "Women and dogs, and other impure animals, are not permitted to enter." Wendell Phillips says, "The best and greatest thing one is capable of doing, that is his sphere." I have confidence in the Father to believe that when He gives us the capacity to do anything He does not make a blunder. Leave women, then, to find their sphere. And do not tell us before we are born even, that our province is to cook dinners, darn stockings, and sew on buttons. We are told woman has all the rights she wants; and even women, I am ashamed to say, tell us so. They mistake the politeness of men for rights— seats while men stand in this hall to-night, and their adulations; but these are mere courtesies. We want rights. The flour-merchant, the house-builder, and the postman charge us no less on account of our sex; but when we endeavor to earn money to pay all these, then, indeed, we find the difference. Man, if he have energy, may hew out for himself a path where no mortal has ever trod, held back by nothing but what is in himself; the world is all before him, where to choose; and we are glad for you, brothers, men, that it is so. But the same society that drives forth the young man, keeps woman at home—a dependent— working little cats on worsted, and little dogs on punctured paper; but if she goes heartily and bravely to give herself to some worthy purpose, she is out of her sphere and she loses caste. Women working in tailor-shops are paid one-third as much as men. Some one in Philadelphia has stated that women make fine shirts for twelve and a half cents apiece; that no woman can make more than nine a week, and the sum thus earned, after deducting rent, fuel, etc., leaves her just three and a half cents a day for bread. Is it a wonder that women are driven to prostitution? Female teachers in New York are paid fifty dollars a year, and for every such situation there are five hundred applicants. I know not what you believe of God, but I believe He gave yearnings and longings to be filled, and that He did not mean all our time should be devoted to feeding and clothing the body. The present condition of woman causes a horrible perversion of the marriage relation. It is asked of a lady, "Has she married well?" "Oh, yes, her husband is rich." Woman must marry for a home, and you men are the sufferers by this; for a woman who loathes you may marry you because you have the means to get money which she cannot have. But when woman can enter the lists with you and make money for herself, she will marry you only for deep and earnest affection. . . .

II

THE ARGUMENT
BECOMES SPECIFIC

WHEN FEMINISTS *demanded a wider sphere for woman, the question naturally arose among women as well as among men whether women were capable of more varied occupations. Anti-feminists of course argued that women's restriction to domestic activities reflected an inborn limitation in their abilities; feminists insisted that the apparent limitation was a result of training. Hence a crucial subject for propaganda on both sides was whether mind has sex; and hence a crucial demand of early feminists was for increased educational opportunities for girls. Feminists also turned their attention to other alleged influences limiting the development of women's talents, and some of them discovered in the Bible and organized religion an implacable enemy. Most feminists, however, were deeply religious and preferred to identify the enemy as the perversion of true Christianity and misinterpretations of the Bible. A third specific grievance, which seemed much more important then than it does now, was feminine attire, which many feminists considered a symbol of women's inferiority. Not only was it unhealthful; it was, they believed, so absurdly decorative as to be unfit for an active, self-respecting human being. The dress-reform movement began in the 1850's with the invention of the bloomer costume, and it received a good deal of attention again in the '80's and '90's. There were always some feminists who refused to believe it was an urgent question and who rightly predicted that a more rational dress would follow rather than pave the way for greater equality.[1] A fourth specific*

---

[1] See Robert E. Riegel, "Women's Clothes and Women's Rights," *American Quarterly*, XV (Autumn 1963), 390–401.

from that feminism took reflected the cult of science popular in the late nineteenth century: some women rejoiced at new discoveries that seemed to give scientific sanction to sex equality. They were particularly delighted with the theories of the sociologist Lester Frank Ward and the anthropologist Lewis Henry Morgan. And, finally, a fifth question to which feminists addressed themselves received much attention throughout this second period, and understandably, for it seemed to be the most important both to the antifeminists and to themselves—namely, the nature of marriage, the home, and the family.

I

INTELLECT AND EDUCATION

Emma Hart Willard, Address to the Public (1819)

Emma Hart Willard (1787–1870), born in Troy, New York, was head of the Middlebury, Vermont, Female Academy from 1807 to 1809, and in 1814 founded the Middlebury Female Seminary to put into practice new methods of educating girls. Seven years later she established the Troy Female Seminary, first college-level school for women in the United States. The document from which the following excerpt is taken resulted in the chartering of the Waterford Academy, but the legislature provided no money for the school. [*Address to the Public: Particularly to the Members of the Legislature of New-York, Proposing a Plan for Improving Female Education* (Middlebury, 1819), pp. 13–17.]

Education should seek to bring its subjects to the perfection of their moral, intellectual and physical nature: in order, that they may be of the greatest possible use to themselves and others: or, to use a different expression, that they may be the means of the greatest possible happiness of which they are capable, both as to what they enjoy, and what they communicate.

Those youth have the surest chance of enjoying and commu-

nicating happiness, who are best qualified, both by internal disposition, and external habits, to perform with readiness, those
duties, which their future life will most probably give them
occasion to practice. . . .

These are the principles, on which systems of male education
are founded; but female education has not yet been systematized.
Chance and confusion reign here. Not even is youth considered
in our sex, as in the other, a season, which should be wholly
devoted to improvement. Among families, so rich as to be entirely
above labour, the daughters are hurried through the routine of
boarding school instruction, and at an early period introduced
into the gay world; and, thenceforth, their only object is amusement.—Mark the different treatment, which the sons of these
families receive. While their sisters are gliding through the mazes
of the midnight dance, they employ the lamp, to treasure up for
future use the riches of ancient wisdom; or to gather strength
and expansion of mind, in exploring the wonderful paths of
philosophy. When the youth of the two sexes has been spent so
differently, is it strange, or is nature at fault, if more mature age
has brought such a difference of character, that our sex have
been considered by the other, as the pampered wayward babies
of society, who must have some rattle put into our hands, to keep
us from doing mischief to ourselves or others?

Another difference in the treatment of the sexes is made in
our country, which, though not equally pernicious to society, is
more pathetically unjust to our sex. How often have we seen a
student, who, returning from his literary pursuits, finds a sister,
who was his equal in acquirements, while their advantages were
equal, of whom he is now ashamed. While his youth was devoted
to study, and he was furnished with the means, she, without
any object of improvement, drudged at home, to assist in the
support of the father's family, and perhaps to contribute to her
brother's subsistence abroad; and now, a being of a lower order,
the rustic innocent wonders and weeps at his neglect. . . .

Another errour is, that it has been made the first object in
educating our sex, to prepare them to please the other. But

reason and religion teach, that we too are primary existencies; that it is for us to move, in the orbit of our duty, around the Holy Centre of perfection, the companions, not the satellites of men; else, instead of shedding around us an influence, that may help to keep them in their proper course, we must accompany them in their wildest deviations.

I would not be understood to insinuate, that we are not, in particular situations, to yield obedience to the other sex. Submission and obedience belong to every being in the universe, except the great Master of the whole. Nor is it a degrading peculiarity to our sex, to be under human authority. Whenever one class of human beings, derive from another the benefits of support and protection, they must pay its equivalent, obedience. . . .

Neither would I be understood to mean, that our sex should not seek to make themselves agreeable to the other. The errour complained of, is that the taste of men, whatever it might happen to be, has been made a standard for the formation of the female character. . . . A system of education, which leads one class of human beings to consider the approbation of another, as their highest object, teaches, that the rule of their conduct should be the will of beings imperfect and erring like themselves, rather than the will of God, which is the only standard of perfection. . . .

It is the duty of a government, to do all in its power to promote the present and future prosperity of the nation, over which it is placed. This prosperity will depend on the character of its citizens. The characters of these will be formed by their mothers; and it is through the mothers, that the government can control the characters of its future citizens, to form them such as will ensure their country's prosperity. If this is the case, then it is the duty of our present legislators to begin now, to form the characters of the next generation, by controling that of the females, who are to be their mothers, while it is yet with them a season of improvement.

But should the conclusion be almost admitted, that our sex too are the legitimate children of the legislature; and, that it is their duty to afford us a share of their paternal bounty; the phantom of a college-learned lady, would be ready to rise up, and destroy every good resolution, which the admission of this truth would naturally produce in our favour.

To shew that it is not a masculine education which is here recommended, and to afford a definite view of the manner in which a female institution might possess the respectability, permanency, and uniformity of operation of those appropriated to males; and yet differ from them, so as to be adapted to that difference of character and duties, to which the softer sex should be formed, is the object of the following imperfect

SKETCH OF A FEMALE SEMINARY

[Under that section title, Mrs. Willard describes the institution she proposes to create. Instruction will fall under four categories: religious and moral, literary, domestic, and ornamental. The literary course includes natural philosophy and resembles more closely than the other three the academic course given male students. The ornamental course comprises "drawing and painting, elegant penmanship, music, and the grace of motion."]

Catherine E. Beecher, Suggestions Respecting Improvements in Education (1829)

Catherine E. Beecher (1800–78) was one of eleven children of the famous preacher Lyman Beecher and sister of Harriet Beecher Stowe and Henry Ward Beecher. From 1823 to 1827 she directed a girls' seminary in Hartford, Connecticut. Although a propagandist for teacher training for women, Miss Beecher opposed woman suffrage and is one of many famous women who were feminists on some subjects but not on others. [*Suggestions Respecting Improvements in Education, Presented to the Trustees of the Hartford Female Seminary, and Published at Their Request* (Hartford, 1829), pp. 49–54.]

Another defect in education has arisen from the fact, that teachers have depended too much upon *authority*, and too little upon *the affections*, in guiding the objects of their care. It is not uncommon to see teachers in their intercourse with pupils, feeling it *necessary*, to maintain a dignity and reserve, which keeps their scholars at such a distance as prevents all assimilation of feeling and interest. . . . [O]ften times teachers are so oppressed with care and responsibility, and their efforts are so constantly needed in discharging other duties, that it is *impossible* to seek a frequent and familiar intercourse with their pupils. Yet still it is believed, that if teachers generally would make this a *definite object* of attention and effort, more than double the influence could be exerted over the minds of their charges; for the *wishes* of a beloved teacher, have unspeakably more influence, than the *authority* of one who is always beheld only at a respectful distance.

For these and other reasons, it seems of great importance that the formation of the female character should be committed to the female hand. It will be long, if ever, before the female mind can boast of the accurate knowledge, the sound judgment, and ready discrimination which the other sex may claim. But if the mind is to be guided chiefly by means of the affections; if the regulation of the disposition, the manners, the social habits and the moral feelings, are to be regarded before the mere acquisition of knowledge, is not *woman* best fitted to accomplish these important objects[?] Beside this, in order to secure the correction and formation of intellectual and moral character which is deemed so important, it is necessary that a degree of familiarity of intercourse, at all times and places, an intimate knowledge of feelings, affections, and weaknesses be sought by a teacher, which is not practicable or proper for one of the other sex to attain.

It may be said, and said truly, that women are not prepared by *sufficient knowledge* to become teachers in many branches. But they *can be prepared*, and where they are not so well qualified as one of the other sex, they so often excel in patience and persevering interest, as to more than counter-balance the deficiency.

The writer cannot but believe, that all female institutions, for these and *many other reasons* ought to be conducted exclusively by females, *so soon as suitable teachers of their own sex can be prepared*. And is it not an indication that such is the will of

Providence, when we see a *profession*, offering influence, respectability and independence, thrown open to women? Until this day no other profession could with propriety admit the female aspirant, nor till this day has the profession of a teacher been the road to honour, influence, and emolument. But the feelings of enlightened society are fast changing on this momentous subject. Men of learning, genius, and enterprize are entering this long neglected profession, bringing the aid of their honours, influence, and talents to render it both lucrative and respectable. The time is not far distant when it will become an honourable profession, and beneath its liberal portal, woman is gladly welcomed to lawful and unsullied honours. Here, all that stimulus of motive which animates the other sex in their several professions, may be applied to quicken and animate her energies. *She* also, can discern before her the road to honourable independence, and extensive usefulness, where she need not outstep the proscribed boundaries of feminine modesty, nor diminish one of those retiring graces that must ever constitute her most attractive charms.

Woman has been but little aware of the high incitements that should stimulate to the cultivation of her noblest powers. The world is no longer to be governed by *physical* force, but by *the influence which mind exerts over mind.* How are the great springs of action in the political world put in motion? Often by the secret workings of a *single mind,* that in retirement plans its schemes, and comes forth to execute them only by presenting motives of prejudice, passion, self-interest, or pride to operate on other minds.

Now the world is chiefly governed by motives that men *are ashamed to own.* When do we find mankind acknowledging that their efforts in political life are the offspring of pride, and the desire of self-aggrandizement, and yet who hesitates to believe that this is true?

But there *is* a class of motives that men are not only willing, but proud to own. Man does not willingly yield to force; he is ashamed to own he can yield to fear; he will not acknowledge his motives of pride, prejudice, or passion. But none are unwilling to own they can be governed by *reason,* even the worst will boast of being regulated by *conscience*, and where is the person who is ashamed to own the influence of the kind and generous emotions of the heart[?] Here then is the only lawful field for the ambition of our sex. Woman in all her relations is bound to "honour and obey" those on whom she depends for protection and support, nor does the truly feminine mind desire to exceed this limitation of Heaven. But where the dictates of authority may never controul, the voice of reason and affection, may ever convince and persuade; and while others govern by motives that mankind are ashamed to own, the dominion of woman may be based on influence that the heart is proud to acknowledge.

And if it is indeed the truth, that reason and conscience guide to the only path of happiness, and if affection will gain a hold on these powerful principles which can be attained no other way, what high and holy motives are presented to woman for cultivating her noblest powers. The development of the reasoning faculties, the fascination of a purified imagination, the charms of a cultivated taste, the quick perceptions of an active mind, the power of exhibiting truth and reason, by perspicuous, and animated conversation and writing, all these can be employed by woman as much as by man. And with these attainable facilities for gaining influence, woman has already received from the hand of her Maker those warm affections and quick susceptibilities, which can most surely gain the empire of the heart.

Woman has never wakened to her highest destinies and holiest hopes. She has yet to learn the purifying and blessed influence she may gain and maintain over the intellect and affections of the human mind. Though she may not teach from the portico, nor thunder from the forum, in her secret retirements she may form and send forth the sages that shall govern and renovate the world. Though she may not gird herself for bloody conflict, nor sound the trumpet of war, she may enwrap herself in the panoply of Heaven, and send the thrill of benevolence through a thousand youthful hearts. Though she may not enter the lists in legal collision, nor sharpen her intellect amid the passions and conflicts of men, she may teach the law of kindness, and hush up the discords and conflicts of life. Though she may not be cloathed as the ambassador of Heaven, nor minister at the altar of God; as a secret angel of mercy she may teach its will, and cause to ascend the humble, but most accepted sacrifice.

Sarah Moore Grimké, Intellect of Woman (1838)

"Intellect of Woman" is Letter X in Sarah M. Grimké's series of essays on the equality of the sexes. The difference between this and the two preceding documents is startling; the Grimké sisters never hedged their claim to complete equality. [The *Liberator*, January 26, 1838.]

MY DEAR SISTER,—It will scarcely be denied, I presume, that, as a general rule, men do not desire the improvement of women. There are few instances of men who are magnanimous enough to be entirely willing that women should know more than themselves, on any subjects except dress and cookery; and, indeed, this necessarily flows from their assumption of superiority. As *they* have determined that Jehovah has placed woman on a lower platform than man, they of course wish to keep her there; and hence the noble faculties of our minds are crushed, and our reasoning powers are almost wholly uncultivated.

. . . Within the last century, it has been gravely asserted that, "chemistry enough to keep the pot boiling, and geography enough to know the location of the different rooms in her house, is learning sufficient for a woman." Byron, who was too sensual to conceive of a pure and perfect companionship between the sexes, would limit a woman's library to a Bible and cookery book. I have myself heard men, who knew for themselves the value of intellectual culture, say they cared very little for a wife who could not make a pudding, and smile with contempt at the ardent thirst for knowledge exhibited by some women.

But all this is miserable wit and worse philosophy. It exhibits that passion for the gratification of a pampered appetite, which is beneath those who claim to be so far above us, and may justly be placed on a par with the policy of the slaveholder, who says that men will be better slaves, if they are not permitted to learn to read. . . .

Matilda Joslyn Gage, Woman as Inventor (1870)

Matilda Joslyn Gage (1826–98), an authority on the history of women's status, lived all her life in upstate New York. Her first public appearance as a feminist was at the 1852 National Woman's Rights Convention in Syracuse, where she was the youngest participant. She helped to organize both the New York State Woman Suffrage Association and the National Woman Suffrage Association in 1869. This thirty-two-page pamphlet discusses inventions by women in various countries and centuries, and ends with an account of ancient goddesses and their attributes. [*Woman as Inventor* (Fayetteville, N.Y., 1870), pp. 3–4, 6–7.]

THE COTTON GIN

It may, perhaps, be unknown to many persons, that the invention of the cotton-gin, one of the greatest mechanical triumphs of modern times, is due to a woman. Although the work on the model was done by the hands of Eli Whitney, yet Mrs. Greene originated the idea, and knowing Whitney to be a practical mechanic, she suggested his doing the work. This was during the winter of 1792–3, when he was a guest at her house, near Savannah.

Mrs. Greene, whose maiden name was Catharine Littlefield, was the widow of Gen. Greene, of Revolutionary memory. After the return of peace Gen. Greene moved with his family from Rhode Island to Mulberry Grove, on the Savannah river, where he soon died, leaving his estate much embar[r]assed and five children for his wife to educate. Shortly after this, Eli Whitney went south to teach in a private family. When he reached Georgia he found his place supplied, and thereupon decided to apply himself to the study of law, making Mrs. Greene's house his home.

The great difficulty of separating cotton from the seed was at that time a staple subject of complaint among cotton-planters. To separate a pound of the black seed variety, to which the lint does not adhere even so closely as to the green, was a negro's task for a day. So slow was the process that it became the regular practice for all the family of a cotton-planter to engage every night in the laborious work; and the task was looked upon as so great that it was the ordinary topic of conversation among those who cultivated cotton, and a fortune was prophesied for the lucky inventor of a machine capable of doing the work.

It was after a conversation of this character, which had been held by some guests in her house, that Mrs. Greene proposed to Whitney the making of such a machine, and upon her idea he commenced.

The work was done in her house, and under her immediate supervision. The wooden teeth first tried did not do the work well, and Whitney, despairing, was about to throw the work aside, when Mrs. Greene, whose confidence in ultimate success never wavered, proposed the substitution of wire. Whitney thereupon replaced the wooden by wire teeth, and within ten days from the first conception of Mrs. Greene's idea a small model was completed.

This primitive little model was of such perfect construction that it has ever since stood as the model of all cotton-gins, and the inventive genius of universal male Yankeedom has not yet been able to suggest any practical improvement in the machine. Mrs. Greene, through her second husband, Mr. Miller, became the partner of Whitney in the manufacture of gins. . . .

It may be asked why Mrs. Greene did not take out the patent in her own name. To have done so would have exposed her to the contumely and ridicule of her friends. Custom, that unwritten law, has for years frowned upon any attempt of woman to take such a step. If she has been gifted with an inventive genius, she has either stifled its exercise, expended it upon style of dress— that being deemed her legitimate province—or, like Mrs. Greene, suffered some man to claim the award her due. She shrunk [*sic*] from the persecution that would have attended her claiming the patent, while by associating herself with Whitney as his partner in the manufacture of the machines, she hoped at least to share in the pecuniary advantages of the invention.

Women have not dared to exercise their faculties except in certain directions, unless in a covert manner. A knowledge of mechanics has been deemed unwomanly, and yet I have known women whose natural tastes led them to be interested in everything pertaining to this science.

I once had a lady friend, who, to use her own words, "had a perfect passion for engineering," and who if she "had been a man, would have been an engineer."

But she was a woman. She had been taught from her earliest childhood that to make use of this talent with which God had endowed her, would be an outrage against society; so she lived for a few years, going through the routine of breakfasts and dinners, journeys and parties, that society demanded of her, and at last sank into her grave, after having been of little use either to the world or herself.

What a benefit she might have been to her sex had she dared to exercise her powers. Her example would have opened the way for hundreds more to find health and wages and freedom in some congenial occupation outside of the prescribed limits.

So of Mrs. Greene. Had the patent of the cotton-gin been taken in her own name, either singly or in union with Whitney, what a wide-spread benefit her example would have been to others of her sex. . . .

M. Carey Thomas, Present Tendencies in Women's College and University Education (1908)

M. Carey Thomas (1857–1935), a Baltimore-born Quaker, was a Phi Beta Kappa graduate of Cornell, class of 1877. She received her Ph.D., summa cum laude, at Zurich, 1882, and returned to become dean and professor of English literature at Bryn Mawr College, where she served as president from 1894 to 1922. This speech was delivered at the twenty-fifth anniversary celebration of the Association of Collegiate Alumnae in November 1907. ["Present Tendencies in Women's College and University Education," *Publications of the Association of Collegiate Alumnae*, Series III, No. 17 (February 1908), 45–50, 54–56, 60–62.]

. . . I doubt if the most imaginative and sympathetic younger women in this audience can form any conception of what it means to women of the old advance guard, among whom you will perhaps allow me to include myself, to be able to say to each other without fear of contradiction that in the twenty-five years covered by the work of the Association of Collegiate Alumnae the battle for the higher education of women has been gloriously, and forever, won.

The passionate desire of the women of my generation for higher education was accompanied throughout its course by the awful doubt, felt by women themselves as well as by men, as to whether women as a sex were physically and mentally fit for it. I think I can best make this clear to you if I refer briefly to my own experience. I cannot remember the time when I was not sure that studying and going to college were the things above all others which I wished to do. I was always wondering whether it could be really true, as everyone thought, that boys were cleverer than girls. Indeed, I cared so much that I never dared to ask any grown-up person the direct question, not even my father or mother, because I feared to hear the reply. I remember often praying about it, and begging God that if it were true that because I was a girl I could not successfully master Greek and go to college and understand things to kill me at once, as I could not bear to live in such an unjust world. When I was a little older I read the Bible entirely through with passionate eagerness, because I had heard it said that it proved that women were inferior to men. Those were not the days of the higher criticism. I can remember weeping over the account of Adam and Eve because it seemed to me that the curse pronounced on Eve might imperil girls' going to college;

and to this day I can never read many parts of the Pauline epistles without feeling again the sinking of the heart with which I used to hurry over the verses referring to women's keeping silence in the churches and asking their husbands at home. I searched not only the Bible, but all other books I could get for light on the woman question. I read Milton with rage and indignation. Even as a child I knew him for the woman hater he was. The splendor of Shakspere was obscured to me then by the lack of intellectual power in his greatest woman characters. Even now it seems to me that only Isabella in *Measure for Measure* thinks greatly, and weighs her actions greatly, like a Hamlet or a Brutus.

I can well remember one endless scorching summer's day when, sitting in a hammock under the trees with a French dictionary, blinded by tears more burning than the July sun, I translated the most indecent book I have ever read, Michelet's famous—were it not now forgotten, I should be able to say infamous—book on woman, *La Femme.* I was beside myself with terror lest it might prove true that I myself was so vile and pathological a thing. Between that summer's day in 1874, and a certain day in the autumn of 1904, thirty years had elapsed. Although during these thirty years I had read in every language every book on women that I could obtain, I had never chanced again upon a book that seemed to me so to degrade me in my womanhood as the seventh and seventeenth chapters on women and women's education of President Stanley Hall's *Adolescence.* Michelet's sickening sentimentality and horrible over-sexuality seemed to me to breathe again from every pseudo-scientific page.

But how vast the difference between then and now in my feelings, and in the feelings of every woman who has had to do with the education of girls! Then I was terror-struck lest I, and every other woman with me, were doomed to live as pathological invalids in a universe merciless to woman as a sex. Now we know that it is not we, but the man who believes such things about us, who is himself pathological, blinded by neurotic mists of sex, unable to see that women form one-half of the kindly race of normal, healthy human creatures in the world; that women, like men, are quickened and inspired by the same great traditions of their race, by the same love of learning, the same love of science, the same love of abstract truth; that women, like men, are immeasurably benefited, physically, mentally, and morally, and are made vastly better mothers, as men are made vastly better fathers, by subordinating the distracting instincts of sex to the simple human fellowship of similar education, and similar intellectual and social ideals.

It was not to be wondered at that we were uncertain in those old days as to the ultimate result of women's education. Before I myself went to college I had seen only one college woman. I had heard that such a woman was staying at the house of an acquaintance. I went to see her with fear. Even if she had appeared in hoofs and horns I was determined to go to college all the same. But it was a relief to find this Vassar graduate tall and handsome and dressed like other women. When, five years later, I went to Leipsig to study after I had been graduated from Cornell, my mother used to write me that my name was never mentioned to her by the women of her acquaintance. I was thought by them to be as much of a disgrace to my family as if I had eloped with the coachman. Now, women who have been to college are as plentiful as blackberries on summer hedges. Even my native city of Baltimore is full of them, and women who have in addition studied in Germany are regarded with becoming deference by the very Baltimore women who disapproved of me.

During the quarter of the century of the existence of the Association of Collegiate Alumnae two generations of college women have reached mature life, and the older generation is now just passing off the stage. We are, therefore, better prepared than ever before to give an account of what has been definitely accomplished, and to predict what will be the tendencies of women's college and university education in the future.

I think I can best tell you in a concrete way what has been accomplished in women's education by describing to you the condition of affairs which I found in 1884, when I returned from Germany, and set about planning the academic organization of Bryn Mawr. The outlook was discouraging except for the delight women were beginning to show in going to college . . . . Women were teaching in Wellesley, Mount Holyoke, and Smith without even the elementary training of a college course behind them. . . . When I protested to the president of the most advanced college for women in regard to this lack of training, he told me that we could never run Bryn Mawr if we insisted on the same scholarly attainments in women professors as in men professors. He . . . and the president of perhaps the greatest university for men in the United States, both told me that there was an intuitive something in ladies of birth and position, which enabled them to do without college training, and to make on the whole better professors for women college students than if they had themselves been to college.

Everyone I consulted prophesied disaster if we carried out our plan of appointing to our professorships young unmarried men of high scientific promise. They said: in the first place, such men will not consent to teach women in a women's college; in the second place, if they should consent, their unmarried students will distract their minds; and in the third place, if by chance they should be able to teach coherently, then surely such will be the charm of their bachelor estate that their girl students will compete with each other for proposals out of the classroom rather than for marks in the classroom. . . .

Unmarried men are now teaching in all colleges for women. The experience of Bryn Mawr has proved that men of the highest scholarly reputation are not only willing to accept positions in a college for women, but that they decline to resign them except for the most tempting posts in colleges for men. . . . Bryn Mawr has also proved that a faculty composed of such men has no hesitation in working under a woman president, or under women scholars as heads of departments when they too are eminent. In the world of intellect eminence is so rare, and excellence of any kind so difficult to attain, that when we are dealing with intellectual values, or genuine scholarly, literary, or artistic excellence, the question of sex tends to become as unimportant to men as to women. . . .

We did not really know anything about even the ordinary everyday intellectual capacity of women when we began to educate them. We were not even sure that they inherited their intellects from their fathers as well as from their mothers. We were told that their brains were too light, their foreheads too small, their reasoning powers too defective, their emotions too easily worked upon to make good students. None of these things has proved to be so. Perhaps the most wonderful thing of all to have come true is the wholly unexpected, but altogether delightful, mental ability shown by women college students. We should have been satisfied if they had been proved to be only a little less good than men college students, but, tested by every known test of examination, or classroom recitation, women have proved themselves equal to men, even slightly superior. It is more like a fairy story than ever to discover that they are not only as good, but even a little better. When this came to be clearly recognized, as was the case early in the movement, we were asked to remember that those first women students were a picked class, and could not fairly be compared to average men students. But now in many colleges, such as Chicago, the numbers of men and women are practically equal, and many of the women who attend college today have not the bread and butter incentive of men to do well in their classes, yet the slight superiority continues. Year after year, for example, Chicago reports fewer absences and fewer conditions incurred by women than by men in the same classes. . . .

And just because women have shown such an aptitude for a true college education and such delight in it, we must be careful to maintain it for them in its integrity. We must see to it that its disciplinary quality is not lowered by the insertion of so-called practical courses which are falsely supposed to prepare for life. . . .

Indeed, I personally have come to regard this vitally important question in education as now settled for most truly intelligent and open-minded people by the very costly method of practical experiment. I am in consequence astounded to see the efforts which have been made within the past few years, and perhaps never more persistently than during the past year, to persuade, I might almost say to compel, those in charge of women's education to riddle the college curriculum of women with hygiene, and sanitary drainage, and domestic science, and child-study, and all the rest of the so-called practical studies.

The argument is a specious one at first sight and seems reasonable. It is urged that college courses for women should be less varied than for men and should fit them primarily for the two great vocations of women, marriage or teaching, the training of children in the home, or in the schoolroom. Nothing more disastrous for women, or for men, can be conceived of than this specialized education for women as a sex. It has been wholly overlooked that any form of specialized education, which differs from men's education, will tend to unfit women in less than a generation to teach their own boys at home, as well as, of course, other boys in the schoolroom. Women so educated will eventually be driven out of the teaching profession, or confined wholly to the teaching of girls. But there is a more far-reaching answer to this short-sighted demand for specialized women's courses. If 50 per cent. of college women are to marry, and nearly 40 per cent. are to bear and rear children, such women cannot conceivably be given an education too broad, too high, too deep, to fit them to become the educated mothers of the future race of men and women to be born of educated parents. Somehow or other such mothers must be made familiar with the great mass of inherited knowledge which is handed on from generation to generation of civilized educated men. . . . If it is true—and it is absolutely true—that all subjects do not train the mind and heart and intellect equally well, it is also true that sanitary and domestic science are not among the great disciplinary race studies. The place for such studies, and they undoubtedly have an important place, is *after* the college course, not during it. They belong with law, medicine, dentistry, engineering, architecture, agriculture in the professional school, not in the college. . . .

And for college women who may be teachers as well as for those who may be mothers, any form of special education is also highly objectionable. If the education of women is directed mainly, or exclusively, toward the profession of teaching, such specialized training will drive women who must support themselves into the teaching profession without regard to their special qualifications for teaching, which will be an overwhelming misfortune for the women themselves as well as for the children they teach. If women are to support themselves, even as generally as they do now, they must be trained so as to find ready admission into the professions and into different kinds of business activity. Their education must be at least as varied, and open to modification, as men's education. . . .

[There follows a long argument in favor of women's colleges' having graduate schools and offering the Doctor of Philosophy degree.]

But there is still another and, as it seems to me, more cogent reason for our women's colleges maintaining graduate schools of philosophy. The highest service which colleges can render to their time is to discover and foster imaginative and constructive genius. Such genius unquestionably needs opportunity for its highest development. This is peculiarly the case with women students. As I watch their gallant struggles I sometimes think that the very stars in their courses are conspiring against them. Women scholars can assist women students, as men cannot, to tide over the first discouragements of a life of intellectual renunciation. Ability of the kind I am speaking of is, of course, very rare, but for this reason it is precious beyond all other human products. If the graduate schools of women's colleges could develop one single woman of Galton's "X" type—say a Madame Curie or a Madame Kovalewsky born under a happier star—they would have done more for human advancement than if they had turned out thousands of ordinary college graduates.

The time has now come for those of us who are in control of women's education to bend ourselves to the task of creating academic conditions favorable for the development of this kind of creative ability. We should at once begin to found research chairs for women at all our women's colleges, with three or four hours a week of research training and the rest of the time free for independent investigation. We should bring pressure on our state universities to give such women opportunities to compete for professors' chairs. In the four woman-suffrage states this can be accomplished in the twinkling of an eye: it will only be necessary for women's organizations to vote for university regents with proper opinions. The Johns Hopkins University situated in conservative Baltimore has two women on its academic staff who are lecturing to men. Why cannot all chairs in the arts departments of universities, that is, in the college and school of philosophy, be thrown open to the competition of women? This is the next advance to be made in women's education—the last and greatest battle to be won.

But have women ability of this highest kind to be developed? Can they compete successfully with men in the field of original and productive scholarship? Before this pertinent question even our dearest friends among college presidents and professors who are generously educating women balk and shy and lose themselves in a maze of platitudes about women's receptive and unoriginal minds.[1] But what do we ourselves, what do we women, think? I for one am sure that women possess this ability. My opinion has been greatly strengthened by the scientific and sociological investigations of the past few years. Recent studies in heredity, including the work on Mendel's law, seem to me to show conclusively that boys and girls inherit equally from both mothers and fathers in mathematical proportion, that a woman's place in the inheritance and transmission of physical and mental and moral qualities is precisely the same as a man's, that she is discriminated against in no way. . . .

It seems to me, then, to rest with us, the college women of this generation, to see to it that the girls of the next generation are given favorable conditions for this higher kind of scholarly development. To advance the boundaries of human knowledge however little is to exercise our highest human faculty. There is no more altruistic satisfaction, no purer delight. I am convinced that we can do no more useful work than this—to make it possible

[1] See President David Starr Jordan, "The Higher Education of Women," *Popular Science Monthly*, December 1902, pp. 97 ff. (See especially pp. 100, 106.) [*Author's note.*]

for the few women of creative and constructive genius born in any generation to join the few men of genius of their generation in the service of their common race.

Anna Garlin Spencer, Woman's Share in Social Culture (1912)

Anna Garlin Spencer (1851–1931) taught in Providence, Rhode Island, public schools, 1870–71, and worked as a journalist for the Providence *Daily Journal*, 1869–78. In 1878 she married a Unitarian minister who encouraged her to preach, and in 1891 she was ordained and installed as minister in an independent church in Providence, where she stayed fourteen years. The book excerpted here is a collection of her articles that appeared originally in *The Forum*. In the following selection, using the medical profession as an example, she discusses the artificial obstacles to the development of genius in women and how some women nevertheless have achieved eminence. [*Woman's Share in Social Culture* (New York, 1912), pp. 66–85, from chap. iii: "The Drama of the Woman of Genius." Footnotes omitted.]

"Talent," says Lowell, "is that which is in a man's power; genius is that in whose power a man is." If genius, even in its lesser ranges, be this irresistible pressure toward some unique self-expression, then women cannot be left out of the charmed circle; especially when we remember Helen Hunt with her solitary but wide approach to love and life, and Emily Dickinson, that hermit thrush among poets. Nor can those unique interpreters of art and literature among women whose vital expression has so enhanced the works of genius as to make them seem new creations, be left out of the count. In modern times, the growing company of musicians, some of them composers, and the artists of pen and brush, and the sculptors among women who swell the secondary ranks of genius in numbers and in power, must have increasing recognition.

All this, however, does not reach the deepest considerations involved in taking account of the intellectual contribution of women to art, science, philosophy and affairs. Whatever may be the reasons in nature for the lower level of women along these lines of man's greatest achievement, there are the gravest reasons in circumstance for the comparatively meagre showing. In addition to the handicap of lack of education, a handicap which no exceptional success of the self-made man or woman can offset for the majority of the talented, there is a no less important deprivation which all women have suffered in the past and most women now suffer. This deprivation is that of the informal but highly stimulating training which the good fellowship of their chosen guild of study and of service gives to men, but which is denied for the most part even to professional women. For example, women have been in the medical profession for a considerable time, and have obtained high distinction in it. They have won just recognition from many influential doctors of the other sex. Yet they can hardly be said to have entered the inner circle of their clan. They may stop to dinner at medical conventions, it is true, provided they make no fuss about smoking and do not mind being in the minority; but there are few men, even in that enlightened group, who can so sink sex-consciousness in professional comradeship as either to give or get the full social value that might be gained from a mixed company of like vocation. The women lawyers and members of the clergy are in even smaller minority, and hence suffer still more from that embarrassment of the "exception" which prevents easy and familiar association. In the teaching profession, where the relative numbers of the sexes are reversed, there is often more adequate professional intercourse; but the woman college professor, or college president, is still that one among many whose reception into her special class, even if courteous and friendly, is too formal and occasional for real guild fellowship.

To this negative deprivation must be added the positive opposition of men to the entrance of women into that professional life and work from which the genius arises as the rare flower from a vast field. The whole course of evolution in industry, and in the achievements of higher education and exceptional talent, has shown man's invariable tendency to shut women out when their activities have reached a highly specialized period of growth. The primitive woman-worker, as Jack-at-all-trades, does not develop any one employment to its height of perfection. Gradually initiating old men and boys, not fitted for war and the chase, into these varied forms of effort, women start the other sex toward that concentration of effort upon one process-activity which finally develops separate arts, sciences and professions. When this point is reached, the "woman's work" usually becomes "man's work"; and when that time comes, men turn round and shut out women from the labor which women themselves have initiated. This monopolistic tendency of men is shown most clearly in the history of the learned professions. Women were seldom, if ever, priests but they participated in religious services when religion was a family affair. When a priestly caste arose and became the symbol of peculiar authority, only men entered its ranks. Woman can reënter her natural place as religious leader only through the Theological Schools and Ordination, and these have been forbidden her until very recently and are now seldom open to her in full measure. . . .

Again, women developed law and its application to life in the germs of family rule and tribal custom quite as much as did men; but when statutes took the place of tradition, and courts superseded personal judgeship, and when a special class of lawyers was needed to define and administer laws, which grew more difficult to understand with growing complexity of social relationship, men alone entered that profession. . . .

This process of differentiating and perfecting intellectual labor, the process in which at most acute periods of specialization and advance, women were wholly shut out of their own ancient work, finds its most complete and its most dramatic illustration in the history of the medical profession. Some phases of the healing art have always been connected in primitive society with the priestly office and, hence, in the hands of men. Three great branches, however, were always, in all forms of social organization of which we have knowledge, in the hands exclusively of women, namely, midwifery, the treatment of diseases of women so far as those were cared for at all, and the diseases of children. . . . The result of this sex-segregation in the care of the sick in these important branches has been that women doctors, unschooled but often not unskilled, have served all the past of human experience in childbirth, in child-care, and in the special illnesses of women. This has been true in our own, as well as in older civilizations up to the 18th century. In our own country, in colonial times, only women ushered into a bleak New England the potential citizens of the new world. We read of Mrs. Wiat, who died in 1705 at the age of 94 years, having assisted as midwife at the birth of more than 1,100 children. And in Rehoboth, one of the oldest communities in Massachusetts, the Town Meeting itself "called" from England "Dr. Sam Fuller and his mother," he to practise medicine and she "as midwife to answer to the town's necessity, which was great." Busied with other matters, the Colonies paid little attention to medical science until the war of the American Revolution betrayed the awful results of ignorance in the slaughter of soldiers by preventable disease. When the healing art began to become a true science and took great strides toward better training and facilities of practice for the student, attention was at once drawn to the need for better service in the fields wholly occupied by women. The opening and improvement of the medical schools, however, was a new opportunity for men alone and the new demand for more scientific care of women in childbirth and for higher medical service to childhood and for the women suffering from special diseases, resulted in the greatest of innovations, namely, the assumption by men of the office of midwife and their entrance into the most intimate relationships with women patients. Dr. James Lloyd, after two years' study in England, began to practise "obstetrics" (the new name that disguised in some degree the daring change in medical practice) in Boston, in 1762. Dr. Shippen, similarly trained abroad, took up the same practice in Philadelphia and added lectures upon the subject. Thus began in our own country the elevation of this important branch of the healing art to a professional standard and the consequent exclusion of women from their immortal rights in the sickroom. It was a poor recognition of the debt the race owed to the mother-sex, both as suffering the pangs of childbirth and as helping to assuage them and in caring for the infants and children of all time! After men entered upon the task of perfecting the medical profession, and incidentally shutting women out of it, it did not take long, however, for the thoughtful to see the propriety of allowing women those advantages of training which would put them back again into their rightful place on the higher plane of science now demanded. What gave sharp point to this feeling was the common opposition to men engaging in these ancient prerogatives of women. This was at first as intense and as bitter as the later opposition to the entrance of women into the co-educational medical schools. . . . The first women who tried to secure training in medical schools in order to reënter those branches of the healing art from which they had so recently been driven, and on the higher plane of science now properly demanded, endured such hardships as made them veritable martyrs. In 1847 Harriot K. Hunt knocked at the door of Harvard Medical School to be persistently refused admission. In 1849 Elizabeth Blackwell graduated from Geneva Medical School, having secured instruction as a special favor, and began her great career, devoted equally to securing the best possible medical training for women, and to elevating to higher standards than had as yet been attained by men the whole area of medical training. Among the heroic figures of these early days are to be found many married women whose husbands, often themselves physicians, helped them to obtain their training. . . . The attitude of the men of the medical profession generally, however, was one of the utmost hostility, showing every form of monopolistic selfishness and injustice. England, which had led the United States in all medical advance, gave belated attention to the needs of women. Not until 1872 was the Medical department of the London University opened to women, and when they were declared eligible for its medical degree many indignant men-graduates of the institution protested that their "property rights had been invaded by this action"; that for women to be able legally to practise medicine "lowered the value of their own diplomas, and, therefore, the University had violated its contract with men by allowing women to share its privileges."

All this was without reference to the intellectual standing or practical efficiency of the women graduates. The mere fact of women entering the profession meant, in the minds of these protestants, degradation to the men already in it! Earlier than this, in 1859, the Medical Society of the County of Philadelphia passed "resolutions of excommunication" against every physician who should "teach in a medical school for women" and every one who should "consult with a woman physician or with a man teaching a woman medical student." In Massachusetts after qualified women physicians were given State certificates to practise, the Massachusetts Medical Society forbade them membership, thus refusing to admit the legality of diplomas already sanctioned by the highest authority. The facts that women medical students, like those of the other sex, required clinic teaching and hospital training for proper preparation, and that, since hospital opportunities could not be adequately duplicated, women must be taught with men in this field, gave the pioneer women medical students a peculiar discipline of hardship. When the gentle Ann Preston and the highly bred and scientifically trained Emmeline Cleveland led their classes of women into the amphitheatre of the operating room of the first hospital opened to women for this clinic training, the men students howled and called vile names and made the women, on leaving the hospital, pass through a lane of riotous men all shouting indecencies at women so far above them in moral height that they could not touch them where their spirits lived, even by personal violence! . . . Nevertheless, the women did reënter their ancient profession of healing after a brief exclusion. So far from permanently lowering the standards of training newly established, their chief pioneer leader, Elizabeth Blackwell, was instrumental in inaugurating modern preventive medicine, by the establishment in the New York Medical College for Women, opened in 1865, of the first chair of Hygiene ever set apart in a medical college in the United States. In 1882 this pioneer medical college for women set forth the bravest and truest of philosophies respecting women's work in the following words: "We call upon all those who believe in the higher education of women to help set the highest possible standards for their medical education; and we call upon those who do not believe in such higher education to help in making such requirements as shall turn aside the incompetent;—not by any exercise of arbitrary power, but by a demonstration of incapacity, which is the only logical, manly reason for refusing to allow women to pursue an honorable calling in an honorable way."

This brief allusion to the heroic struggle of woman to reënter the healing art against the positive opposition of men already entrenched in all the coigns of vantage in professional training and organized professional guilds, furnishes a flashlight picture of the whole course of woman's entrance into the more modern types of differentiated labor. . . .

In addition to these handicaps must be named the well-known but scarcely adequately measured interruptions to both study and self-expression which the women of talent and specialized power have always experienced. Anyone can see that to write *Uncle Tom's Cabin* on the knee in the kitchen, with constant calls to cooking and other details of housework to punctuate the paragraphs, was a more difficult achievement than to write it at leisure in a quiet room. And when her biographer says of an Italian woman poet, "during some years her Muse was intermitted," we do not wonder at the fact when he casually mentions her ten children. No record, however, can even name the women of talent who were so submerged by child-bearing and its duties, and by "general housework," that they had to leave their poems and stories all unwritten. Moreover, the obstacles to intellectual development and achievement which marriage and maternity interpose (and which are so important that they demand a separate study) are not the only ones that must be noted. It is not alone the fact that women have generally had to spend most of their strength in caring for others that has handicapped them in individual effort; but also that they have almost universally had to care wholly for themselves. Women even now have the burden of the care of their belongings, their dress, their home life of whatever sort it may be, and the social duties of the smaller world, even if doing great things in individual work. A successful woman preacher was once asked "what special obstacles have you met as a woman in the ministry?" "Not one," she answered, "except the lack of a minister's wife." When we read of Charles Darwin's wife not only relieving him from financial cares but seeing that he had his breakfast in his room, with "nothing to disturb the freshness of his morning," we do not find the explanation of Darwin's genius, but we do see how he was helped to express it. Men geniuses, even of second grade, have usually had at least one woman to smooth their way, and often several women to make sure that little things, often even self-support itself, did not interfere with the development and expression of their talent. On the other hand, the obligation of all the earlier women writers to prepare a useful cook-book in order to buy their way into literature, is a fitting symbol of the compulsion laid upon women, however gifted, to do all the things that women in general accomplish before entering upon their special tasks. That brave woman who wanted to study medicine so much that not even the heaviest family burdens could deter her from entering the medical school first opened to her sex, but who "first sewed steadily until her entire family was fitted with clothes to last six months," is a not unusual type.

Added to all this, the woman of talent and of special gifts has had until very lately, and in most countries has still, to go against the massed social pressure of her time in order to devote herself to any particular intellectual task. The expectation of society has long pushed men toward some special work; the expectation of society has until recently been wholly against women's choosing any vocation beside their functional service in the family. This is a far more intense and all-pervading influence in deterring women from success in intellectual work than is usually understood. . . . No book has yet been written in praise of a woman who let her husband and children starve or suffer while she invented even the most useful things, or wrote books, or expressed herself in art, or evolved philosophic systems. On the contrary, the mildest approach on the part of a wife and mother, or even of a daughter or sister, to that intense interest in self-expression which has always characterized genius has been met with social disapproval and until very recent times with ostracism fit only for the criminal. Hence her inner impulsion has needed to be strong indeed to make any woman devote herself to ideas.

In view of these tremendous obstacles, it is fair to assume that when women in the past have achieved even a second or third place in the ranks of genius they have shown far more native ability than men have needed to reach the same eminence. Not excused from the more general duties that constitute the cement of society, most women of talent have had but one hand free with which to work out their ideal conceptions. Denied, at cost of "respectability" itself, any expression of that obstinate egotism which is nature's protection of the genius in his special task, and in the preparation for it, they have had to make secret and painful experiments in self-expression after spending first strength in the commonplace tasks required of all their sex.

The genius is at once the most self-centred and the most universal of human beings. He sees only himself and the world of thought or of affairs he would master for his special work. All that lies between, family, friends, social groups, is but material for his elect service. Delight in his own personality, absorbed attention to the processes of his own mind, have made him generally the master shirker in respect to the ordinary duties of life. He has been often "ill to live with," and greedy in demand upon the support and care of others. He is so rare and precious, however, that "with all his faults we love him still" when he enriches the commonwealth of thought, imagination or action with some new gift. But, alas, the "near" genius has too often the character frailties of the genuine great one without his power of achievement. We see therefore the social advantage of the poverty and hardships and lack of immediate appreciation which have so often weeded out from the lists, in advance, all but the giants in intellectual power. Seeing how many small people mistake their own strongly individualized taste for great talent, and feel justified in declining all disagreeable tasks of "menial" work on the plea of absorption in some form of effort which is mainly self-indulgence, we realize that nature has done well to discipline the would-be genius severely. The "artistic temperament" so often drops the final syllables to become mere vulgar "temper" that family life could not well bear the strain of greatly multiplying the type that for the most part only enjoys but does not produce masterpieces. But to suppress in wholesale fashion, and at the outset, all troublesome "variations" in women, while leaving men free to show what they can become and giving them besides a good chance to prove their quality, is to make that discipline too one-sided. The universal social pressure upon women to be all alike, and do all the same things, and to be content with identical restrictions, has resulted not only in terrible suffering in the lives of exceptional women, but also in the loss of unmeasured feminine values in special gifts. The Drama of the Woman of Genius has been too often a tragedy of misshapen and perverted power. Col. Higginson said that one of the great histories yet to be written is that of the intellectual life of women. When that is accomplished, those truly great women whose initiative was choked by false ideals of feminine excellence, whose natures were turned awry for want of "space to burgeon out their powers," whose very purpose to "aggrandize the human mind by cultivating their own" was made a cross for their crucifixion, will be given just honor.

2

RELIGION AND
WOMAN'S STATUS

Debate at Woman's Rights Convention (1854)

The following debate on the relation of religion to women's status contains expressions of opinions typical in that period. Most of the participants were leading abolitionists, including the antifeminist Rev. Henry Grew of Philadelphia. It took place during the Fifth National Woman's Rights Convention, October 1854, in Philadelphia. [*HWS* I, 379–83.]

. . . The Rev. HENRY GREW, of Philadelphia, then appeared upon the platform, and said he was sorry to differ from the general tone of the speakers present, but he felt it to be his duty to give his views on the questions under consideration. His opinions as to woman's rights and duties were based on the Scriptures. He quoted numerous texts to show that it was clearly the will of God that man should be superior in power and authority to woman; and asserted that no lesson is more plainly and frequently taught in the Bible, than woman's subjection.

Mrs. [HANNAH TRACY] CUTLER [of Illinois] replied at length, and skillfully turned every text he had quoted directly against the reverend gentleman, to the great amusement of the audience. She showed that man and woman were a simultaneous creation, with equal power and glory on their heads, and that dominion over the fowl of the air, the fish of the sea, and every creeping thing on the earth was given to *them*, and not to man alone. The time has come for woman to read and interpret Scripture for herself; too long have we learned God's will from the lips of man and closed our eyes on the great book of nature, and the safer teaching of our own souls. It is a pity that those who would recommend the Bible as the revealed will of the all-wise and benevolent Creator, should uniformly quote it on the side of tyranny and oppression. I think we owe it to our religion and ourselves to wrest it from such hands, and proclaim the beautiful spirit breathed through all its commands and precepts, instead of dwelling so much on isolated texts that have no application to our day and generation.

Mrs. [LUCRETIA] MOTT [of Pennsylvania] said: It is not Christianity, but priestcraft that has subjected woman as we find her. . . .

Blame is often attached to the position in which woman is found. I blame her not so much as I pity her. So circumscribed have been her limits that she does not realize the misery of her condition. Such dupes are men to custom that even servitude, the worst of ills, comes to be thought a good, till down from sire to son it is kept and guarded as a sacred thing. Woman's existence is maintained by sufferance. The veneration of man has been misdirected, the pulpit has been prostituted, the Bible has been ill-used. It has been turned over and over as in every reform. The temperance people have had to feel its supposed denunciations. Then the anti-slavery, and now this reform has met, and still continues to meet, passage after passage of the Bible, never intended to be so used. Instead of taking the truths of the Bible in corroboration of the right, the practice has been, to turn over its pages to find example and authority for the wrong, for the existing abuses of society. For the usage of drinking wine, the example of the sensualist Solomon, is always appealed to. In reference to our reform, even admitting that Paul did mean preach, when he used that term, he did not say that the recommendation of that time was to be applicable to the churches of all after-time. We have been so long pinning our faith on other people's sleeves that we ought to begin examining these things daily ourselves, to see whether they are so; and we should find on comparing text with text, that a very different construction might be put upon them. Some of our early Quakers not seeing how far they were to be carried, became Greek and Hebrew scholars, and they found that the text would bear other translations as well as other constructions. All Bible commentators agree that the Church of Corinth, when the apostle wrote, was in a state of great confusion. They fell into discussion and controversy; and in order to quiet this state of things and bring the Church to greater propriety, the command was given out that women should keep silence, and it was not permitted them to speak, except by asking questions at home. In the same epistle to the same Church, Paul gave express directions how women shall prophesy, which he defines to be preaching, "speaking to men," for "exhortation and comfort." He recognized them in prophesying and praying. The word translated "servant," is applied to a man in one part of the Scripture, and in another it is translated "minister." Now that same word you will find might be applied to Phebe, a deaconess. . . .

It is not so Apostolic to make the wife subject to the husband as many have supposed. It has been done by law and public opinion since that time. There has been a great deal said about sending missionaries over to the East to convert women who are immolating themselves on the funeral pile of their husbands. I know this may be a very good work, but I would ask you to look at it. How many women are there now immolated upon the shrine of superstition and priestcraft, in our very midst, in the assumption that man only has a right to the pulpit, and that if a woman enters it she disobeys God; making woman believe in the misdirection of her vocation, and that it is of divine authority that she should be thus bound. Believe it not, my sisters. In this same epistle the word "prophesying" should be "preaching"—"preaching godliness," etc. On the occasion of the first miracle which it is said Christ wrought, a woman went before Him and said, "Whatsoever he biddeth you do, that do." The woman of Samaria said, "Come and see the man who told me all the things that ever I did."

These things are worthy of note. I do not want to dwell too much upon Scripture authority. We too often bind ourselves by authorities rather than by the truth. We are infidel to truth in seeking examples to overthrow it. The very first act of note that is mentioned when the disciples and apostles went forth after Jesus was removed from them, was the bringing up of an ancient prophecy to prove that they were right in the position they assumed on that occasion, when men and women were gathered together on the holy day of Pentecost, when every man heard and saw those wonderful works which are recorded. Then Peter stood forth—some one has said that Peter made a great mistake in quoting the prophet Joel—but he stated that "the time is come, this day is fulfilled the prophecy, when it is said, I will pour out my spirit upon all flesh, and your sons and your daughters shall prophesy," etc.—the language of the Bible is beautiful in its repetition—"upon my servants and my handmaidens I will pour out my spirit and they shall prophesy." Now can anything be clearer than that?

Rev. Henry Grew again quoted Scripture in reply to Mrs. Mott, and said the coming of Christ into the world did not restore man and woman to the original condition of our first parents. If the position assumed by the women be true, then must the Divine Word from Genesis to Revelation be set aside as untrue, that woman may be relieved from the, perhaps, unfortunate limitations that hold her back in this age of progress. . . .

Mr. [William Lloyd] Garrison [of Massachusetts] said: Consulting the Bible for opinions as to woman's rights, is of little importance to the majority of this Convention. We have gone over the whole ground, and placed our cause upon the decrees of nature. We *know* that man and woman are equal in the sight of God. We know that texts and books are of no importance, and have no taste for the discussion of dry doctrinal points.

But with the American people the case is different. The masses believe the Bible directly from God; that it decrees the inequality of the sexes; and that settles the question. There is no doubt that there are many persons connected with the Protestant churches who would be with the movement were it not for the supposed Bible difficulty. They shudder at anything they think against the Bible, as against the will of God. Take away this incubus, and these persons would experience a change in their views; they would be with us.

In regard to Mr. Grew, Mr. G. said he had long known him and loved him. He was a man of purity and charity, and he was glad he had given his views. Yet this kindly man did not stand upon a solid foundation.

Why go to the Bible to settle this question? As a nation, we have practically ignored the Bible. The assertion of the equality and inalienability of the rights of man, in the Declaration of Independence, includes the whole of the human race. He would never attempt to prove to an American the right of any man to liberty. He asserted the fact; and considered that in holding slaves while they proclaimed liberty to all men, the American people were hypocrites and tyrants. Mr. Grew goes to St. Paul to prove that woman is not equal to man. Why go to the Bible? What question was ever settled by the Bible? What Question of theology or any other department? None that I ever heard of! With this same version of the Bible, and the same ability to read it, we find that it has filled all Christendom with theological confusion. All are Ishmaelites; each man's hand against his neighbor.

The human mind is greater than any book. The mind sits in judgment on every book. If there be truth in the book, we take it; if error, we discard it. Why refer this to the Bible? In this country, the Bible has been used to support slavery and capital punishment; while in the old countries, it has been quoted to sustain all manner of tyranny and persecution. All reforms are anti-Bible. We must look at all things rationally. We find woman endowed with certain capacities, and it is of no importance if any book denies her such capacities. Would Mr. Grew say that woman can not preach, in the face of such a preacher as LUCRETIA MOTT?

Mrs. MOTT begged leave to substitute friend Grew's own daughter, Mary Grew, who has already spoken on this platform!! and said, Mr. Grew himself does not take all the Bible as inspiration, in which most of the speakers concurred. She expressed her attachment to the Scriptures, and said many excellent lessons could be learned from them. She showed the misinterpretations of the texts quoted by Mr. Grew and others against the equality of the sexes. Mr. Grew does not take the Bible for his guide, altogether. Mrs. Mott then quoted St. Paul in regard to marriage, and said: Why in opposition to that text has Mr. Grew married a second time? It was because he did not really believe that the Scriptures were entirely inspired.

EMMA R. COE made a few remarks on the position of the clergy generally toward this reform, the most beneficent in its results of any, man has ever yet been called upon to consider. We often hear it remarked that woman owes so much to Christianity. It can not be the Christianity that the clergy have proclaimed on our platform. From them we hear only of woman's degradation and subjection. We have certainly nothing to be thankful for if such are the principles Christ came into the world to declare; the subjection of one half of the race to the other half, as far as we are concerned, is no improvement upon the religions of all nations and ages.

Elizabeth Cady Stanton, The Woman's Bible (1895)

In 1895 *The Woman's Bible*—a series of commentaries on those parts of the Bible that refer to women—caused an uproar within the suffragist movement, which was aspiring to respectability and feared alienating orthodox people who could be won to its cause. The movement itself was coming to be dominated by young women who were more conventional in their beliefs than the founders. The following excerpts are all by Elizabeth Cady Stanton (1815–1902), one of the organizers of the first woman's-rights convention, first president of the National American Woman Suffrage Association (1890–92), mother of seven children, and the boldest thinker and most outstanding leader of the first generation of feminists. She differed from most feminists in her insistence that women could achieve equality only when the pernicious influence of organized religion had been destroyed. [Elizabeth Cady Stanton and others, *The Woman's Bible*, Part I: Comments on Genesis, Exodus, Leviticus, Numbers, and Deuteronomy (New York, 1895), pp. 7–13 (Introduction), 20–22, 66, 83.]

From the inauguration of the movement for woman's emancipation the Bible has been used to hold her in the "divinely ordained sphere," prescribed in the Old and New Testaments.

The canon and civil law; church and state; priests and legislators; all political parties and religious denominations have alike taught that woman was made after man, of man, and for man, an inferior being, subject to man. . . .

The Bible teaches that woman brought sin and death into the world, that she precipitated the fall of the race, that she was arraigned before the judgment seat of Heaven, tried, condemned and sentenced. Marriage for her was to be a condition of bondage, maternity a period of suffering and anguish, and in silence and subjection, she was to play the role of a dependent on man's bounty for all her material wants, and for all the information she might desire on the vital questions of the hour, she was commanded to ask her husband at home. Here is the Bible position of woman briefly summed up.

Those who have the divine insight to translate, transpose and transfigure this mournful object of pity into an exalted, dignified personage, worthy our worship as the mother of the race, are to be congratulated as having a share of the occult mystic power of the eastern Mahatmas.

The plain English to the ordinary mind admits of no such liberal interpretation. The unvarnished texts speak for themselves. The canon law, church ordinances and Scriptures, are homogeneous, and all reflect the same spirit and sentiments.

These familiar texts are quoted by clergymen in their pulpits, by statesmen in the halls of legislation, by lawyers in the courts, and are echoed by the press of all civilized nations, and accepted by woman herself as "The Word of God." So perverted is the religious element in her nature, that with faith and works she is the chief support of the church and clergy; the very powers that make her emancipation impossible. . . .

Listening to the varied opinions of women, I have long thought it would be interesting and profitable to get them clearly stated in book form. To this end six years ago I proposed to a committee of women to issue a Woman's Bible, that we might have women's commentaries on women's position in the Old and New Testaments. . . .

Those who have undertaken the labor are desirous to have some Hebrew and Greek scholars, versed in Biblical criticism, to gild our pages with their learning. Several distinguished women have been urged to do so, but they are afraid that their high reputation and scholarly attainments might be compromised by taking part in an enterprise that for a time may prove very unpopular. Hence we may not be able to get help from that class. . . .

The large number of letters received, highly appreciative of the undertaking, is very encouraging. . . . But we have the usual array of objections to meet and answer. One correspondent conjures us to suspend the work, as it is "ridiculous" for "women to attempt the revision of the Scriptures." I wonder if any man wrote to the late revising committee of Divines to stop their work on the ground that it was ridiculous for men to revise the Bible. Why is it more ridiculous for woman to protest against her present status in the Old and New Testament, in the ordinances and discipline of the church, than in the statutes and constitutions of the state? . . . Why is it more audacious to review Moses than Blackstone, the Jewish code of laws, than the English system of jurisprudence? . . . Forty years ago it seemed as ridiculous to timid, time-serving and retrograde folk for women to demand an expurgated edition of the laws, as it now does to demand an expurgated edition of the Liturgies and the Scriptures. Come, come, my conservative friend, wipe the dew off your spectacles, and see that the world is moving. . . .

Others say it is not *politic* to rouse religious opposition. This much-lauded policy is but another word for *cowardice*. How can woman's position be changed from that of a subordinate to an equal, without opposition, without the broadest discussion of all the questions involved in her present degradation? . . .

Let us remember that all reforms are interdependent, and that whatever is done to establish one principle on a solid basis, strengthens all. . . .

Bible historians claim special inspiration for the Old and New Testaments containing most contradictory records of the same events, of miracles opposed to all known laws, of customs that degrade the female sex of all human and animal life, stated in most questionable language that could not be read in a promiscuous assembly, and call this "The Word of God."

The only points in which I differ from all ecclesiastical teaching are that I do not believe that any man ever saw or talked with God, I do not believe that God inspired the Mosaic Code, or told the historians what they say he did about woman, for all the religions on the face of the earth degrade her, and so long as woman accepts the position that they assign her, her emancipation is impossible. Whatever the Bible may be made to do in Hebrew or Greek, in plain English it does not exalt and dignify woman. My standpoint for criticism is the revised edition of 1888. I will so far honor the revising committee of wise men who have given us the best exegesis they can according to their ability, although Disraeli said the last one before he died, contained 150,000 blunders in the Hebrew, and 7,000 in the Greek.

But the verbal criticism in regard to woman's position amounts to little. The spirit is the same in all periods and languages, hostile to her as an equal.

There are some general principles in the holy books of all religions that teach love, charity, liberty, justice and equality for all the human family, there are many grand and beautiful passages, the golden rule has been echoed and re-echoed around the world. There are lofty examples of good and true men and women, all worthy our acceptance and imitation whose lustre cannot be dimmed by the false sentiments and vicious characters bound up in the same volume. The Bible cannot be accepted or rejected as a whole. . . . In criticising the peccadilloes of Sarah, Rebecca and Rachel, we would not shadow the virtues of Deborah, Huldah and Vashti. In criticising the Mosaic Code we would not question the wisdom of the golden rule and the Fifth Commandment. . . .

The canon law, the Scriptures, the creeds and codes and church discipline of the leading religions bear the impress of fallible man, and not of our ideal great first cause, "the Spirit of all Good," that set the universe of matter and mind in motion, and by the immutable law holds the land, the sea, the planets, revolving around the great centre of light and heat, each in its own elliptic, with millions of stars in harmony all singing together, the glory of Creation forever and ever.

[From chap. ii, on Genesis ii:21–25, the story of the creation of Eve from Adam's rib:]

There is something sublime in bringing order out of chaos, light out of darkness; giving each planet its place in the solar system; oceans and lands their limits; wholly inconsistent with a petty surgical operation, to find material for the mother of the race. It is on this allegory that all the enemies of woman rest their battering rams, to prove her inferiority.

[From chap. xii, on Genesis xxxix, concerning Joseph in Egypt:]

Indeed the Pentateuch is a long, painful record of war, corruption, rapine, and lust. Why Christians who wished to convert the heathen to our religion should send them these books, passes all understanding. It is most demoralizing reading for children and the unthinking masses, giving all alike the lowest possible idea of womanhood, having no hope nor ambition beyond conjugal unions with men they scarcely knew, for whom they could not have had the slightest sentiment of friendship, to say nothing of affection. There is no mention of women except when the advent of sons is announced. . . . To begin with Abraham, and go through to Joseph, leaving out all conjugal irregularities, we find Abraham and Sarah had Isaac, Isaac and Rebekah had Jacob and Esau. Jacob and Rachel (for she alone was his true wife), had Joseph and Benjamin. Joseph and Asenath had Manasseh and Ephraim. Thus giving the Patriarchs just seven legitimate descendants in the first generation. If it had not been for polygamy and concubinage, the great harvest so recklessly promised would have been meagre indeed.

[From comments on the Book of Exodus, the section on the Ten Commandments:]

The fifth commandment will take the reader by surprise. It is rather remarkable that the young Hebrews should have been told to honor their mothers, when the whole drift of the teaching thus far has been to throw contempt on the whole sex. In what way could they show their mothers honor? All the laws and customs forbid it. Why should they make any such manifestations? Scientists claim that the father gives the life, the spirit, the soul, all there is of most value in existence. Why honor the mother, for giving the mere covering of flesh[?] It was not her idea, but the father's to start their existence. He thought of them, he conceived them. You might as well pay the price of a sack of wheat to the field, instead of the farmer who sowed it, as to honor the mother for giving life. . . . In the midst of such teachings and examples of the subjection and degradation of all womankind, a mere command to honor the mother has no significance.

Elizabeth Cady Stanton, Letter to the Editor, *The Critic* (1896)

Elizabeth Cady Stanton replied to the critics of *The Woman's Bible* in this letter to the editor of *The Critic*, March 28, 1896, pp. 218–19.

Reading the Book with our own unassisted common sense, we do not find that the Mother of the race is exalted and dignified in the Pentateuch. The female half of humanity rests under the ban of general uncleanness. Even a female kid is not fit for a burnt offering to the gods. Women are denied the consecrated bread and meat, and not allowed to enter the holy places in the temples. Woman is made the author of sin, cursed in her maternity, subordinated in marriage, and a mere afterthought in creation. It is very depressing to read such sentiments emanating from the brain of man, but to be told that the good Lord said and did all the monstrous things described in the Pentateuch, makes woman's position sorrowful and helpless. . . . The first step in the elevation of women under all systems of religion is to convince them that the great Spirit of the Universe is in no way responsible for any of these absurdities. If the Bible is a message from Heaven to Humanity, neither language nor meaning should be equivocal. If the salvation of our souls depends on obedience to its commands, it is rank injustice to make scholars and scientists the only medium of communication between God and the mass of the people. "The Woman's Bible" comes to the ordinary reader like a real benediction. It tells her the good Lord did not write the Book; that the garden scene is a fable; that she is in no way responsible for the laws of the Universe. The Christian scholars and scientists will not tell her this, for they see she is the key to the situation. Take the snake, the fruit-tree and the woman from the tableau, and we have no fall, nor frowning Judge, no Inferno, no everlasting punishment,—hence no need of a Savior. Thus the bottom falls out of the whole Christian theology. Here is the reason why in all the Biblical researches and higher criticisms, the scholars never touch the position of women.

Elizabeth Cady Stanton, February 29, 1896.

Catharine Waugh McCulloch, The Bible on Women Voting

Catharine Waugh McCulloch (1862–1945), mother of four, was the first woman elected to a judicial office in the United States (Justice of the Peace in Illinois). A graduate of Rockford College and Northwestern University Law School, she practiced law in partnership with her husband and was a national leader of the National American Woman Suffrage Association. Her pamphlet excerpted below is far more typical of suffragist writings on the Bible than is *The Woman's Bible*, in its contention that the Bible rightly interpreted supports woman's claim to equality and that the apparently male-supremacist portions can be explained away metaphorically or historically. [*The Bible on Women Voting* (Evanston, Ill., n.d., but by 1910).]

There are many modern problems to which no Bible Concordance can give us a clew. There are social questions today pressing for solution which Christ never named in words. He never said specifically that we should drag the little girl widows in India from the funeral pyre; that we should unbind the tortured feet of Chinese women; that we should make sanitary our prisons or do Red Cross work. Nor did Jesus say in so many words, "Let women vote."

But Christianity will solve these newer problems if we study the spirit of Christ's words and then apply the treatment most in accord with His life and teachings. . . .

The Jews to whom Christ came were better prepared than any other existing nation for a just recognition of women. They had learned in the books of Moses that men and women were made of the same flesh and blood, and that over the newly created world they had been given joint dominion.

They easily explained woman's subservient position as a punishment for sin, and every Jewish mother hoped her coming child might lift the curse from her sex. Perhaps some thought the Genesis statement, that woman should bring forth her children in sorrow and be subject to her husband, a divine command for all ages. Some early Christian teachers so construed it when they forbade the use of any anesthetic by a woman in childbirth, on the ground that God wanted women to suffer. Who could worship or love so cruel a God? Our God never wanted women to suffer, to be humiliated, to be degraded. Some one's sin, doubtless the sin and neglect of many, are responsible for women's physical suffering and social degradation. This statement in Genesis was not a law, but a prophecy of what the future held for women—a prophecy fulfilled by the sufferings of millions of wives and mothers through thousands of years. This prophecy should no more be called a command of God than the statement made at the same time to man, that he should eat his bread in the sweat of his face and that he should eat the herb of the field. If that also is a command to endure through countless generations, then any man who eats meat is wicked, for it was said that he would eat herbs, and any man who eats without perspiring is flying in the face of his Creator. This is no more absurd than to claim that God ordained women to suffer and to obey.

The scientists of today quite agree with the Genesis parable concerning creation; that creation was in the ascending scale, first the lower creatures, then the higher animals, then man, and last at the apex the more complex woman. The order of creation affords no argument why women should obey men, though Paul in I. Tim. 2:13 so seems to regard it. It might rather be a reason why men should obey women. The question as to joint government was foreshadowed in the Genesis statement, "to them," that is male and female humanity, "gave he dominion.". . .

Some have claimed that Paul wholly opposed women's preaching and recommended to them only humble tasks. But a careful reading of all his letters will show that he was only trying to conform somewhat to the customs of the day then prevalent among Eastern peoples, and was advising a line of conduct which might draw toward Christian women the least possible criticism. . . .

We must admit that Christianity has been the inspiration which has already partly lifted women out of the degradation of heathenism and the bondage of the dark ages. But it has not yet brought woman full freedom for self-development and helpfulness. It has not yet made her man's political equal throughout Christendom. There are more important matters before us today than whether a woman should speak veiled or unveiled, whether she should wear jewels or not, and whether her hair should be braided or not. . . .

3

THE RELATION OF
WOMEN'S FASHIONS
TO WOMAN'S STATUS

Sarah Moore Grimké, Dress of Women (1838)

Sarah M. Grimké wrote the following article, "Dress of Women," as Letter XI of her series on the equality of the sexes. It is an example of her insistence that the same criteria of morality and propriety be applied to both men and women. [The *Liberator*, January 26, 1838.]

My Dear Sister,— . . . "Woman," says Adam Clarke, "has been invidiously defined, *an animal of dress*. How long will they permit themselves to be thus degraded?" I have been an attentive observer of my sex, and I am constrained to believe that the passion for dress, which so generally characterizes them, is one cause why there is so little of that solid improvement and weight of character which might be acquired under almost any circumstances, if the mind were not occupied by the love of admiration, and the desire to gratify personal vanity. . . .

. . ."It has been observed," says Scott, "that foppery and extravagance as to dress *in men* are most emphatically condemned by the apostle's silence on the subject, for this intimated that surely *they* could be under no temptation to such a childish vanity." But even those men who are superior to such a childish vanity in themselves, are, nevertheless, ever ready to encourage it in women. They know that so long as we submit to be dressed like dolls, we never can rise to the stations of duty and usefulness from which they desire to exclude us; and they are willing to grant us paltry indulgences, which forward their own design of keeping us out of our appropriate sphere, while they deprive us of essential rights. . . .

. . . May we not form some correct estimate of dress, by asking ourselves how we should feel, if we saw ministers of the gospel rise to address an audience with ear-rings dangling from their ears, glittering rings on their fingers, and a wreath of artificial flowers on their brow, and the rest of their apparel in keeping? If it would be wrong for a minister, it is wrong for every professing Christian. God makes no distinction between the moral and religious duties of ministers and people. We are bound to be "a chosen generation, a royal priesthood, a peculiar people, a holy nation; that we should show forth the praises of him who hath called us out of darkness into his marvellous light."

Thine in the bonds of womanhood,

SARAH M. GRIMKÉ.

Elizabeth Smith Miller, On the Bloomer Costume

Elizabeth Smith Miller (1822–1911), a relative of Elizabeth Cady Stanton, was the designer of the "bloomer" costume which was made famous by Mrs. Amelia Bloomer in her paper *The Lily*. In the following undated and untitled manuscript in the Smith Family Papers, Mrs. Miller tells how and why she designed and wore the costume. [Courtesy of the Manuscript Division, The New York Public Library; Astor, Lenox, and Tilden Foundations.]

It was in the fall of 1850 [1] that I adopted the short skirt, after

[1] In another document in the same collection she gives the date as spring 1851.—*Ed.*

years of annoyance in wearing the long, heavy skirt, and of dissatisfaction with myself for submitting to such bondage. Working in my garden—weeding & transplanting in bedraggled skirts that clung in fettering folds about my feet & ankles, I became desperate and resolved on immediate release.

With the short skirt I wore Turkish trousers, but these soon gave place to the straight pantaloon which was much better adapted to walking through the snow drifted roads of my country home.

My father & husband fully approved of this change of costume, but with scarcely an exception, my relatives & friends were sadly grieved. One of them said to me: "it would be a suitable dress for a journey to California" (this was before the day of western railways)—"What," thought I, ["]is *Life*, but a journey to California—to that Eldorado of higher development in pursuit of which one should cast off every impediment.["]

I wore the dress in Washington during my father's congressional term—'52–53. It excited less curiosity there than in New York owing to the more cosmopolitan character of the city. My walking dress consisted of a dark maroon corded silk, a graceful French wrap of black velvet & sable furs. The costume was completed by a broad brimmed beaver hat with a long plume.

I wore this costume for several years, enjoying its many advantages, but was always more or less tried by its exceedingly awkward effect in sitting. I gave up the pantaloons & lengthened the skirt half way to the boot-tops. The descent of the skirt continued until, at the end of seven years, I was again enthralled. I had sacrificed the useful to the beautiful.

Correspondence Between Gerrit Smith and Elizabeth Cady Stanton (1855)

Could women win equality before they reformed their style of dress, or would that reform be a result of the winning of equality? This question is here debated in an exchange of letters between

Elizabeth Cady Stanton and her cousin Gerrit Smith, father of Elizabeth Smith Miller. Smith (1797–1874) was a rich landowner and merchant of upstate New York, who became an abolitionist in 1835 and throughout his life was interested in many reform movements, including feminism. [*HWS* I, 836–42.]

PETERBORO, *December* 1, 1855.
ELIZABETH CADY STANTON.—*My Dear Friend:*— . . . The object of the "Woman's Rights Movement" is nothing less than to recover the rights of woman—nothing less than to achieve her independence. . . . I rejoice in this object; and my sorrow is, that they, who are intent upon it, are not capable of adjusting themselves to it—not high-souled enough to consent to those changes and sacrifices in themselves, in their positions and relations, essential to the attainment of this vital object.

What if a nation in the heart of Europe were to adopt, and uniformly adhere to, the practice of cutting off one of the hands of all their new-born children? It would from this cause be reduced to poverty, to helpless dependence upon the charity of surrounding nations, and to just such a measure of privileges as they might see fit to allow it, in exchange for its forfeited rights. Very great, indeed, would be the folly of this strange nation. But a still greater folly would it be guilty of, should it, notwithstanding this voluntary mutilation, claim all the wealth, and all the rights, and all the respect, and all the independence which it enjoyed before it entered upon this systematic mutilation.

Now, this twofold folly of this one-hand nation illustrates the similar twofold folly of some women. Voluntarily wearing, in common with their sex, a dress which imprisons and cripples them, they nevertheless, follow up this absurdity with the greater one of coveting and demanding a social position no less full of admitted rights, and a relation to the other sex no less full of independence, than such position and relation would naturally and necessarily have been, had they scorned a dress which leaves them less than half their personal power of self-subsistence and usefulness. I admit that the mass of women are not chargeable with this latter absurdity of cherishing aspirations and urging claims so wholly and so glaringly at war with this voluntary imprisonment and this self-degradation. They are content in their helplessness and poverty and destitution of rights. Nay, they are so deeply deluded as to believe that all this belongs to their natural and unavoidable lot. But the handful of women of whom I am here complaining—the woman's rights women—persevere just as blindly and stubbornly as do other women, in wearing a dress that both marks and makes their impotence, and yet, O amazing inconsistency! they are ashamed of their dependence, and remonstrate against its injustice. They claim that the fullest measure of rights and independence and dignity shall be accorded to them, and yet they refuse to place themselves in circumstances corresponding with their claim. . . .

I admit that the dress of woman is not the primal cause of her helplessness and degradation. That cause is to be found in the false doctrines and sentiments of which the dress is the outgrowth and symbol. On the other hand, however, these doctrines and sentiments would never have become the huge bundle they now are, and they would probably have all languished, and perhaps all expired, but for the dress. For, as in many other instances, so in this, and emphatically so in this, the cause is made more efficient by the reflex influence of the effect. Let woman give up the irrational modes of clothing her person, and these doctrines and sentiments would be deprived of their most vital aliment by being deprived of their most natural expression. In no other practical forms of folly to which they might betake themselves, could they operate so vigorously and be so invigorated by their operation.

Were woman to throw off the dress, which, in the eye of chivalry and gallantry, is so well adapted to womanly gracefulness and womanly helplessness, and to put on a dress that would leave her free to work her own way through the world, I see not but that chivalry and gallantry would nearly or quite die out. No longer would she present herself to man, now in the bewitching character of a plaything, a doll, an idol, and now in the degraded character of his servant. But he would confess her transmutation into his equal; and, therefore, all occasion for the display of chivalry and gallantry toward her on the one hand, and tyranny on the other, would have passed away. Only let woman attire her person fitly for the whole battle of life—that great and often rough battle, which she is as much bound to fight as man is, and the common sense expressed in the change will put to flight all the nonsensical fancies about her superiority to man, and all the nonsensical fancies about her inferiority to him. No more will then be heard of her being made of a finer material than man is made of; and, on the contrary, no more will then be heard of her being but the complement of man, and of its taking both a man and a woman (the woman, of course, but a small part of it) to make up a unit. No more will it then be said that there is sex in mind—an original sexual difference in intellect. What a pity that so many of our noblest women make this foolish admission! It is made by the great majority of the women who plead the cause of woman.

I am amazed that the intelligent women engaged in the "Woman's Rights Movement," see not the relation between their dress and the oppressive evils which they are striving to throw off. I am amazed that they do not see that their dress is indispensable to keep in countenance the policy and purposes out of which those evils grow. I hazard nothing in saying, that the relation between the dress and degradation of an American woman, is as vital as between the cramped foot and degradation of a Chinese woman; as vital as between the uses of the inmate of the harem and the apparel and training provided for her. More-over, I hazard nothing in saying, that an American woman will never have made her most effectual, nor, indeed, any serviceable protest against the treatment of her sex in China, or by the lords of the harem, so long as she consents to have her own person clothed in ways so repugnant to reason and religion, and graceful only to a vitiated taste, be it in her own or in the other sex.

Women are holding their meetings; and with great ability do they urge their claim to the rights of property and suffrage. But, as in the case of the colored man, the great needed change is in him-self, so, also, in the case of woman, the great needed change is in herself. Of what comparative avail would be her exercise of the right of suffrage, if she is still to remain the victim of her present false notions of herself and of her relations to the other sex?—

false notions so emphatically represented and perpetuated by her dress? Moreover, to concede to her the rights of property would be to benefit her comparatively little, unless she shall resolve to break out from her clothes-prison, and to undertake right earnestly, as right earnestly as a man, to get property. . . .

I am not unaware that such views as I have expressed in this letter will be regarded as serving to break down the characteristic delicacy of woman. I frankly admit that I would have it broken down; and that I would have the artificial and conventional, the nonsensical and pernicious thing give place to the natural delicacy which would be common to both sexes. As the delicacy, which is made peculiar to one of the sexes, is unnatural, and, therefore, false, this, which would be common to both, would be natural, and, therefore, true. I would have no characteristic delicacy of woman, and no characteristic coarseness of man. On the contrary, believing man and woman to have the same nature, and to be therefore under obligation to have the same character, I would subject them to a common standard of morals and manners. The delicacy of man should be no less shrinking than that of woman, and the bravery of woman should be one with the bravery of man. Then would there be a public sentiment very unlike that which now requires the sexes to differ in character, and which, therefore, holds them amenable to different codes—codes that, in their partiality to man, allow him to commit high crimes, and that, in their cruelty to woman, make the bare suspicion of such crimes on her part the justification of her hopeless degradation and ruin. . . .

But if woman is of the same nature and same dignity with man, and if as much and as varied labor is needed to supply her wants as to supply the wants of man, and if for her to be, as she so emphatically is, poor and destitute and dependent, is as fatal to her happiness and usefulness and to the fulfillment of the high purposes of her existence, as the like circumstances would be to the honor and welfare of man, why then put her in a dress which compels her to be a pauper—a pauper, whether in ribbons or rags? Why, I ask, put her in a dress suited only to those occasional and brief moods, in which man regards her as his darling, his idol, and his angel; or to that general state of his mind in which he looks upon her as his servant, and with feelings certainly much nearer contempt than adoration. Strive as you will to elevate woman, nevertheless the disabilities and degradation of this dress, together with that large group of false views of the uses of her being and of her relations to man, symbolized and perpetuated, as I have already said, by this dress, will make your striving vain. . . .

Affectionately yours,

GERRIT SMITH.

SENECA FALLS, *Dec.* 21, 1855.

MY DEAR COUSIN:— . . . I thank you, in the name of woman, for having said what you have on so many vital points. You have spoken well for a man whose convictions on this subject are the result of reason and observation; but they alone whose souls are fired through personal experience and suffering can set forth the height and depth, the source and center of the degradation of women; they alone can feel a steadfast faith in their own native energy and power to accomplish a final triumph over all adverse surroundings, a speedy and complete success. You say you have but little faith in this reform, because the changes we propose are so great, so radical, so comprehensive; whilst they who have commenced the work are so puny, feeble, and undeveloped. The mass of women are developed at least to the point of discontent, and that, in the dawn of this nation, was considered a most dangerous point in the British Parliament, and is now deemed equally so on a Southern plantation. In the human soul, the steps between discontent and action are few and short indeed. . . .

We who have spoken out, have declared our rights, political and civil; but the entire revolution about to dawn upon us by the acknowledgment of woman's social equality, has been seen and felt but by the few. The rights, to vote, to hold property, to speak in public, are all-important; but there are great social rights, before which all others sink into utter insignificance. The cause of woman is, as you admit, a broader and a deeper one than any with which you compare it; and this, to me, is the very reason why it must succeed. It is not a question of meats and drinks, of money and lands, but of human rights—the sacred right of a woman to

her own person, to all her God-given powers of body and soul. . . .
[W]hen woman shall stand on an even pedestal with man—when
they shall be bound together, not by withes of law and gospel, but
in holy unity and love, then, and not till then, shall our efforts at
minor reforms be crowned with complete success. Here, in my
opinion, is the starting-point; here is the battleground where our
independence must be fought and won. A true marriage relation
has far more to do with the elevation of woman than the style and
cut of her dress. Dress is a matter of taste, of fashion; it is change-
able, transient, and may be doffed or donned at the will of the
individual; but institutions, supported by laws, can be overturned
but by revolution. We have no reason to hope that pantaloons
would do more for us than they have done for man himself. The
negro slave enjoys the most unlimited freedom in his attire, not
surpassed even by the fashions of Eden in its palmiest days; yet
in spite of his dress, and his manhood, too, he is a slave still. Was
the old Roman in his toga less of a man than he now is in swal-
low-tail and tights? Did the flowing robes of Christ Himself render
His life less grand and beautiful? In regard to dress, where you
claim to be so radical, you are far from consistent. . . .

I fully agree with you that woman is terribly cramped and
crippled in her present style of dress. I have not one word to utter
in its defense; but to me, it seems that if she would enjoy entire
freedom, she should dress just like man. Why proclaim our sex
on the house-tops, seeing that it is a badge of degradation, and
deprives us of so many rights and privileges wherever we go? Disguised as a man, the distinguished French woman, "George Sand,"
has been able to see life in Paris, and has spoken in political meetings with great applause, as no woman could have done. In male
attire, we could travel by land or sea; go through all the streets and
lanes of our cities and towns by night and day, without a protector; get seven hundred dollars a year for teaching, instead of
three, and ten dollars for making a coat, instead of two or three, as
we now do. All this we could do without fear of insult, or the
least sacrifice of decency or virtue. If nature has not made the sex
so clearly defined as to be seen through any disguise, why should
we make the difference so striking? Depend upon it, when men

and women in their every-day life see and think less of sex and more of mind, we shall all lead far purer and higher lives. . . .

. . . Talk not to us of chivalry, that died long ago. . . . In social life, true, a man in love will jump to pick up a glove or bouquet for a silly girl of sixteen, whilst at home he will permit his aged mother to carry pails of water and armfuls of wood, or his wife to lug a twenty-pound baby, hour after hour, without ever offering to relieve her. . . . If a short dress is to make the men less gallant than they now are, I beg the women at our next convention to add at least two yards more to every skirt they wear. . . .

Affectionately yours, ELIZABETH CADY STANTON.

Tennie C. Claflin, Constitutional Equality a Right of Woman (1871)

Tennie C. (or Tennessee) Claflin (1846–1923) was the younger sister of Victoria Woodhull, the beautiful stockbroker, protégée of Commodore Vanderbilt, candidate for President in 1872, and defier of conventional morality. The sisters published *Woodhull & Claflin's Weekly* from 1870 on, advocating women's rights, a single standard of morality, and free love. [Tennie C. Claflin, *Constitutional Equality a Right of Woman*: Or a Consideration of the Various Relations Which She Sustains as a Necessary Part of the Body of Society and Humanity; With Her Duties to Herself—Together with a Review of the Constitution of the United States, Showing That the Right to Vote Is Guaranteed to All Citizens. Also a Review of the Rights of Children (New York, 1871), pp. 56, 89–93.]

Women dress to make themselves appear attractive to men; marriage with them is the one and only thing they are educated to; hence, this attractiveness with them has a first and second intention—first, to appear generally attractive to the other sex as a whole, and thereby to gain general admiration; second, that each woman may be able to be especially attractive to him whom she

shall decide to allow the opportunity of wooing her. By these artificial means she is assisted to win the man whom she consents to
become attached to. Thus far the matter progresses finely; but how
about the sequel! Those of you who have gained husbands thus
must expect to lose them after the same fashion, by the charms of
some other than yourselves; and we assert that you deserve to thus
lose them, or to be subjected to some other righteous judgment.

It is scarcely to be wondered that so many men regard with a
supreme contempt women who assert privileges beyond those included in a genuinely wifely subjection. They know that women
generally are born, grow up, and are educated with the one idea
of becoming the wife of somebody who shall be able to take care
of her physical needs. Why should they not affect and really feel
disdain when some woman stands gloriously forth as independent
and free—as entirely above depending upon anybody for anything; and competent to choose for herself whom she shall marry,
or whether she will marry at all, and determined never to be
under the necessity of so doing if her preferences shall decide
otherwise. . . .

The truth of the matter is, that "young ladies" are set up, ad-
vertised and sold to the highest cash bidder, and where a mutual
attraction does not exist, a strict analysis finds no difference between it and the other association of the sexes denominated prostitution. . . . A woman rigged with the entire paraphernalia of fashion is only a fit subject for a show. There is so much of artificial
ornamentation that nature, whatever her beauties are, retires in
disgust, before superfluity on the one extreme and brazenness upon
the other. Ladies who would affect to blush when subjects are
spoken of which are of the greatest interest to humanity generally,
and who would hide their faces behind their handkerchiefs to
cover the blushes they would have it supposed were there, appear
at balls and receptions and at the opera, with the most perfect
self-assurance, virtually naked to the waists, and if by such exposure
of their persons some admirer is made bold enough to presume
upon it, the "big brother" has business on hand to punish the insult. These things bespeak a superficiality and a mock-modesty
that is robbing the sex of all its natural beauty and its real
attractiveness.

Practically, the present styles of dress for women of business, so far as convenience is concerned, are simply absurd, not to say ridiculous, while from the health point of view they are suicidal. While women remain mere dolls, to be admired for the external appearance they can present, it does not matter very much how they dress; but when any of them shake off the shackles of dependence, and become their own support, they should certainly have the right to accommodate their dress to their new modes of life, without being exposed to the ridicule of the fashion apes of either sex. . . .

It may be thought far-fetched, by some, to assert that the subject of dress has any legitimate bearing upon the Sixteenth Amendment Question; [1] if so, it comes from lack of thought and attention to the many-sided bearings of the Woman Question. Taken as a whole, it must be considered as one of the most important Humanitarian movements of the age, and every part of it which is not already based on fixed principles of right, or upon demonstrated facts, should be analyzed, to the end that *the right* may be separated from *the wrong*, so that the latter may be discarded or supplanted by something better. It is more than a privilege; it is more than a right—it is a duty, stern and imperative, that if there are any hindrances hanging around, which prevent the legitimate use of their newly-acquired freedom, woman should shake them off.

But how does dress relate to woman's freedom? We have said that it was impossible for a single argument to be offered in favor of the style of skirts now almost universally worn by women of refinement and intelligence (?) and just as little for all other external parts of their dress. One of the first principles of dress, regarding health, is, *that all portions of the body should be evenly covered,* so that there shall always be a free and uninfluenced circulation of blood. As women dress now, the great amount of clothing worn about the lumbar regions of the body, which at all times keeps that portion of the body warm, even when the extremities may be nearly frozen, produces a powerful determination

---

[1] By 1871 only fifteen amendments had been added to the Constitution; the proposed woman-suffrage amendment was, accordingly, referred to as the sixteenth.—*Ed.*

of blood to those parts. These parts being a large part of the time kept at a very much higher temperature than any other portion of the body, the extremities are deprived of the vitality requisite to continue healthy conditions. It is a well known fact, that since the present fashions of padding and bustle-wearing came in vogue, the class of complaints known as Female Weakness have increased a hundred fold. While it would not be true that this increase is entirely owing to this overheating process, it is true that it will reasonably account for a very large proportion of it. And when we remember that with this overdress of central parts of the body, the neck, shoulders, and upper parts of the breast and back have been almost deprived of covering, which, when allowed, has been of the nearest approach to nothing, we need not wonder that there are so many frail women, weakly wives, and fragile or scrubby children. . . .

These practices, if allowable or reasonable at all for women of fashion, who are never obliged to expose themselves, cannot be tolerated a moment by the sensible business woman. She requires the same degree of protection, and even more care, than man; but women who, from choice or necessity, become regularly attendant upon business, have not, as a rule, been sensible enough, or independent enough, to meet the situation. . . .

Again: What sense is there in long skirts for business women at any time. 'Tis true that they are pretty nearly all the dressing or protection the lower limbs have; but what kind of protection? Sufficient, perhaps, when worn for nothing but to hide the limbs, but what against dampness, dust and the bleak wintry winds. Against these, clothing more nearly adjusted to the limbs is required; so that it comes down to this at last: that long skirts are worn, not for clothing, but for the purpose of hiding the limbs. Dress is either for the purpose of protection or for disguise. If for the last—and it is indelicate or revolting to the nature of woman to so dress her legs that they can be free to perform the functions of locomotion—why should it not be just as indelicate to go with arms naked to the shoulder, as thousands do who would scream if their leg to the knee were exposed? And why should it not be considered a hundred fold more indelicate to expose, virtually, their breasts to the waist, as thousands do, than it is to tastefully and reasonably dress their legs?

The fact of the case in this matter of female dress is, that a blind and foolish custom has decreed that women must wear skirts to hide their legs, while they may, almost *ad libitum*, expose their arms and breasts. For our part, we can see no more indelicacy in a properly clad leg than in a properly clad arm; but we can see a deal of sentimental and hypocritical mock modesty in the custom which demands skirts and allows bare arms, shoulders and breasts. It is time to call things by their right names, and to be honest enough to speak the truth about these things, which are fettering and diseasing women and producing a generation of sickly children. If those who affect a great deal more modesty and delicacy than they are willing to allow that those have who are bold enough to discuss this question truthfully, vent their spleen and show their virtuous indignation, by calling us bad names, we simply assure them that our estimation of truth, and our desire to promote the true interests of our sex, rises far above all care for whatever they may say or think, and that we are perfectly willing to intrust the vindication of our course to the next ten years, when such unsightly and health-destroying things as our present system of dressing presents will be among the things which were. . . .

Thorstein Veblen, Theory of the Leisure Class (1899)

The topic of woman's fashions received the attention of some male social scientists, too—notable among them Thorstein Veblen (1857–1929). [*Theory of the Leisure Class*, first published in 1899 (New York, 1953), pp. 126–27.]

As has been seen in the discussion of woman's status under the heads of Vicarious Leisure and Vicarious Consumption, it has in the course of economic development become the office of the woman to consume vicariously for the head of the household; and her apparel is contrived with this object in view. It has come about that obviously productive labor is in a peculiar degree derogatory to respectable women, and therefore special pains should be taken in the construction of women's dress, to impress upon the beholder the fact (often indeed a fiction) that the wearer does not and can not habitually engage in useful work. . . . Her sphere is within the household, which she should "beautify," and of which she should be the "chief ornament." The male head of the household is not currently spoken of as its ornament. . . .

[T]he high heel, the skirt, the impracticable bonnet, the corset, and the general disregard of the wearer's comfort which is an obvious feature of all civilized women's apparel, are so many items of evidence to the effect that in the modern civilized scheme of life the woman is still, in theory, the economic dependent of the man—that, perhaps in a highly idealized sense, she still is the man's chattel. The homely reason for all this conspicuous leisure and attire on the part of women lies in the fact that they are servants to whom, in the differentiation of economic functions, has been delegated the office of putting in evidence their master's ability to pay.

There is a marked similarity in these respects between the apparel of women and that of domestic servants, especially liveried servants. In both there is a very elaborate show of unnecessary expensiveness, and in both cases there is also a notable disregard of the physical comfort of the wearer. But the attire of the lady goes farther in its elaborate insistence on the idleness, if not on the physical infirmity of the wearer, than does that of the domestic. And this is as it should be; for in theory, according to the ideal scheme of the pecuniary culture, the lady of the house is the chief menial of the household.

4

SCIENCE ENLISTED IN THE CAUSE OF FEMINISM

Matilda Joslyn Gage, Address at a Convention (1884)

Matilda Joslyn Gage delivered this speech at the 1884 convention of the National American Woman Suffrage Association in Washington. In keeping with the fascination of her generation with science, it cites several sciences in support of sex equality. [*HWS* IV, 28–30.]

We must bear in mind the old theologic belief that the earth was flat, the center of the universe, around which all else revolved —that all created things, animate and inanimate, were made for man alone—that woman was not part of the original plan of creation but was an after-thought for man's special use and benefit. So that a science which proves the falsity of any of these theological conceptions aids in the overthrow of all.

The first great battle fought by science for woman was a Geographical one lasting for twelve centuries. But finally, Columbus, sustained and sent on his way by Isabella in 1492, followed by

Magellan's circumnavigation of the globe twenty years later, settled the question of the earth's rotundity and was the first step toward woman's enfranchisement.

Another great battle was in progress at the same time and the second victory was an Astronomical one. Copernicus was born, the telescope discovered, the earth sank to its subordinate place in the solar system and another battle for woman was won.

Chemistry, long opposed under the name of Alchemy, at last gained a victory, and by its union of diverse atoms began to teach man that nature is a system of nuptials, and that the feminine is everywhere present as an absolute necessity of life.

Geology continued this lesson. It not only taught the immense age of creation, but the motherhood of even the rocks.

Botany was destined for a fierce battle, as when Linnaeus declared the sexual nature of plants, he was shunned as having degraded the works of God by a recognition of the feminine in plant life.

Philology owes its rank to Catherine II of Russia, who, in assembling her great congress of deputies from the numerous provinces of her empire, gave the first impetus to this science. Max Müller declares the evidence of language to be irrefragable, and it is the only history we possess prior to historic periods. Through Philology we ascend to the dawn of nations and learn of the domestic, religious and governmental habits of people who left neither monuments nor writing to speak for them. From it we learn the original meaning of our terms, father and mother. Father, says Müller, who is a recognized philological authority, is derived from the root "Pa," which means to protect, to support, to nourish. Among the earliest Aryans, the word *mater* (mother), from the root "Ma," signified maker; creation being thus distinctively associated with the feminine. Taylor, in his Primitive Culture says the husband acknowledged the offspring of his wife as his own as thus only had he a right to claim the title of father.

While Philology has opened a new fount of historic knowledge, Biology, the seventh and most important witness, the latest science in opposition to divine authority, is the first to deny the theory of man's original perfection. Science gained many triumphs, conquered many superstitions, before the world caught a glimpse of the result toward which each step was tending—the enfranchisement of woman.

Through Biology we learn that the first manifestation of life is feminine. The albuminous protoplasm lying in silent darkness on the bottom of the sea, possessing within itself all the phenomena exhibited by the highest forms of life, as sensation, motion, nutrition and reproduction, produces its like, and in all forms of life the capacity for reproduction undeniably stamps the feminine. Not only does science establish the fact that primordial life is feminine, but it also proves that a greater expenditure of vital force is required for the production of the feminine than for the masculine.

The experiments of Meehan, Gentry, Treat, Herrick, Wallace, Combe, Wood and many others, show sex to depend upon environment and nutrition. A meager, contracted environment, together with innutritious or scanty food, results in a weakened vitality and the birth of males; a broad, generous environment together with abundant nutrition, in the birth of females. The most perfect plant produces feminine flowers; the best nurtured insect or animal demonstrates the same law. From every summary of vital statistics we gather further proof that more abundant vitality, fewer infantile deaths and greater comparative longevity belong to woman. It is a recognized fact that quick reaction to a stimulus is proof of superior vitality. In England, where very complete vital statistics have been recorded for many years, it is shown that while the mean duration of man's life within the last thirty years has increased five per cent. that of woman has increased more than eight per cent. Our own last census (tenth) shows New Hampshire to be the State most favorable for longevity. While one in seventy-four of its inhabitants is eighty years old, among native white men the proportion is but one to eighty, while among native white women, the very great preponderance of one to fifty-eight is shown.

That the vitality of the world is at a depressed standard is proven by the fact that more boys are born than girls, the per cent. varying in different countries. Male infants are more often deformed, suffer from abnormal characteristics, and more speedily succumb to infantile diseases than female infants, so that within a few years, notwithstanding the large proportion of male births, the balance of life is upon the feminine side. Many children are born to a rising people, but this biological truth is curiously supplemented by the fact that the proportion of girls born among such people, is always in excess of boys; while in races dying out, the very large proportion of boys' births over those of girls is equally noticeable.

From these hastily presented scientific facts it is manifest that woman possesses in a higher degree than man that adaptation to the conditions surrounding her which is everywhere accepted as evidence of superior vitality and higher physical rank in life; and when biology becomes more fully understood it will also be universally acknowledged that the primal creative power, like the first manifestation of life, is feminine.

Elizabeth Cady Stanton, The Matriarchate (1891)

Mrs. Stanton, relying on then current but now discredited theories of anthropology, here argues that in primitive matrilineal societies women had been the rulers and the inventors of all the arts of civilization. [Elizabeth Cady Stanton, "The Matriarchate, or Mother-Age," in *Transactions of the National Council of Women of the United States* (Philadelphia, 1891), pp. 218–27.]

Without going into any of the fine calculations of historians as to the centuries of human growth, I would simply state that some agree on about eighty-five thousand years. They assign sixty thousand to savagery, twenty thousand to barbarism, and five thousand to civilization.

For my present purpose, these facts are only interesting to show for how long a period, in proportion, women reigned supreme; the arbiters of their own destiny, the protectors of their children, the acknowledged builders of all there was of home life, religion, and later, from time to time, of government.

All along from the beginning until the sixteenth century, when Luther eliminated the feminine element wholly from the Protestant religion and brought the full power of the Church to enforce woman's complete subjection, we find traces of the matriarchate. Karl Pearson, in a series of deeply interesting essays, gives us the result of his researches into the works of modern historians, and the startling facts they unearth, from what to most of us is the dead, unknown, eternal past, shadowed in mystery. The publication of Wilkeson's "Ancient Egypt" in 1836, of "Das Mutter-[r]echt," by Bachofen in 1861, of Morgan's "Ancient Society" in 1877, with other lesser lights pursuing the same trend of investigation, all show the leading, independent position women held for ages.

What is often said, and repeated from time to time and never contradicted, is accepted as truth. Thus, the assertion that women have always been held in a subject condition, has been universally believed.

This view has furnished the opponents to woman's emancipation their chief arguments for holding her in bondage, and logically so, for if at all periods and in all latitudes and longitudes woman had held the same subordinate position, men would naturally infer that what we choose to call Providence, for wise purposes, had made woman the slave of man. The worst feature of these assumptions is that women themselves believe them, and feel that to strive for their own emancipation is simply an attempt at the impossible. Fortunately, historical research has at last proved the fallacy of these assumptions and all the arguments that grow out of them. Mankind may be traced by a chain of necessary inferences back to a time when, ignorant of fire, without articulate language, without artificial weapons, they depended, like the wild animals, upon the spontaneous fruits of the earth.

Through all this period woman was left to protect herself and forage for her children. Morgan, in his "Ancient Society," gives many remarkable examples of the superior position of women among different tribes in the latter part of the period of barbarism. Among the greater number of the American aborigines the descent of property and children were in the female line. Women sat in the councils of war and peace, and their opinions had equal weight on all questions. Among the Winnebagoes that occupied the territory now known as Wisconsin, a woman was at the head of the nation. The same was true among the early tribes or gens in the Eastern Hemisphere. In the councils of the Iroquois gens every adult male or female member had a voice upon all questions brought before it. . . .

At the epoch of European Discovery, the American Indian tribes generally were organized into gentes, with descent in the female line. Before paterfamilias was known, the family was nowhere considered a unit around which society centred. . . . During these early periods the property of woman was in her own line and gens, and man's property was in his own line and gens. . . .

Mr. Morgan knows, too, that the early tribes in Greece, like the American aborigines, were essentially democratic in their government. Historians, accustomed to monarchial governments, would naturally interpret words and actions in harmony with their ideas. Thus, Mr. Grote has a memorable dictum of Ulysses in the *Iliad* to prove that the Greeks had a one-man government. "The rule of many is not a good thing; let us have one ruler only,—one king,—him to whom Zeus hath given the sceptre with the tutelary sanctions." But this saying has no significance as applied to government. Ulysses, from whose address the quotation is taken, was speaking of the command of an army before a besieged city. There was no occasion for Ulysses to discuss or endorse any plan of government; but he had sufficient reason for advocating obedience to a single commander of the army before a besieged city.

As thus we have seen that Grote, in his "History of Greece," writing from his own true inwardness, mistook the spirit of the times of which he wrote, it behooves us women to question all historians, sacred or profane, who teach by examples or precepts any philosophy that lowers the status of the mothers of the race, or favors the one-man power in government.

As far back into the shadowy past as human thought has penetrated, and been able by a process of reason to substantiate the facts of primeval life, we behold woman in all her native dignity, self-poised and self-supporting, her own head and hands her guidance and protection. The instincts of motherhood gave her the first thought of privacy and seclusion, and led her to make a home for herself and children in the caves of the earth, safe from the wild beasts of the forests, and the wily hunter, who lived on uncooked food and slept on the ground, wherever night found him. While his rude activities developed but few of his faculties, the woman, in solitude, was learning the great lessons of life. A new birth! What a mystery for her to ponder! What love and tenderness helpless infancy calls out; what intelligence and activity its necessities compel; what forethought and responsibility, in providing for herself and children it involves! Sex relations being transitory and promiscuous, the idea of fatherhood was unknown. As men naturally have no sense of paternal responsibility, no one knew or cared about the father of the child. To know one's mother was deemed all-sufficient for a legitimate name and an abiding place.

The period of woman's supremacy lasted through many centuries,—undisputed, accepted as natural and proper wherever it existed, and was called the matriarchate, or mother-age. It was plainly traceable among the Aryans, the Germans, the Persians, and indications of it are still seen among the uncivilized tribes and nations.

Careful historians now show that the greatest civilizing power all along the pathway of natural development has been found in the wisdom and tender sentiments growing out of motherhood. For the protection of herself and her children woman made the first home in the caves of the earth; then huts with trees in the sunshine. She made the first attempts at agriculture; raised grain, fruits, and herbs which she learned to use in sickness. She was her own physician; all that was known of the medical art was in her hands. She domesticated the cow and goat, and from the necessities of her children learned the use of milk. The women cultivated

the arts of peace, and the sentiments of kinship, and all there was
of human love and home-life. The necessities of motherhood were
the real source of all the earliest attempts at civilization.

Thus, instead of being a "disability," as unthinking writers are
pleased to call it, maternity has been the all-inspiring motive or
force that impelled the first steps towards a stable home and
family life. Clearly the birth of civilization must be sought in the
attempt of woman at self-preservation during the period of preg-
nancy and lactation.

What man achieved at that period was due to the contest for
food with his fellows and the wild beasts. He simply invented and
improved weapons of warfare; but the woman, handicapped as
she appeared to be by child-bearing, became on this very account
the main factor in human progress. The man's contributions at
this early period are nothing as compared to woman's. Her varied
responsibilities as mother, bread-winner, protector, defender of a
group of helpless children, raised her intellectual and inventive
supremacy and made her the teacher and ruler of man. . . .

With such personal independence and superiority, such authority in the national councils, in religious faith, and at the fireside,
with the absolute control of her own home, property, and children, how did it come to pass that the mother was at last dethroned and womanhood degraded in every nation of the globe?

The mother's labors had from an early period been re-enforced
by those of her sons whose tastes led them to agriculture and
the herding of cattle, to domestic life rather than that of the
wandering nomad existence of the wily hunter, but this class was
proportionally small. However, in process of time,—as the home
with its increasing comforts and attractions, fire, cooked food, and
woman's tender care in old age, sickness, and death, the innocent
prattle of children, the mother's songs and stories, her religious
faith and services, all appealed to the better feelings of the wily
hunter also,—men began to think, when weary of the battle and
the chase, that they would like a permanent foothold in some
family group besides the one into which they were born.

As soon as monogamic marriage appeared with property and
descent in the male line, and men found themselves comfortably

ensconced in a home of their own, they began little by little to make their aggressions, and in time completely dominated woman, leaving her no remnant of authority anywhere, neither in the home, nor at the altar, nor in the councils of the nation.

Having no paternal instinct, no natural love for children, the devices of men to establish the rights of paternity were as varied as ridiculous. It was the custom at one time when the mother gave birth to a child for the acknowledged father to take to his bed to pretend that he had shared in the perils of labor, and thus prove his identity, while the wife waited on him; for the women, accustomed to agricultural work, were so hardened by it that they did not suffer in childbirth.

On this point Karl Pearson tells us the transition from the mother to the father-age was marked by the appearance of women of gigantic stature. The old legends of contests between men and women for supremacy are not such idle figures as some would have us believe. Very dark shadows indeed do such figures as those of Ildico, Fredegunde, and Brunhilde cast across the pages of history. Such women were only paralleled by the Clytemnestra and Medea of a like phase of Greek development. Among the Germans, too, the poets represent the contest between men and women for the mastery. Wuodan replaces Hellja; Siegfried conquers Brunhilde; Beovulf, the offspring of Grindel and Thor, fights with Gialp and Griep, the daughters of Geirrod. One great element of physical and mental vigor is freedom, which women have never enjoyed except under the Matriarchate. . . .

The victory of man over women was not easily accomplished. It took long centuries to fully confirm it, and traces of the mother-age remain throughout the Mediaeval times. The permanency of sex relations among the agriculturists and the necessity for organization in matters of defence, which must be intrusted mainly to men, were the beginnings of the father-age.

For though women had been compelled to fight for their own protection, and were abundantly able to maintain the contest, yet wars for territory and conquests over other tribes and nations were opposed by all the tenderest sentiments of their nature. Hence they naturally of their own accord would withdraw from the

councils of war and the battle-field, but [they would return?] as
angels of mercy to minister to the wounded and the dying. Thus
man became ruler, tribal organizer, tribal father, before his position of sexual father was recognized. While the mother still ruled
the house, "the Alvater" ruled the fight, though ofttimes guided
by the woman.

Driven from the commanding position of home mother, and
deprived of her rights to property and children, the last fortress of
the Teutonic woman was her sacerdotal privileges. She remained
holy as priestess. She had charge of the tribal sacrifices and the
tribal religion.

From this last refuge she was driven by the introduction of the
Christian religion, with its narrow Pauline doctrine, which made
woman mentally and physically the inferior of man, and lawfully
in subjection to him.

The spirit of the Church in its contempt for women, as shown
in the Scriptures, in Paul's epistles and the Pentateuch, the hatred
of the fathers, manifested in their ecclesiastical canons, and in
the doctrines of asceticism, celibacy, and witchcraft, destroyed
man's respect for woman and legalized the burning, drowning, and
torturing of women by the thousand.

Women and their duties became objects of hatred to the Christian missionaries and of alternate scorn and fear to pious ascetics
and monks. The priestess mother became something impure, associated with the devil, and her lore an infernal incantation, her
very cooking a brewing of poison, nay, her very existence a source
of sin to man. Thus woman, as mother and priestess, became
woman as witch. The witch trials of the Middle Ages, wherein
thousands of women were condemned to the stake, were the very
real traces of the contest between man and woman. Christianity
putting the religious weapon into man's hand made his conquest
complete. . . . It was this wholesale, violent suppression of the
feminine element, in the effort to establish the Patriarchate, that,
more than any other one cause, produced the Dark Ages.

Morgan, in his "Ancient Society," attributes the premature destruction of ethnic life, in the societies of Greece and Rome, to
their failure to develop and utilize the mental and moral conserva-

tive forces of the female intellect, which were not less essential than those of men to their progress.

In closing, I would say that every woman present must have a new sense of dignity and self-respect, feeling that our mothers, during some periods in the long past, have been the ruling power, and that they used that power for the best interests of humanity. As history is said to repeat itself, we have every reason to believe that our turn will come again, it may not be for woman's supremacy, but for the as yet untried experiment of complete equality, when the united thought of man and woman will inaugurate a just government, a pure religion, and happy home, a civilization at last in which ignorance, poverty, and crime will exist no more. . . .

5

MARRIAGE, DIVORCE, AND THE HOME

Marriage Documents: Robert Dale Owen and Mary Robinson (1832); Henry B. Blackwell and Lucy Stone (1855)

Many feminists were fortunate in having the approval of their husbands for their activities in behalf of sex equality. Robert Dale Owen and Henry B. Blackwell were two of several men who at their marriage signed statements in which they renounced the legal superiority granted them by law. Owen (1801–77), son of Robert Owen, was a leader of the Workingmen's Party, founded in New York in 1829. Blackwell (1825–1909) was Lucy Stone's husband and a lifelong worker for woman suffrage. [HWS I, 294–95, 260–61.]

New York, Tuesday, *April* 12, 1832.

This afternoon I enter into a matrimonial engagement with Mary Jane Robinson, a young person whose opinions on all important subjects, whose mode of thinking and feeling, coincide more intimately with my own than do those of any other individual with whom I am acquainted. . . . We have selected the simplest ceremony which the laws of this State recognize. . . . This ceremony involves not the necessity of making promises regarding that over which we have no control, the state of human affections in the distant future, nor of repeating forms which we deem offensive, inasmuch as they outrage the principles of human liberty and equality, by conferring rights and imposing duties unequally on the sexes. The ceremony consists of a simply written contract in which we agree to take each other as husband and wife according to the laws of the State of New York, our signatures being attested by those friends who are present.

Of the unjust rights which in virtue of this ceremony an iniquitous law tacitly gives me over the person and property of another, I can not legally, but I can morally divest myself. And I hereby distinctly and emphatically declare that I consider myself, and earnestly desire to be considered by others, as utterly divested, now and during the rest of my life, of any such rights, the barbarous relics of a feudal, despotic system, soon destined, in the onward course of improvement, to be wholly swept away; and the existence of which is a tacit insult to the good sense and good feeling of this comparatively civilized age.

ROBERT DALE OWEN.

I concur in this sentiment.

MARY JANE ROBINSON.

PROTEST

While acknowledging our mutual affection by publicly assuming the relationship of husband and wife, yet in justice to ourselves and a great principle, we deem it a duty to declare that this act on our part implies no sanction of, nor promise of voluntary obedience to such of the present laws of marriage, as refuse to recognize the wife as an independent, rational being, while they confer upon the husband an injurious and unnatural superiority, investing him with legal powers which no honorable man would exercise, and which no man should possess. We protest especially against the laws which give to the husband:

1. The custody of the wife's person.
2. The exclusive control and guardianship of their children.

3. The sole ownership of her personal, and use of her real estate, unless previously settled upon her, or placed in the hands of trustees, as in the case of minors, lunatics, and idiots.

4. The absolute right to the product of her industry.

5. Also against laws which give to the widower so much larger and more permanent an interest in the property of his deceased wife, than they give to the widow in that of the deceased husband.

6. Finally, against the whole system by which "the legal existence of the wife is suspended during marriage," so that in most States, she neither has a legal part in the choice of her residence, nor can she make a will, nor sue or be sued in her own name, nor inherit property.

We believe that personal independence and equal human rights can never be forfeited, except for crime; that marriage should be an equal and permanent partnership, and so recognized by law; that until it is so recognized, married partners should provide against the radical injustice of present laws, by every means in their power.

We believe that where domestic difficulties arise, no appeal should be made to legal tribunals under existing laws, but that all difficulties should be submitted to the equitable adjustment of arbitrators mutually chosen.

Thus reverencing law, we enter our protest against rules and customs which are unworthy of the name, since they violate justice, the essence of law.

(Signed), HENRY B. BLACKWELL,
LUCY STONE.

Antoinette Brown Blackwell, Relation of Woman's Work in the Household to the Work Outside (1873)

Antoinette Brown Blackwell (1825–1921) studied theology at Oberlin and for a year had her own Congregational church in South Butler, New York, but later became a Unitarian. The wife of Samuel C. Blackwell and sister-in-law of Lucy Stone, she was the mother of six children as well as an author, a lecturer (on women's rights, prohibition, and abolitionism), and an excellent speaker. This remarkably modern-sounding speech deplores the depressing effects, on women's bodies and minds, of their restriction to the home day after day, without change of scene or activities. ["The Relation of Woman's Work in the Household to the Work Outside," in *Papers and Letters Presented at the First Woman's Congress of the Association for the Advancement of Woman, . . . New York, October, 1873* (New York, 1874), pp. 178–84.]

There is one dogma, I believe, which has been taught and accepted universally. It asserts that the paramount social duties of women are household duties, avocations arising from their relations as wives and mothers, and as the natural custodians of home. I make haste to endorse this dogma; fully, and without equivocation. The work nearest and clearest before the eyes of average womanhood is work within family boundaries,—work within a sphere which men cannot enter; surrounded by a still wider area of duties and privileges that very few of us desire to relinquish. I yield to none in the earnestness of my faith that to women preeminently has been committed the happiness, the usefulness, and the dignity of the homes of Christendom.

But does it follow that there is no work equally imperative awaiting women outside the household? As reasonably insist that because Peter Cooper owes allegiance to the State of New York, therefore, that he is not a citizen of the General Government. . . . All agree in admitting that there is a special woman's sphere; yet every dogmatist who attempts to limit its boundary lines varies of necessity from every other . . . , because every woman must find the domain of her work to be widely different from her neighbor's, as defined by her differing circumstances, tastes and capacities. . . . Each sphere is personal, not the limits of a class. . . .

What would be the consequence if mechanics could be compelled to live and die in their workshops—forbidden all rights of occupation of citizens outside? When the weaver has watched his shuttle through the weary ten hours, he has no desire to camp beneath his loom to eat and sleep. Home on the other side of the village, with the walk to and fro, is vastly more refreshing. His garden, if he will dig in it, is a better rest than idleness. . . . The more pleasant and diversified his interests, the happier and stronger the man.

If the majority of women could be hemmed in, day and night, by home duties, never quite freed from the world of care, and seldom looking outside for other occupation, this would be utter destruction. Better any amount of outside frivolity and extravagance. Better the lot of the washerwoman who spends some portion of her time in other laundries than her own. She breathes another atmosphere, though it be misty with soap suds. She has change of food and surroundings to occupy attention and relax the overstrained nerves. . . .

The newspapers tell of an old lady who walked over a bridge marked "dangerous" without seeing the sign, and when informed of the fact on the other side, turned back in great alarm and hastily recrossed. The *Woman's Journal* calls the story a "joke" which illustrates the "barbarous contempt" felt for woman's intellect. Very likely, yet it may be true all the same. Any woman of fifty, after thirty years of omniscient supervision in a large household, or of unceasing toil in a smaller one, should be sufficiently broken down in body and mind to do things equally absurd.

Our country*men* have also nerves fairly developed—as witness the late financial panic. Men, even in high places, are reported to have turned back affrighted and recrossed bridges marked very dangerous indeed. Some diseases may descend only in the female line; but irritability of nerves apparently is not so narrowly limited. Sleeplessness is becoming the national disease, paralysis following stealthily in its wake. We may attribute the evil to over-pressure in our modes of doing business, male and female alike. A thousand side causes will swell the result; yet we must trace the baleful stream back at last to parental influence upon the impressible child.

Here, action and reaction clash endlessly, like waves against the sea shore. A modern baby, keeping its mother awake half the night by restless tossing in his little crib may be descended from four grand-parents, all of whom were able to sleep soundly eight or ten hours upon a stretch. But not so the father or mother. The former may take a next day's tonic of change and fresh air; but how with the mother? Yet human nature cannot stay twenty-four hours daily in the nursery and either live the beautitudes [*sic*] or teach them properly to childhood. The evening return of the husband must be about as refreshing morally as the unchanged atmosphere is physically to the imprisoned occupants.

Where, then, is the remedy? Can it lie in adding kitchen to nursery for relaxation? Is attaching plain sewing and dressmaking establishments to every household a good sanitary measure? The most thrifty American women are out-vieing all other nationalities by attempting to do everything which an exacting household needs to have done for it, single-handed, or at best, by superintending its being done within their own domiciles. The plan is economical of money, but utterly destructive to all higher interests. An English woman in the same rank would give up tucking and ruffling, and be content to dress her household simply in strong plain clothing. With us it is fine clothing *versus* nerves, and the clothes always win.

Shall we cry out, then, that women have already too much to do in the household, and therefore prohibit all work outside? Exactly the reverse. It would be as reasonable to decree that because the baby tosses in his little crib all night that, therefore, as he has had exercise more than enough, it will be proper and desirable to keep him tied in his high chair all day to give him rest and quiet. Many mothers have learned that plenty of play, and out of doors are excellent sleep producers for children; but they are slow to prescribe some remedy for their own infirmities.

So far from admitting that women have occupation enough in their family duties, I maintain unqualifiedly, that every woman, rich or poor, not actually an invalid, confined to one room, is in imperative need of a daily distinct change of thought and employment. The change of mere recreation is not sufficient. None but very young children can find adequate satisfaction, or even health, in unlimited play.

Women need a purpose; a definite pursuit in which they are interested, if they expect to gather from it tone and vigor, either of mind or body. If their necessities compel this, let them seek for the stimulus of pecuniary gain, with the hopeful feeling that they can earn more abroad than they can possibly save at home. If one is unskillful and yet very poor, better to go out every day as a rag-picker, than to pinch and pine at home in unbroken weariness. . . . Two poor neighbors might help each other, one superintending the children of both in the morning, and the other in the afternoon, that each family may receive a double advantage. Wife and husband could be mutual helpers with admirable effect. Let her take his place in garden or field or workshop an hour or two daily, learning to breathe more strongly, and exercising a fresh set of muscles in soul and body. To him baby-tending and bread-making would be most humanizing in their influence, all parties gaining an assured benefit, and the whole family might be expected to rest well at night.

The application of this mutual-exchange principle could be varied indefinitely. It might be made to abolish needle-work, the present baneful method of eking out a scanty income. It would promote a cure of the hurtful sentiment, that the women of the family have a right to be supported; comfortably if possible, but otherwise that they must endure a meagre fare inertly, to the detriment of all higher interests. Wives and daughters not only may starve rather than earn, but they still must do so or lose caste. Our "Woman Movement" is changing this sentiment, yet to-day ten thousand women would gladly be self-supporting if they could do so with no more loss of position than their brothers. Genius can make its own place honorable; but this seems infinitely harder to the great body of womanhood. As an alternative they double the time required in making each new garment, and quadruple it by altering over each old one, tempting their already over-worked sisters into the same destructive fashion-seeking.

Women are in less need of more work than of a more sensible

class of occupations on which to wisely spend their energies. To this end, also, we need a general reconstruction in the division of labor. Let no women give all their time to household duties, but require nearly all women, and all men also, since they belong to the household, to bear some share of the common household burdens. Many hands make light work, and hearts would be lightened in proportion. I would seek to have society so readjusted, that every man and every woman could feel that from three to six hours of each day were absolutely at his or her own disposal; and that the machinery of business or of the family would go on unimpeded meantime.

This systematic leisure is essential. . . . This is a duty to one's self, to the family, to society, and to posterity. The work done would gain in quality vastly more than it could lose in quantity. . . . The majority of people now, probably, get much more than three hours daily of comparative leisure; but it is only comparative. A thousand cares hang suspended above their heads; their occupations are not going on to completion, but waiting their return; and the claims of social life, instead of aiding to make their time really available for good, fritter it away, often to their hurt.

I should rejoice to see springing up in every city, distinct classes of three to five hour industries, with a fresh relay of workers at stated intervals, arranged for the express benefit of men and women, who desire to give but a small portion of their time to outside pursuits. . . .

That division of labor which makes skilled artisans into ten-hour machines, that exercise only one set of muscles, may teach them to do their work well. But it would be difficult to convince me that an engraver or a worker in fine jewelry all the morning would not find an immense advantage from out-door gardening, or from the use of the carpenter's saw and plane, in the afternoon. . . . If required to work many hours a day to support one's helpless dependents, most laborers of every degree would gain vastly by choosing two complementary occupations, each of which would be a relief against the other. Let the tailor and the blacksmith enter into practical partnership—each working alternately at both trades. Twelve hours would be less wearing than ten hours now. If the wife and daughters would add each—say a quarter of a day's earnings in addition to their houshold duties—the entire family might fall back upon the eight-hour system, yet live comfortably, surrounded by luxury and leisure, with the temptation to unwise speculation in fancy railroad stocks and other lotteries reduced to its minimum. . . .

Womanhood gives no more claim to a life of idleness than does manhood. Daughters would have little more right than sons to be provided for by fathers, if custom did not force them into this most uncomfortable position. It is our duty to change all this, and to enforce a greater equality of work between the sexes.

Still, I am ready to concede, most fully, that the mothers of young children ought not to be considered the bread-winners. Their leisure should be largely play, recreation—the most perfect freedom to follow whatever personal bent will injure neither themselves nor their offspring. They, more than any others, should secure their daily leisure. No well-to-do household, where there are children under ten years, if it would consult its own interests, can afford to let the mother toil for many hours daily, in kitchen, laundry, or sewing-room; and her nursery should secure some competent and trustworthy supervision during the hours when she needs rest and change—a complete laying down of all family cares. It may not be desirable that she should be entirely an idler, even in her most unfettered moments, but that is for herself to determine. Let her secure fresh air and exercise, among new scenes, as her necessities require. Our physiologists should teach her the laws of life in early girlhood, giving special heed to the maternal duty of being always fresh and vigorous, at whatever cost; not selfishly, but for the sake of her children, and in the interest of the peace and quietness of the home to which the husband should come as to a haven of comfort.

It was conceded in the beginning of my essay, that the nearest social work of average womanhood was our work in the household. But there is the earlier, the equally imperative duty of self-culture, beginning in infancy, but never ending, not if one should live, as I think all women ought, in excellent health and vigor, for nearly a century. One is weary of hearing that men outgrow their wives mentally, and that women fade, sicken, and deteriorate from the over-burden of rearing half a dozen children. . . . Facts will prove that the most active, as well as the most sensible workers, who have maintained a steady balance between work and rest, are both the longest and most vigorous livers, physically and mentally. . . . [W]ith social life properly adjusted, women should have a positive advantage over men, both in health and in gaining a longer term than they, for active usefulness.

Take notice: I do not claim that they should have equal strength with men, or that they have [equal] working capacity in early and middle life, but only that all the functions peculiar to womanhood are healthful and invigorating—while at the same time they demand that rest and relaxation from work which leaves both mind and body at fifty in the state of reaction which must make work thenceforward towards ninety easier for average women than for average men.

Circulation is checked, not destroyed, in deciduous trees in winter, but every spring they leaf out into a new freshness of beauty, which the evergreens are destined never to experience. The work of manhood is evergreen. There are not ten or twenty years in which he has a right to be an idler, while nature works within and around him at will—he content to be the grateful, re-joicing and almost passive recipient of her highest beneficence. But women, the mothers of the race, often serve humanity the best when they only rest and wait. They may freely accept of all the best gifts under heaven, of the freshest air, of the choicest food, of the most comfortable surroundings, and, above all, they have not only the right, but it is their imperative duty to live in the most invigorating and elevating mental atmosphere which it is within their limits to command. Music, art, literature, science, phi-losophy, every pursuit that strengthens instead of enervates, they may enjoy without selfishness, accumulating steadily, though slowly, in middle life, a wealth of material, which, in the autumn, should be bound in sheaves and freely offered to all who may choose to accept, privately or publicly as choice may dictate.

May not physiology be called on, then, to confirm my position, that fifty or fifty-five should be but the prime—the very crown and summit of a woman's life? Thenceforward she should aim at vigorous personal achievements, with a reach beyond the household—not at the sacrifice of the best family claims, but still in obedience to the highest home instincts. Women too often seem aged at fifty. Their only harvest, the earlier and more fleeting fruits, has passed already beyond their keeping; and their work, such as it is, is accomplished. But these have been the aimless women who indulged in slow lingering suicide—the mistaken women who over-burdened themselves with endless cares, breathing no higher and more bracing atmosphere as a perpetual alternative, or women whom accident or inheritance have made hopeless invalids. . . .

Then, after fifty, when the children have grown, allow the stateswomen who can prove their wisdom and ability to their constituents, to hold any office to which they may be elected, from town-school superintendent up to President. Why not? If the husbands are content, who else has a right to object?

Doubtless, a very competent woman might prove herself, at once a good mother, a housekeeper, and yet act as merchant, physician, or pastor of a church. A family of young children need not wholly supersede her chosen business relations, though one should freely concede her especial temptation in that case to burn the life-candle at both ends. But she would be required simply to modify her modes of working—not the work done. . . .

No home can be thoroughly attractive without intelligence, without a thousand wide-spreading interests, reaching out towards places of human weal the most remote from personal and family details, and the broader the sympathies, the efforts, both of father and mother, the better for the whole household, the better for the whole world. The co-operation of both sexes must reach everywhere, into industries, science, art, religion, and into the conduct and government of the State. Family interests, instead of suffering from this widening of womanly influence, must be surely ennobled and benefited proportionately with the wider sympathies of a more enlightened motherhood. Tenderness is not incompatible with a reach of intellect, nor have head and heart been so constituted by the All-father that they must dwell in perpetual rivalry. Nature is full of compensations. Women have no disabilities which are not equitably balanced by commensurate privileges, and men and women are equals but not identicals, associates but not rivals.

Susan B. Anthony, Social Purity (1875)

Susan B. Anthony (1820–1906) was the foremost agitator for woman suffrage in the nineteenth century. Unlike her close friend Mrs. Stanton, she considered disfranchisement the single most important cause of woman's inferiority. She was president of the National American Woman Suffrage Association from 1892 to 1900. The following address on "Social Purity," delivered in Chicago in 1875, argues that the prevalence of prostitution, sex crimes, and wife murders proves men's incapacity to cope with social problems, that their basic cause is woman's dependence, and that their cure will be woman's economic independence and political equality. [Ida Husted Harper, *The Life and Work of Susan B. Anthony*, II (Indianapolis, 1898), 1004–12.]

. . . Though women, as a class, are much less addicted to drunkenness and licentiousness than men, it is universally conceded that they are by far the greater sufferers from these evils. Compelled by their position in society to depend on men for subsistence, for food, clothes, shelter, for every chance even to earn a dollar, they have no way of escape from the besotted victims of appetite and passion with whom their lot is cast. They must endure, if not endorse, these twin vices, embodied, as they so often are, in the person of father, brother, husband, son, employer. No one can doubt that the sufferings of the sober, virtuous woman, in legal subjection to the mastership of a drunken, immoral husband and father over herself and children, not only from physical abuse, but from spiritual shame and humiliation, must be such as the man himself can not possibly comprehend. . . .

The roots of the giant evil, intemperance, are not merely moral and social; they extend deep and wide into the financial and political structure of the government; and whenever women, or men, shall intelligently set themselves about the work of uprooting the liquor traffic, they will find something more than tears and prayers needful to the task. Financial and political power must be combined with moral and social influence, all bound together in one earnest, energetic, persistent force. . . .

The prosecutions in our courts for breach of promise, divorce, adultery, bigamy, seduction, rape; the newspaper reports every day of every year of scandals and outrages, of wife murders and paramour shootings, of abortions and infanticides, are perpetual reminders of men's incapacity to cope successfully with this monster evil of society.

The statistics of New York show the number of professional prostitutes in that city to be over twenty thousand. Add to these the thousands and tens of thousands of Boston, Philadelphia, Washington, New Orleans, St. Louis, Chicago, San Francisco, and all our cities, great and small, from ocean to ocean, and what a holocaust of the womanhood of this nation is sacrificed to the insatiate Moloch of lust. And yet more: those myriads of wretched women, publicly known as prostitutes, constitute but a small portion of the numbers who actually tread the paths of vice and crime. For, as the oft-broken ranks of the vast army of common drunkards are steadily filled by the boasted moderate drinkers, so are the ranks of professional prostitution continually replenished by discouraged, seduced, deserted unfortunates, who can no longer hide the terrible secret of their lives. . . .

Nor is it womanhood alone that is thus fearfully sacrificed. For every betrayed woman, there is always the betrayer, man. For every abandoned woman, there is always *one* abandoned man and oftener many more. It is estimated that there are 50,000 professional prostitutes in London, and Dr. Ryan calculates that there are 400,000 men in that city directly or indirectly connected with them, and that this vice causes the city an annual expenditure of $40,000,000. . . .

Man's legislative attempts to set back this fearful tide of social corruption have proved even more futile and disastrous than have those for the suppression of intemperance—as witness the Contagious Diseases Acts of England and the St. Louis experiment. And yet efforts to establish similar laws are constantly made in our large cities, New York and Washington barely escaping last winter. . . .

The work of woman is not to lessen the severity or the certainty of the penalty for the violation of the moral law, but to prevent this violation by the removal of the causes which lead to it. These causes are said to be wholly different with the sexes. The acknowledged incentive to this vice on the part of man is his own abnormal passion; while on the part of women, in the great majority of cases, it is conceded to be destitution—absolute want of the necessaries of life. . . . Hence, there is no escape from the conclusion that, while woman's want of bread induces her to pursue this vice, man's love of the vice itself leads him into it and holds him there. While statistics show no lessening of the passional demand on the part of man, they reveal a most frightful increase of the temptations, the necessities, on the part of woman.

In the olden times, when the daughters of the family, as well as the wife, were occupied with useful and profitable work in the household, getting the meals and washing the dishes three times in every day of every year, doing the baking, the brewing, the washing and the ironing, the whitewashing, the butter and cheese and soap making, the mending and the making of clothes for the entire family, the carding, spinning and weaving of the cloth—when everything to eat, to drink and to wear was manufactured in the home, almost no young women "went out to work." But now, when nearly all these handicrafts are turned over to men and to machinery, tens of thousands, nay, millions of the women of both hemispheres are thrust into the world's outer market of work to earn their own subsistence. Society, ever slow to change its conditions, presents to these millions but few and meager chances. Only the barest necessaries, and oftentimes not even those, can be purchased with the proceeds of the most excessive and exhausting labor.

Hence, the reward of virtue for the homeless, friendless, penniless woman is ever a scanty larder, a pinched, patched, faded wardrobe, a dank basement or rickety garret, with the colder, shabbier scorn and neglect of the more fortunate of her sex. Nightly, as weary and worn from her day's toil she wends her way through the dark alleys toward her still darker abode, where only cold and hunger await her, she sees on every side and at every turn the gilded hand of vice and crime outstretched, beckoning her to food and clothes and shelter; hears the whisper in softest accents, "Come with me and I will give you all the comforts, pleasures and luxuries that love and wealth can bestow." Since the vast multitudes of human beings, women like men, are not born to the courage or conscience of the martyr, can we wonder that so many poor girls fall, that so many accept material ease and comfort at the expense of spiritual purity and peace? Should we not wonder, rather, that so many escape the sad fate?

Clearly, then, the first step toward solving this problem is to lift this vast army of poverty-stricken women who now crowd our cities, above the temptation, the necessity, to sell themselves, in marriage or out, for bread and shelter. To do that, girls, like boys, must be educated to some lucrative employment; women, like men, must have equal chances to earn a living. If the plea that poverty is the cause of woman's prostitution be not true, perfect equality of chances to earn honest bread will demonstrate the falsehood by removing that pretext and placing her on the same plane with man. Then, if she is found in the ranks of vice and crime, she will be there for the same reason that man is and, from an object of pity, she, like him, will become a fit subject of contempt. From being the party sinned against, she will become an equal sinner, if not the greater of the two. Women, like men, must not only have "fair play" in the world of work and self-support, but, like men, must be eligible to all the honors and emoluments of society and government. Marriage, to women as to men, must be a luxury, not a necessity; an incident of life, not all of it. And the only possible way to accomplish this great change is to accord to women equal power in the making, shaping and controlling of the circumstances of life. That equality of rights and privileges is vested in the ballot, the symbol of power in a republic. Hence, our first and most urgent demand—that women shall be protected in the exercise of their inherent, personal, citizens' right to a voice in the government, municipal, state, national.

Alexander Hamilton said one hundred years ago, "Give to a man the right over my subsistence, and he has power over my whole moral being." No one doubts the truth of this assertion as between man and man; while, as between man and woman, not only does almost no one believe it, but the masses of people deny it. And yet it is the fact of man's possession of this right over woman's subsistence which gives to him the power to dictate to her a moral code vastly higher and purer than the one he chooses for himself. Not less true is it, that the fact of woman's dependence on man for her subsistence renders her utterly powerless to exact from him the same high moral code she chooses for herself. . . .

Whoever controls work and wages, controls morals. Therefore, we must have women employers, superintendents, committees, legislators; wherever girls go to seek the means of subsistence, there must be some woman. Nay, more; we must have women preachers, lawyers, doctors—that wherever women go to seek counsel—spiritual, legal, physical—there, too, they will be sure to find the best and noblest of their own sex to minister to them.

Independence is happiness. . . . In one of our western cities I once met a beautiful young woman, a successful teacher in its public schools, an only daughter who had left her New England home and all its comforts and luxuries and culture. Her father was a member of Congress and could bring to her all the attractions of Washington society. That young girl said to me, "The happiest moment of my life was when I received my first month's salary for teaching." Not long after, I met her father in Washington, spoke to him of his noble daughter, and he said: "Yes, you woman's rights people have robbed me of my only child and left the home of my old age sad and desolate. Would to God that the notion of supporting herself had never entered her head!" Had that same lovely, cultured, energetic young girl left the love, the luxury, the protection of that New England home for marriage, instead of self-support; had she gone out to be the light and joy of a husband's life, instead of her own; had she but chosen another man, instead of her father, to decide for her all her pleasures and occupations; had she but taken another position of dependence, instead of one of independence, neither her father nor the world would have felt the change one to be condemned. . . .

Fathers should be most particular about the men who visit their daughters, and, to further this reform, pure women not only must refuse to meet intimately and to marry impure men, but, finding themselves deceived in their husband, they must refuse to continue in the marriage relation with them. We have had quite enough of the sickly sentimentalism which counts the woman a heroine and a saint for remaining the wife of a drunken, immoral husband, incurring the risk of her own health and poisoning the life-blood of the young beings that result from this unholy alliance. Such company as ye keep, such ye are! must be the maxim of married, as well as unmarried, women. . . .

In a western city the wives conspired to burn down a house of ill-fame in which their husbands had placed a half-dozen of the demi-monde. Would it not have shown much more womanly wisdom and virtue for those legal wives to have refused to recognize their husbands, instead of wreaking their vengeance on the heads of those wretched women? But how could they without finding themselves, as a result, penniless and homeless? The person, the services, the children, the subsistence, of each and every one of those women belonged by law, not to herself, but to her unfaithful husband.

Now, why is it that man can hold woman to this high code of morals, like Caesar's wife—not only pure but above suspicion— and so surely and severely punish her for every departure, while she is so helpless, so powerless to check him in his license, or to extricate herself from his presence and control? His power grows out of her dependence on him for her food, her clothes, her shelter.

Marriage will never cease to be a wholly unequal partnership until the law recognizes the equal ownership in the joint earnings and possessions. The true relation of the sexes never can be attained until woman is free and equal with man. Neither in the making nor executing of the laws regulating these relations has woman ever had the slightest voice. The statutes for marriage and divorce, for adultery, breach of promise, seduction, rape, bigamy, abortion, infanticide—all were made by men. They, alone, decide who are guilty of violating these laws and what shall be their punishment, with judge, jury and advocate all men, with no woman's voice heard in our courts, save as accused or witness, and in many cases the married woman is denied the poor privilege of testifying as to her own guilt or innocence of the crime charged against her.

Since the days of Moses and the prophets, men and ministers have preached the law of "visiting the iniquity of the fathers upon the children and the children's children, to the third and fourth generations." But with absolute power over woman and all the conditions of life for the whole 6,000 years, man has proved his utter inability either to put away his own iniquities, or to cease to hand them down from generation to generation; hence, the only hope of reform is in sharing this absolute power with some other than himself, and that other must be woman. When no longer a subject, but an equal—a free and independent sovereign, believing herself created primarily for her own individual happiness and development and secondarily for man's, precisely as man believes himself created first for his own enjoyment and second for that of woman—she will constitute herself. sole umpire in the sacred domain of motherhood. Then, instead of feeling it her Christian duty to live with a drunken, profligate husband, handing down to her children his depraved appetites and passions, she will *know* that God's curse will be upon her and her children if she flee not from him as from a pestilence.

It is worse than folly, it is madness, for women to delude themselves with the idea that their children will escape the terrible penalty of the law. The taint of their birth will surely follow them. For pure women to continue to devote themselves to their man-appointed mission of visiting the dark purlieus of society and struggling to reclaim the myriads of badly-born human beings swarming there, is as hopeless as would be an attempt to ladle the ocean with a teaspoon; as unphilosophical as was the undertaking of the old American Colonization Society, which, with great labor and pains and money, redeemed from slavery and transported to Liberia annually 400 negroes, or the Fugitive Slave Societies, which succeeded in running off to Canada, on their "under-ground railroads," some 40,000 in a whole quarter of a century. While those good men were thus toiling to rescue the 400 or the 40,000 individual victims of slavery, each day saw hundreds and each year thousands of human beings born into the terrible condition of chattelism. All see and admit now what none but the Abolitionists saw then, that the only effectual work was the entire overthrow of the system of slavery; the abrogation of the law which sanctioned the right of property in man. . . .

. . . [W]herever you go, you find the best women, in and out of the churches, all absorbed in establishing or maintaining benevolent or reform institutions; charitable societies, soup-houses, ragged schools, industrial schools, mite societies, mission schools— at home and abroad—homes and hospitals for the sick, the aged, the friendless, the foundling, the fallen; asylums for the orphans, the blind, the deaf and dumb, the insane, the inebriate, the idiot. The women of this century are neither idle nor indifferent. They are working with might and main to mitigate the evils which stare them in the face on every side, but much of their work is without knowledge. It is aimed at the effects, not the cause; it is plucking the spoiled fruit; it is lopping off the poisonous branches of the deadly upas tree, which but makes the root more vigorous in sending out new shoots in every direction. A right understanding of physiological law teaches us that the cause must be removed; the tree must be girdled; the tap-root must be severed.

The tap-root of our social upas lies deep down at the very foundations of society. It is woman's dependence. It is woman's subjection. Hence, the first and only efficient work must be to emancipate woman from her enslavement. The wife must no longer echo the poet Milton's ideal Eve, when she adoringly said to Adam, "God thy law; thou, mine!" She must feel herself accountable to God alone for every act, fearing and obeying no man, save where his will is in line with her own highest idea of divine law. . . .

I am a full and firm believer in the revelation that it is through woman that the race is to be redeemed. And it is because of this faith that I ask for her immediate and unconditional emancipation from all political, industrial, social and religious subjection. . . . Ralph Waldo Emerson says, "Men are what their mothers made them." But I say, to hold mothers responsible for the character of their sons while you deny them any control over the surroundings of their lives, is worse than mockery, it is cruelty! Responsibilities grow out of rights and powers. Therefore, before mothers can be held responsible for the vices and crimes, the wholesale demoralization of men, they must possess all possible rights and powers to control the conditions and circumstances of their own and their children's lives.

Harriot Stanton Blatch, Voluntary Motherhood (1891)

Harriot Stanton Blatch (1856–1940) was Elizabeth Cady Stanton's daughter and a graduate of Vassar. She married an Englishman and moved to England in 1882, but returned soon after the turn of the century and became active in the suffragist movement in New York City. Her address, excerpted below, argues that "race improvement" depends on lengthened infancy and thus on the wisdom and philoprogenitiveness of the mothers. Women must therefore have the right to decide whether and when to become mothers. ["Voluntary Motherhood," *Transactions of the National Council of Women of the United States, Assembled in Washington, D.C., February 22 to 25, 1891* (Philadelphia, 1891), pp. 278–85.]

"The truth is, we are in the midst of such terrible errors on the subject of woman and her veritable rights that it is frightful to think of."—*Tolstoi's "Kreutzer Sonata."*

The difficulty of approaching the subject of the relation of the sexes is tenfold, if the prerogatives of the dominant sex are challenged. It is because of its attack upon men that Tolstoi's "Kreutzer Sonata" has raised so much opposition. To decry this last publication of the Russian novelist as immoral is merely a little dust-throwing to blind women to the truths in the book, and it is hoped that neither this abuse nor the author's own religious beliefs and Eastern philosophy will obscure for his readers the gospel set forth. True, Tolstoi is extreme; but humanity has been so misguided by the average man's thought, or rather passion, that it is scarcely ground for wonder that a sensitive thinker should regard as an ideal, entire continence.

Tolstoi aims to reach a solution of life for men; as to the feelings of women, he admits he is not informed. In this object he resembles most writers who deal with the relation of the sexes; for all look at this matter from the man's point of view, and seldom if ever from the side of the rights and duties of the mother and the interests of the child. These weighty considerations are buffeted about according to the opinions upon other subjects held by the persons handling them. The political economist of the Mill school tells the working-man that his trouble does not come from unequal distribution of wealth, but from his large family. The labor market is overstocked, and poverty results. The Malthusian, while foretelling terrible consequences if human increase is not limited, advocates various artificial checks, not to human license, but to race productivity. Many a socialist denies all these forebodings, and proclaims that even England now "has too small a population for a really high civilization."

Now, these contradictory theories resemble one another in one particular,—those who propound them think that economic considerations alone should settle this matter of population. In contrast to this, the man's commercial view of race production, stands the woman's intuition backed by reason. She asks, first, will the child be welcome? second, what will be its inheritance of physical, mental, and moral character? third, can the child be provided for in life? Every conscientious mother replies to the socialist and to the Malthusian that satisfactory answers must be given to the woman's first and second demands, and that with satisfactory answers to those questions the third consideration may safely be left to take care of itself.

In animal life, as soon as we get conscious motherhood, the strides in evolution become greater and more rapid.

Below the birds "the animal takes care of himself as soon as he begins to live. He has nothing to learn, and his career is a simple repetition of the careers of countless ancestors." Among higher birds and mammals a great change takes place: the life of the creature becomes so varied and complex that habits cannot be fully organized in the nervous system before birth. The antenatal period is too short to allow of such development. So we get a period of infancy, a time of plasticity, of teachableness. Of this time Fiske truly says, "The first appearance of infancy in the animal world heralded the new era which was to be crowned by the development of man." From this point in evolution the period of infancy lengthens,—indeed, this is the condition of progress. To reach a higher stage of development a longer time must be given to immaturity or growth, and that period will be one of greater or less dependence according as the adult being is of higher or lower species. What chiefly distinguishes the human being from the lower animals is the increase in the former of cerebral surface and organization, and the necessary accompaniment of this development, a lengthened period of infancy.

Now, this increased time of immaturity is a direct tax upon the mother in any species; so to her is due each step in evolution. Men talk of the sacredness of motherhood, but judging from their acts it is the last thing that is held sacred in the human species. Poets sing and philosophers reason about the holiness of the mother's sphere, but men in laws and customs have degraded the woman in her maternity. Motherhood is sacred,—that is, voluntary motherhood; but the woman who bears unwelcome children is outraging every duty she owes the race. The mothers of the human species should turn to the animals, and from the busy caretakers, who are below them in most things, learn the simple truths of procreation. Let women but understand the part unenforced maternity has played in the evolution of animal life, and their reason will guide them to the true path of race development.

Let them note that natural selection has carefully fostered the maternal instinct. The offspring of the fondest females in each animal species, having of course the most secure and prolonged infancy, are "naturally selected" to continue their kind. The female offspring gains by inheritance in philoprogenitiveness, and thus is built up the instinct which prepares the females of a higher species for a more developed altruism. Through countless ages mother-love has been evolved and been working out its mission; surely women should recognize the meaning of the instinct, and should refuse to prostitute their creative powers, and so jeopardize the progress of the human race. Upon the mothers must rest in the last instance the development of any species.

In this work women need not hope for help from men. The sense of obligation to offspring, men possess but feebly; there has not been developed by animal evolution an instinct of paternity. They are not disinherited fathers; they are simply un-evolved parents. There is no ground for wonder that this is so; for in but a few species among the lower animals is even a suggestion of paternal instinct found. The male bird often occupies itself with the hatching and feeding of the brood, and the lion is a pattern father; but usually we find no hint of paternal instinct in the male, and sometimes antagonism towards the young of the species. Evidently nature tried her hand on paternity, it did not fulfil the hopes she had of it, and she turned a cold shoulder upon its development. The paternal instinct is not a factor in evolution.

If, then, the law of natural selection is of weight, we should expect to find very little, if any, instinct of paternity in the male of the human species. Not only by such *a priori* reasoning is this conclusion reached, but *a posteriori* reasoning emphasizes the same truth. Men like to accumulate, and hand down their accumulation with their name. This is a method of securing some sort of immortality, and gives rise to the neglect of illegitimate children, the preference of male to female offspring, the law of primo-geniture, and the selection, in case of male heirs failing, of some distant relation to inherit the property provided he will adopt the name of his benefactor. The masculine tendencies which have crystallized themselves in these customs bear no resemblance to paternal love. A woman does not discriminate between her legitimate and illegitimate child; and had mothers been instrumental in making legal codes there would not have been a law of entail.

But perhaps the strongest proof of the feebleness of philoprogenitiveness in men is the existence of their system of prostitution, with the accompanying thoughtlessness in which parenthood is risked, and the indifference with which rich fathers leave their children to a life of hardship, if not of crime. When Henry Ward Beecher made his famous assertion, in the Presidential campaign of '88, that if all the men who, like Grover Cleveland, had carried on illicit relations with women, voted for him, the Democratic candidate would sweep New York by an overwhelming majority, his words called forth no resentment. But does not such a statement, if it be a fact, imply a more vital truth? It means that but a handful of men could solemnly swear that they are certain no child of theirs is rotting out its life in some tenement or gutter. Could there be a more unanswerable argument against the existence of paternal feeling than the brief statement, that of the seventy thousand illegitimate children born each year in France, only five thousand are acknowledged by the fathers? And our very attitude toward men of the type of the other sixty-five thousand shows that we do not expect strong paternal feeling in men. No one feels that George Eliot drew an abnormal creature in Godfrey Cass. When he fails to acknowledge his child and leaves it with the despised weaver, the author does not describe his conduct as that of a brutal man. Again, no thoughtful person could fail to be struck in reading Darwin's Life and Letters, by the fact that the greatest student of heredity of our time, though himself the victim of an incurable and hereditary disease, never questioned his right to become the father of many children. And yet he was fully aware of the probability of ill health for his offspring; for in letters to friends he pours out his fears: "My dread is hereditary ill health. *Even death is better for them.*" Is it only a woman's logic that would lead to the opposite conclusion: *Better had they never been born?* Now, no one could say that Darwin was a bad man; on the contrary, if report speaks truly, we may look upon him as exceptionally good. The conclusion then forces itself upon us that even the best of men are lacking in that nice conscience which recognizes the sacredness of life and the responsibility of its creation. But humanity would suffer the minimum of evil from this cause, were not laws based upon the extraordinary assumption that, "by the law of nature and the law of God," the father is the sole guardian of the child, and the suicidal custom followed of giving the power of legislation and the social dominance, in all sex matters, into the hands of that half of the race which is unfitted by nature for any just comprehension of these questions.

Ever since the patriarchate was established, there has been a tendency to cramp the mother in her maternal rights; so we see no race improvement comparable with our advance in material science. Those who could improve humanity have been hindered by those who prefer to improve steam-engines. The sex which has been laboriously evolved by nature for the arduous work of race-building is handicapped; so more and more the best women turn from the work of motherhood and join the ranks of competitive labor, or seek in society and politics a field for the free play of their ambitions. And now certain of our thinkers forebode evil for a people whose women turn from the home to the frivolities of fashion and the excitement of the political arena. Their forebodings are not without foundation; but the remedy does not lie in depriving women of public freedom, but in according them absolute domestic liberty. The world must act, as well as talk, as if motherhood were important and sacred, before women will give full allegiance to that office. But so to act requires a complete right-about-face.

. . . The need is that the race be lifted up. But how is a species raised? Always by lengthening the period of infancy. And at whose expense must this be done? At the mother's; more and more of her thought, more and more of her time must be given to the period of immaturity in her offspring; later and later should the child be brought into contact with the practical demands of life. This work requires as its first condition voluntary maternity; for the unwelcome child is mentally and physically below the average; and it is a direct drag upon the mother in the efficient performance of already assigned maternal duties. The evolution of humanity and enforced maternity are antagonistic.

A second condition of race-improvement is a broader education of women. It is amazing that the nineteenth century holds that any sort of education is good enough for girls. It indicates, too, how low an opinion we have of motherhood, that when a woman does receive superior training it is considered lost, unless she enters upon a competitive career. In a recent speech before a girls' school, Mr. Gladstone, commenting on the success women had achieved in education, said that as a result places of work would have to be thrown open to them; that "of course they could not be given the training, and be debarred from the use of that training." But surely is it not equally a matter *of course* that even if women were debarred from public life, they would not be debarred a very important use for all the knowledge of the universe in their sphere of race-builders? The fact is, few women and fewer men regard maternity in its true light; traced down to finalities, the birth of most human beings is a sexual accident. Of course, the person playing the chief *rôle* in this game of haphazard is neither self-respecting nor respected; for a matter of chance is never held as holy, however much poets and philosophers, popes and bishops may declare the reverse.

A third condition of race progress is that women should divide with no other person authority over the child. When the work of race-building is left wholly to women, we may look for better results; for then the ambition of the best mothers will find a congenial field for action in their so-called "sphere." As the human being is always of more real value than the work, so to rear an astronomer is perchance a higher labor than to discover a comet. . . . If nature has intended women for a special career, the way to defeat the object is to limit their responsibility and authority so completely that they turn to freer fields of work. . . .

The first step toward making maternity voluntary is to secure for all women financial independence. There are those who think this can be done by women entering the world of competitive work. Now, there is no doubt that the female of the human species could win her way, if free of artificial hinderances [*sic*]. The female among the lower animals supports herself and her offspring; she is competent both as bread-winner and mother. Under present sex relations women have been enfeebled in two ways,—they have lost the mental training gained in bread-winning, and have been physically depleted by playing a double *rôle* of mother and mistress. But undoubtedly in freedom, women could again be self-supporting and efficient mothers, just as they were in the time of the matriarchate; but we may well doubt whether, in our dire need for the elevation of our species, it would be economy to make the mothers of the race enter the field of competition to gain their bread and cheese. However, if the choice lies between this and the financial dependence of one woman upon one man, then every well-wisher to the race must say, let the woman be self-supporting. But educated thought upon this subject will desire to make better terms with women, and the latter will finally make better terms with civilization. Undoubtedly the tendency at present is to seek independence by undertaking competitive work, rather than to demand that work done in the home shall be recognized and command money return. Just where this tendency is to lead is not plain; but if with self-support should come an increasing neglect of maternal duties, the result will be race decadence; but if self-support leads women to the conditions, in some co-operative form, of life in the time of the Mutterrecht, human improvement may be carried to a high point of perfection. But the field of race production is so fundamental in its importance, so broad in its possibilities, it opens an arena so wide for the play of the loftiest ambitions and of the most varied talents, that time and leisure to be secured, on honorable terms, to those cultivating this field, seems but justice the most meagre and wisdom the most evident.

The solution most often offered for our social difficulties is divorce. But it is a solution which does not touch the real source of the trouble, and its agitation diverts attention from more vital questions. It is because divorce merely shifts the disease from one home to another, because it in no way lessens our trouble—

the financial dependence of women, and enforced maternity—
that the carrying of legislation upon the lines of easier dissolution
of the marriage contract proves but a barren victory. . . . As public
opinion grows upon our two great needs, legislation will probably
take more the line of securing to the woman her fair share of the
family income, and giving her absolute right to her children.

Charlotte Perkins Gilman, Economic Basis of the Woman Question (1898)

Just as Mrs. Stanton was the boldest thinker of the first generation of feminists, Charlotte Perkins Gilman was the boldest of
those who dominated the movement between the 1890's and
World War I. Born in 1860, she was a poet, novelist, essayist,
and journalist. Suffragism, however, was never quite as important
to her as it was to most of her contemporaries in the movement.
She died by suicide in 1935, a victim of cancer. The theme in the
following article is one that appears again and again throughout
her writings, namely the contrast between the progressive, indus-
trializing world and the stagnant, primitive home. [Charlotte
Perkins Stetson (Gilman), "Economic Basis of the Woman Question," *Woman's Journal*, October 1, 1898.]

The question before women is how best to do their duty upon
earth. To define individual duty is difficult; but the collective
duty of a class or sex is clear. It is the duty of women to develop
and improve themselves; to bring children into the world who
are superior to their parents; and to forward the progress of the
race. . . .

A peculiar condition of women is that their environment has
been almost wholly that of the home; and the home is the most
ancient of human institutions; the most unalterably settled in its
ideals and convictions; the slowest and last to move. . . .

The progressive changes and social evolution accomplish wonders in those fields of life open to their influence; but the motion-less, sheltered, inner places remain unchanged among us, like the frozen mastodons, confronting us with their complacent presence, an immense anachronism. So in our social world to-day, men and women who are familiar with liquefied air and Roentgen rays, who have accepted electric transit and look forward with com-placence to air-ships, people who are as liberal and progressive in mechanical lines as need be hoped, remain sodden and buried in their prehistoric sentiment as to the domestic relations. The world of science and invention may change; art, religion, govern-ment may change; industry, commerce and manufacturing may change; but women and the home are supposed to remain as they are, forever. . . .

The development of humanity can not proceed far through one sex only; and in this age it [nature] has at last succeeded in stir-ring the heavy, hidden centres of our lives, the home, and in rousing woman to face life at last.

This movement among women, so characteristic of this century, has many faces, many voices, and many aims. It has been upheld and defended, it has been vilified and opposed by many honest persons of both sexes, and has made wonderful progress withal; yet it is still possible that the true basis and purpose of the great change are unknown to many of the supporters and opponents alike. Without attempting an exhaustive study of this enormous social change, one most important factor is here put forward, the economic conditions which underlie the previous position of woman, and the changes in economic condition which must ac-company her change.

Human creatures, in proportion to their degree of social develop-ment, obtain their livings by the interchange of social services. . . . What work it is that we do for one another, and what manner of living we achieve thereby—these are the economic conditions of humanity.

The economic position of women in the world heretofore has been that of the domestic servant. . . . Do not confuse with this the sex activities of women as wives and mothers, or their "social" activities in the limited sense of entertainment given and received.

Human beings are animals. Animals must eat. Food is produced by labor. Those who do not labor for their food must have it given to them—or steal it. So far as women, taken the world over, throughout history, have labored, it has been mainly in domestic service.

Domestic service is the lowest grade of labor remaining extant. It belongs to an earlier social era. . . . When a man marries a housemaid, makes a wife of his servant, he alters her social status; but if she continues in the same industry he does not alter her economic status. When he makes a servant of his wife, or she of herself by choice, whatever her social, civil, mental or moral status may be, her economic status is that of domestic service. What she is entitled to receive from society for her labor is the wages of the housemaid. What she gets more than that is given her by her husband without any economic equivalent. She is supported by him on account of her sex. It is a low position in this mighty world so complex and stirring, so full of noble activities, to earn no higher place than was open to the slave of countless centuries ago, but it is a far lower position to be fed and clothed as a sex-dependent, a creature without economic usefulness.

This economic dependence is the underlying ground of the helplessness of women. . . . [N]o human creatures can be free whose bread is in other hands than theirs. . . . Husband, father or brother may give wealth to wife, daughter or sister—but that does not make her economically independent in the true sense. As well pile your canary's cage with seed and sugar and say he is independent of your care. . . .

A man might be the noblest and best of husbands, fathers or sons; but if his wife, his daughter or his mother supported him for life on account of his value in these relations, he would not be economically free, but sex-dependent. . . .

Only in a large, well-managed business combination can these matters of heating, lighting, feeding, clothing and cleaning be rightly carried out; and only in the ample scope of such orderly industry, in its regular hours of labor and free time of rest, and in its well earned, liberal payment for each grade of service, can women fulfill their duties in this line and be free human creatures too. We shall have far cleaner, stiller, healthier, happier homes, when their long outgrown industries are at last cut loose and sent where they belong; and women will enjoy their homes, places of pure rest and loving companionship, far more than is possible to the overworked housewife or idle housemistress of to-day.

Against all this so visible trend of change rises the great cry of frightened motherhood; the protest that women must stay alone at home and do their housework because only so can they do their duty by their children.

How do we know this? How do we know that the care of children by one individual mother in the personally conducted home is the best thing for the world?

There is nothing to reply except that it is "natural"—that it always was so and always will be—the same old dead weight of blank feeling without one glimmering flash of thought. Without trying to argue—it is useless to reason against feeling—let it be flatly asserted, first that the vast majority of children are very ill cared for and ill trained by their most loving mothers; that they die in vast proportion; that they are most unnecessarily sick; that they are not conspicuously happy; that they grow up—such of them as survive—to be the kind of tired, timid, selfish, unprogressive people of whom the world is all too full. . . . Only an independent motherhood, working wisely in well-organized businesses, will grow to see that the care of children is a profession in itself— the noblest and most important of all human work, and not to be lightly undertaken and bunglingly struggled through by every female who can bear young. . . . We need people with larger hearts and larger minds, knowing and caring for other interests than their own immediate physical necessities and relations. Only as we learn to work and care for each other in the largest sense shall we grow towards better living for ourselves and those dearest to us. And with all the negative moral superiority of women, there is nothing more absolutely in the way of social progress to-day than the huge, blind, sluggish mass and primitive prejudice embodied in the economically dependent woman.

III

WOMAN AND GOVERNMENT

F ROM 1848 ON, *feminists increasingly emphasized those griev-ances and demands that pertained to woman's relation to govern-ment. At first the chief stress was on securing married women's property laws and other legislation, to wipe out legal inequi-ties. More and more, however, they focused on the demand for the vote. Owing to tactical and personal differences among leaders, two organizations—the National Woman Suffrage Association and the American Woman Suffrage Association—were founded in 1869. In 1890 they merged to form the National American Woman Suffrage Association, which campaigned for woman suf-frage unremittingly until the ratification of the Nineteenth Amendment in 1920, when the NAWSA became the League of Women Voters. During those fifty years suffragists also cam-paigned for the enfranchisement of women by state legislation. By August 1920, when the amendment was ratified, twenty-eight of the forty-eight states already had either full or presidential suffrage. Thus the common remark that the Nineteenth Amend-ment "enfranchised American women" is misleading; the majority of American women—the overwhelming majority outside the South and New England—could already vote at least in elections for President.*

The amendment, rather than working a revolution in women's political status, was the final stage in a continuing process by which women voters had been added to the electorate state by state, beginning with Wyoming in 1890. Women did not vote as a bloc; nor did their entrance into the electorate infuse a feminine influence into American political life, as many people had hoped and others had feared. In fact, except for some early tendencies to vote "dry" more often than men, women voters have been divided, as men have, on all issues and among all parties. It is now clear that Charlotte Perkins Gilman, Elizabeth Cady Stanton, and a few others were correct in their judgment that the feminist movement diverted far too much of its energy and attributed far too much significance to suffragism.

I

DECLARATION OF SENTIMENTS AND RESOLUTIONS, SENECA FALLS CONVENTION (1848)

The Declaration of Sentiments, adopted in July 1848 at Seneca Falls, New York, at the first woman's-rights convention, is the most famous document in the history of feminism. Like its model, the Declaration of Independence, it contains a bill of particulars. Some people at the meeting thought the inclusion of disfranchisement in the list of grievances would discredit the entire movement, and when the resolutions accompanying the Declaration were put to a vote, the one calling for the suffrage was the only one that did not pass unanimously. But it did pass and thus inaugurated the woman-suffrage movement in the United States. [*HWS* I, 70–73.]

DECLARATION OF SENTIMENTS

When, in the course of human events, it becomes necessary for one portion of the family of man to assume among the people of the earth a position different from that which they have hitherto occupied, but one to which the laws of nature and of nature's God entitle them, a decent respect to the opinions of mankind requires that they should declare the causes that impel them to such a course.

We hold these truths to be self-evident: that all men and women are created equal; that they are endowed by their Creator with certain inalienable rights; that among these are life, liberty, and the pursuit of happiness; that to secure these rights governments are instituted, deriving their just powers from the consent of the governed. Whenever any form of government becomes destructive of these ends, it is the right of those who suffer from it to refuse allegiance to it, and to insist upon the institution of a new government, laying its foundation on such principles, and organizing its powers in such form, as to them shall seem most likely to effect their safety and happiness. Prudence, indeed, will dictate that governments long established should not be changed for light and transient causes; and accordingly all experience hath shown that mankind are more disposed to suffer, while evils are sufferable, than to right themselves by abolishing the forms to which they were accustomed. But when a long train of abuses and usurpations, pursuing invariably the same object, evinces a design to reduce them under absolute despotism, it is their duty to throw off such government, and to provide new guards for their future security. Such has been the patient sufferance of the women under this government, and such is now the necessity which constrains them to demand the equal station to which they are entitled.

The history of mankind is a history of repeated injuries and usurpations on the part of man toward woman, having in direct object the establishment of an absolute tyranny over her. To prove this, let facts be submitted to a candid world.

He has never permitted her to exercise her inalienable right to the elective franchise.

He has compelled her to submit to laws, in the formation of which she had no voice.

He has withheld from her rights which are given to the most ignorant and degraded men—both natives and foreigners.

Having deprived her of this first right of a citizen, the elective franchise, thereby leaving her without representation in the halls of legislation, he has oppressed her on all sides.

He has made her, if married, in the eye of the law, civilly dead.

He has taken from her all right in property, even to the wages she earns.

He has made her, morally, an irresponsible being, as she can commit many crimes with impunity, provided they be done in the presence of her husband. In the covenant of marriage, she is compelled to promise obedience to her husband, he becoming, to all intents and purposes, her master—the law giving him power to deprive her of her liberty, and to administer chastisement.

He has so framed the laws of divorce, as to what shall be the proper causes, and in case of separation, to whom the guardianship of the children shall be given, as to be wholly regardless of the happiness of women—the law, in all cases, going upon the false supposition of the supremacy of man, and giving all power into his hands.

After depriving her of all rights as a married woman, if single, and the owner of property, he has taxed her to support a government which recognizes her only when her property can be made profitable to it.

He has monopolized nearly all the profitable employments, and from those she is permitted to follow, she receives but a scanty remuneration. He closes against her all the avenues to wealth and distinction which he considers most honorable to himself. As a teacher of theology, medicine, or law, she is not known.

He has denied her the facilities for obtaining a thorough education, all colleges being closed against her.

He allows her in Church, as well as State, but a subordinate position, claiming Apostolic authority for her exclusion from the ministry, and, with some exceptions, from any public participation in the affairs of the Church.

He has created a false public sentiment by giving to the world a different code of morals for men and women, by which moral delinquencies which exclude women from society, are not only tolerated, but deemed of little account in man.

He has usurped the prerogative of Jehovah himself, claiming it as his right to assign for her a sphere of action, when that belongs to her conscience and to her God.

He has endeavored, in every way that he could, to destroy her confidence in her own powers, to lessen her self-respect, and to make her willing to lead a dependent and abject life.

Now, in view of this entire disfranchisement of one-half the people of this country, their social and religious degradation—in view of the unjust laws above mentioned, and because women do feel themselves aggrieved, oppressed, and fraudulently deprived of their most sacred rights, we insist that they have immediate admission to all the rights and privileges which belong to them as citizens of the United States.

In entering upon the great work before us, we anticipate no small amount of misconception, misrepresentation, and ridicule; but we shall use every instrumentality within our power to effect our object. We shall employ agents, circulate tracts, petition the State and National legislatures, and endeavor to enlist the pulpit and the press in our behalf. We hope this Convention will be followed by a series of Conventions embracing every part of the country.

RESOLUTIONS

WHEREAS, The great precept of nature is conceded to be, that "man shall pursue his own true and substantial happiness." Blackstone in his Commentaries remarks, that this law of Nature being coeval with mankind, and dictated by God himself, is of course superior in obligation to any other. It is binding over all the globe, in all countries and at all times; no human laws are of any validity if contrary to this, and such of them as are valid, derive all their force, and all their validity, and all their authority, mediately and immediately, from this original; therefore,

Resolved, That such laws as conflict, in any way, with the true and substantial happiness of woman, are contrary to the great precept of nature and of no validity, for this is "superior in obligation to any other."

Resolved, That all laws which prevent woman from occupying such a station in society as her conscience shall dictate, or which place her in a position inferior to that of man, are contrary to the great precept of nature, and therefore of no force or authority.

Resolved, That woman is man's equal—was intended to be so by the Creator, and the highest good of the race demands that she should be recognized as such.

Resolved, That the women of this country ought to be enlightened in regard to the laws under which they live, that they may no longer publish their degradation by declaring themselves satisfied with their present position, nor their ignorance, by asserting that they have all the rights they want.

Resolved, That inasmuch as man, while claiming for himself intellectual superiority, does accord to woman moral superiority, it is pre-eminently his duty to encourage her to speak and teach, as she has an opportunity, in all religious assemblies.

Resolved, That the same amount of virtue, delicacy, and refinement of behavior that is required of woman in the social state, should also be required of man, and the same transgressions should be visited with equal severity on both man and woman.

Resolved, That the objection of indelicacy and impropriety, which is so often brought against woman when she addresses a public audience, comes with a very ill-grace from those who encourage, by their attendance, her appearance on the stage, in the concert, or in feats of the circus.

Resolved, That woman has too long rested satisfied in the circumscribed limits which corrupt customs and a perverted application of the Scriptures have marked out for her, and that it is time she should move in the enlarged sphere which her great Creator has assigned her.

Resolved, That it is the duty of the women of this country to secure to themselves their sacred right to the elective franchise.

Resolved, That the equality of human rights results necessarily from the fact of the identity of the race in capabilities and responsibilities.

Resolved, therefore, That, being invested by the Creator with the same capabilities, and the same consciousness of responsibility for their exercise, it is demonstrably the right and duty of woman, equally with man, to promote every righteous cause by every righteous means; and especially in regard to the great subjects of morals and religion, it is self-evidently her right to participate with her brother in teaching them, both in private and in public, by writing and by speaking, by any instrumentalities proper to be used, and in any assemblies proper to be held; and this being a self-evident truth growing out of the divinely implanted principles of human nature, any custom or authority adverse to it, whether modern or wearing the hoary sanction of antiquity, is to be regarded as a self-evident falsehood, and at war with mankind.

[All the above resolutions had been drafted by Elizabeth Cady Stanton. At the last session of the convention Lucretia Mott offered the following, which, along with all the other resolutions except the ninth, was adopted unanimously.—*Ed.*]

Resolved, That the speedy success of our cause depends upon the zealous and untiring efforts of both men and women, for the overthrow of the monopoly of the pulpit, and for the securing to woman an equal participation with men in the various trades, professions, and commerce.

2

THE ANTISUFFRAGISTS: WOMAN'S SPHERE IS HOME, NOT GOVERNMENT

Editorial, New York *Herald* (1852)

"The Woman's Rights Convention—The Last Act of the Drama," editorial, New York *Herald*, September 12, 1852. [HWS I, 853–54.]

The farce at Syracuse has been played out. . . .

Who are these women? What do they want? what are the motives that impel them to this course of action? The *dramatis personae* of the farce enacted at Syracuse present a curious conglomeration of both sexes. Some of them are old maids, whose personal charms were never very attractive, and who have been sadly slighted by the masculine gender in general; some of them women who have been badly mated, whose own temper, or their husbands', has made life anything but agreeable to them, and they are therefore down upon the whole of the opposite sex; some, having so much of the virago in their disposition, that nature appears to have made a mistake in their gender—mannish women, like hens that crow; some of boundless vanity and egotism, who believe that they are superior in intellectual ability to "all the world and the rest of mankind," and delight to see their speeches and addresses in print; and man shall be consigned to his proper sphere—nursing the babies, washing the dishes, mending stockings, and sweeping the house. This is "the good time coming." Besides the classes we have enumerated, there is a class of wild enthusiasts and visionaries—very sincere, but very mad—having the same vein as the fanatical Abolitionists, and the majority, if not all of them, being, in point of fact, deeply imbued with the anti-slavery sentiment. Of the male sex who attend these Conventions for the purpose of taking part in them, the majority are hen-pecked husbands, and all of them ought to wear petticoats. . . .

How did woman first become subject to man as she now is all over the world? By her nature, her sex, just as the negro is and always will be, to the end of time, inferior to the white race, and, therefore, doomed to subjection; but happier than she would be in any other condition, just because it is the law of her nature. The women themselves would not have this law reversed. . . .

What do the leaders of the Woman's Rights Convention want? They want to vote, and to hustle with the rowdies at the polls. They want to be members of Congress, and in the heat of debate to subject themselves to coarse jests and indecent language. . . . They want to fill all other posts which men are ambitious to occupy—to be lawyers, doctors, captains of vessels, and generals in the field. How funny it would sound in the newspapers, that Lucy Stone, pleading a cause, took suddenly ill in the pains of parturition, and perhaps gave birth to a fine bouncing boy in court! Or that Rev. Antoinette Brown was arrested in the middle of her sermon in the pulpit from the same cause, and presented a "pledge" to her husband and the congregation; or, that Dr. Harriot K. Hunt, while attending a gentleman patient for a fit of the gout or *fistula in ano*, found it necessary to send for a doctor,

there and then, and to be delivered of a man or woman child—
perhaps twins. A similar event might happen on the floor of
Congress, in a storm at sea, or in the raging tempest of battle, and
then what is to become of the woman legislator?

New York State Legislative Report (1856)

This Report on Woman's Rights, made to the New York State
Legislature and concerning a petition for political equality for
women, was printed in an Albany paper in March 1856. [*HWS* I,
629–30.]

Mr. Foote, from the Judiciary Committee, made a report on
Women's rights that set the whole House in roars of laughter:

"The Committee is composed of married and single gentlemen.
The bachelors on the Committee, with becoming diffidence, having left the subject pretty much to the married gentlemen, they
have considered it with the aid of the light they have before
them and the experience married life has given them. Thus aided,
they are enabled to state that the ladies always have the best
place and choicest titbit at the table. They have the best seat in
the cars, carriages, and sleighs; the warmest place in the winter,
and the coolest place in the summer. They have their choice on
which side of the bed they will lie, front or back. A lady's dress
costs three times as much as that of a gentleman; and, at the present time, with the prevailing fashion, one lady occupies three
times as much space in the world as a gentleman.

"It has thus appeared to the married gentlemen of your
Committee, being a majority (the bachelors being silent for the
reason mentioned, and also probably for the further reason that
they are still suitors for the favors of the gentler sex), that, if
there is any inequality or oppression in the case, the gentlemen
are the sufferers. They, however, have presented no petitions for
redress; having, doubtless, made up their minds to yield to an
inevitable destiny. . . ."

Orestes A. Brownson, The Woman Question (1869 and 1873)

The following document consists of two articles by Orestes A. Brownson: "The Woman Question. Article I [from the *Catholic World*, May 1869]," in Henry F. Brownson, ed., *The Works of Orestes A. Brownson*, XVIII (Detroit, 1885), 388–89; and "The Woman Question. Article II [a review of Horace Bushnell, *Women's Suffrage: The Reform against Nature* (New York, 1869), from *Brownson's Quarterly Review* for October 1873]," in Henry F. Brownson, *op. cit.*, p. 403.

The conclusive objection to the political enfranchisement of women is, that it would weaken and finally break up and destroy the Christian family. The social unit is the family, not the individual; and the greatest danger to American society is, that we are rapidly becoming a nation of isolated individuals, without family ties or affections. The family has already been much weakened, and is fast disappearing. We have broken away from the old homestead, have lost the restraining and purifying associations that gathered around it, and live away from home in hotels and boarding-houses. We are daily losing the faith, the virtues, the habits, and the manners without which the family cannot be sustained; and when the family goes, the nation goes too, or ceases to be worth preserving. . . .

Extend now to women suffrage and eligibility; give them the political right to vote and to be voted for; render it feasible for them to enter the arena of political strife, to become canvassers in elections and candidates for office, and what remains of family union will soon be dissolved. The wife may espouse one political party, and the husband another, and it may well happen that the husband and wife may be rival candidates for the same office, and one or the other doomed to the mortification of defeat. Will the husband like to see his wife enter the lists against him, and triumph over him? Will the wife, fired with political ambition for place or power, be pleased to see her own husband enter the lists against her, and succeed at her expense? Will political rivalry and the passions it never fails to engender increase the mutual affection of husband and wife for each other, and promote domestic union and peace, or will it not carry into the bosom of the family all the strife, discord, anger, and division of the political canvass? . . .

Woman was created to be a wife and a mother; that is her destiny. To that destiny all her instincts point, and for it nature has specially qualified her. Her proper sphere is home, and her proper function is the care of the household, to manage a family, to take care of children, and attend to their early training. For this she is endowed with patience, endurance, passive courage, quick sensibilities, a sympathetic nature, and great executive and administrative ability. She was born to be a queen in her own household, and to make home cheerful, bright, and happy.

We do not believe women, unless we acknowledge individual exceptions, are fit to have their own head. The most degraded of the savage tribes are those in which women rule, and descent is reckoned from the mother instead of the father. Revelation asserts, and universal experience proves that the man is the head of the woman, and that the woman is for the man, not the man for the woman; and his greatest error, as well as the primal curse of society is that he abdicates his headship, and allows himself to be governed, we might almost say, deprived of his reason, by woman. It was through the seductions of the woman, herself seduced by the serpent, that man fell, and brought sin and all our woe into the world. She has all the qualities that fit her to be a help-meet of man, to be the mother of his children, to be their nurse, their early instructress, their guardian, their life-long friend; to be his companion, his comforter, his consoler in sorrow, his friend in trouble, his ministering angel in sickness; but as an independent existence, free to follow her own fancies and vague longings, her own ambition and natural love of power, without masculine direction or control, she is out of her element, and a social anomaly, sometimes a hideous monster, which men seldom are, excepting through a woman's influence. This is no excuse for men, but it proves that women need a head, and the restraint of father, husband, or the priest of God.

Remarks of Senator George G. Vest in Congress (1887)

The following remarks of Senator George G. Vest (Democrat, Missouri) may be found in the *Congressional Record*, 49th Congress, 2d Session, January 25, 1887, p. 986.

Mr. VEST. . . . If this Government, which is based on the intelligence of the people, shall ever be destroyed it will be by injudicious, immature, or corrupt suffrage. If the ship of state launched by our fathers shall ever be destroyed, it will be by striking the rock of universal, unprepared suffrage. . . .

The Senator who last spoke on this question refers to the successful experiment in regard to woman suffrage in the Territories of Wyoming and Washington. Mr. President, it is not upon the plains of the sparsely settled Territories of the West that woman suffrage can be tested. Suffrage in the rural districts and sparsely settled regions of this country must from the very nature of things remain pure when corrupt everywhere else. The danger of corrupt suffrage is in the cities, and those masses of population to which civilization tends everywhere in all history. Whilst the country has been pure and patriotic, cities have been the first cancers to appear upon the body-politic in all ages of the world.

Wyoming Territory! Washington Territory! Where are their large cities? Where are the localities in those Territories where the strain upon popular government must come? The Senator from New Hampshire [Henry W. Blair—*Ed.*], who is so conspicuous in this movement, appalled the country some months since by his ghastly array of illiteracy in the Southern States. . . . That Senator proposes now to double, and more than double, that illiteracy. He proposes now to give the negro women of the South this right of suffrage, utterly unprepared as they are for it.

In a convention some two years and a half ago in the city of Louisville an intelligent negro from the South said the negro men could not vote the Democratic ticket because the women would not live with them if they did. The negro men go out in the hotels and upon the railroad cars. They go to the cities and by attrition they wear away the prejudice of race; but the women remain at home, and their emotional natures aggregate and compound the race-prejudice, and when suffrage is given them what must be the result? . . .

I pity the man who can consider any question affecting the influence of woman with the cold, dry logic of business. What man can, without aversion, turn from the blessed memory of that dear old grandmother, or the gentle words and caressing hand of that dear blessed mother gone to the unknown world, to face in its stead the idea of a female justice of the peace or township constable? For my part I want when I go to my home—when I turn from the arena where man contends with man for what we call the prizes of this paltry world—I want to go back, not to be received in the masculine embrace of some female ward politician, but to the earnest, loving look and touch of a true woman. I want to go back to the jurisdiction of the wife, the mother; and instead of a lecture upon finance or the tariff, or upon the construction of the Constitution, I want those blessed, loving details of domestic life and domestic love.

. . . I speak now respecting women as a sex. I believe that they are better than men, but I do not believe they are adapted to the political work of this world. I do not believe that the Great Intelligence ever intended them to invade the sphere of work given to men, tearing down and destroying all the best influences for which God has intended them.

The great evil in this country to-day is in emotional suffrage. The great danger to-day is in excitable suffrage. If the voters of this country could think always coolly, and if they could deliberate, if they could go by judgment and not by passion, our institutions would survive forever, eternal as the foundations of the continent itself; but massed together, subject to the excitements of mobs and of these terrible political contests that come upon us from year to year under the autonomy of our Government, what would be the result if suffrage were given to the women of the United States?

Women are essentially emotional. It is no disparagement to them they are so. It is no more insulting to say that women are emotional than to say that they are delicately constructed physically and unfitted to become soldiers or workmen under the sterner, harder pursuits of life.

What we want in this country is to avoid emotional suffrage, and what we need is to put more logic into public affairs and less feeling. There are spheres in which feeling should be paramount. There are kingdoms in which the heart should reign supreme. That kingdom belongs to woman. The realm of sentiment, the realm of love, the realm of the gentler and the holier and kindlier attributes that make the name of wife, mother, and sister next to that of God himself.

I would not, and I say it deliberately, degrade woman by giving her the right of suffrage. I mean the word in its full signification, because I believe that woman as she is to-day, the queen of the home and of hearts, is above the political collisions of this world, and should always be kept above them. . . .

It is said that the suffrage is to be given to enlarge the sphere of woman's influence. Mr. President, it would destroy her influence. It would take her down from that pedestal where she is to-day, influencing as a mother the minds of her offspring, influencing by her gentle and kindly caress the action of her husband toward the good and pure.

Remarks of Abraham L. Kellogg in New York State Constitutional Convention (1894)

These remarks were made by Abraham L. Kellogg, Republican, in the New York State Constitutional Convention in 1894. [*Revised Record of the Constitutional Convention of the State of*

New York, May 8, 1894, to September 29, 1894 (Albany, 1900), II, 433–36.]

. . . Oh, woman, poets have sung of you, and men gone mad over thy beauty, but before you decide to divorce yourselves from the sphere over which you have held undisputed sway from time immemorial, let me remind you of the sweet words of John Howard Payne—"Home, Sweet Home, there is no place like home." Let me recall to you before you further pursue the empty baubles of ambition and fame of the immortal words of Gray:

> "The boast of heraldry, the pomp of power,
>   All that beauty, all that wealth ere [sic] gave,
> Await alike the inevitable hour,
>   The paths of glory lead but to the grave."

It is said, however, that a woman convinced against her will is of the same opinion still, and I repeat, as a consolation for the adverse report of the committee, the priceless stanza—

> "Full many a gem of purest ray serene,
>   The dark unfathomed caves of ocean bear;
> Full many a flower is born to blush unseen
>   And waste its sweetness on the desert air."

No, Mr. President, the true glory of womanhood is not in sitting upon the jury, not in being clothed in judicial ermine, not in being sent to the halls of legislation, not in following the example of the publican, who prayed aloud in public places to be seen and heard of men, but rather by such fond devotion in that sacred place where she stands as a queen in the eyes of all mankind, unrivaled and unsurpassed, as will enshrine her forever in the hearts of the father, the husband and the son. Their pathway to enduring fame is in teaching their daughters lessons of virtue and their sons to be manly, self-reliant and independent. Would the sons of Sparta have been more heroic or patriotic, had their noble women possessed the ballot when they uttered the historic words: "Come back rather upon your armor than without it"? Would the influence of the noble women of the late war, God preserve the memory of their heroic deeds, have been more refining, had they been educated in the mire of politics? Would it have added delicacy to the touch of the hand upon the fevered brow of the dying soldier? No, Mr. President, a thousand times no! It would have robbed the flower of its beauty and fragrance.

With my last breath will I defend from the realm of politics and partisan strife, the institution which has cost untold suffering, heroic sacrifice and the priceless blood of patriots to preserve. . . .

Women of the great State of New York, the diffusion of christianity, no matter of what creed, will emancipate you more than the ballot can possibly do. Let the hand which rocks the cradle teach the coming young men and women of America the Lord's Prayer and the Ten Commandments, and you will do more for your emancipation and for every right which you may possess in the whole realm of human rights, than you can do with both hands full of white ballots. Do this and it will not be necessary for you to teach them political ethics or shine in the political firmament, to make them love you, fight for you and die for you. Do this and they will revere their country and love their flag.

A few of the excellent and worthy women who are in this Convention demanding the right to vote, I concede would do so. There are thousands of bad women who would also vote, at least, upon some questions, thus enforcing upon millions of modest and retiring mothers responsibilities from which they shrink, and rightly so. . . .

For a number of years the best minds of our State have been engaged in solving the question how shall we purify our politics, how best can honest government be attained and how shall we defend the suffrage against bribery and corruption? That some progress has been made in the right direction, I think all good men will admit. But, sir, before doubling twice over the voting population of the State, with its untold possibility of corruption, before we burden our taxpayers with a great expense to pay for such extension of the suffrage, let, rather, this Convention . . . use its time and bend its efforts towards purifying the Augean stables which we now have to contend with, rather than to incur the possibility of new evils which we know not of, and which it is not possible for the wisdom of man at this time to comprehend.

Gentlemen of the Convention, let us not at this time, by woman suffrage, or by its submission to the people, but rather by such wise efforts for entire religious liberty, for the diffusion of knowledge and the maintenance of our institutions of learning, for dispensing the greatest charity possible, consistent with the cause of good government, by demanding the strictest honesty in the discharge of all public affairs and by defending the sanctity and purity of the fireside, preserve this lovely land, this glorious liberty, this priceless legacy of freedom transmitted to us by our fathers. (Applause.)

Grover Cleveland, Would Woman Suffrage Be Unwise? (1905)

This article by a former President of the United States evoked angry replies by suffragists in many periodicals. [Grover Cleveland, "Would Woman Suffrage Be Unwise?" *Ladies' Home Journal*, XXII (October 1905), 7–8. Subtitles have been omitted.]

. . . Thoughtful and right-minded men base their homage and consideration for woman upon an instinctive consciousness that her unmasculine qualities, whether called weaknesses, frailties, or what we will, are the sources of her characteristic and especial strength within the area of her legitimate endeavor. They know that if she is not gifted with the power of clear and logical reasoning she has a faculty of intuition which by a shorter route leads her to abstract moral truth; that if she deals mistakenly with practical problems it is because sympathy or sentiment clouds her perception of the relative value of the factors involved; that if she is unbusinesslike her trustfulness and charitableness stand in the way of cold-blooded calculation; that if she is occasionally stubborn it is because her beliefs take a strong hold upon her; and that if she is sometimes fitful and petulant it is but the prelude to bright smiles and sunny endearments. They know she is loving, long-suffering, self-sacrificing and tender, because God has made her so and with it all they gratefully realize that whatever she has or lacks, the influence and ministrations of woman give firm rooting and sure growth to man's best efforts.

It is a mistake to suppose that any human reason or argument is needful or adequate to the assignment of the relative positions to be assumed by man and woman in working out the problems of civilization. This was done long ago by a higher intelligence than ours. I believe that trust in Divine wisdom, and ungrudging submission to Divine purposes, will enable dutiful men and women to know the places assigned to them, and will incite them to act well their parts in the sight of God. It should also be easy for such as these to see how wisely the work of human progress has been distributed, and how exactly the refining, elevating influence of woman, especially in her allotted sphere of home and in her character of wife and mother, supplements man's strenuous struggles in social and political warfare. In actual war it is the men who go to battle, enduring hardship and privation, and suffering disease and death for the cause they follow. They are deservedly praised for bravery and patriotism. It is the mothers, wives and maids betrothed, who, neither following the camp nor fighting in battle, constitute at home an army of woman's constancy and love, whose yearning hearts make men brave and patriotic. They teach from afar lessons of patient fortitude, and transmit through mysterious agencies, to soldiers in the field, the spirit of endurance and devotion. Soldiers who have fought, and those who praise or eulogize them, never forget to accord to woman the noble service of inspiration she has thus wrought with womanly weapons wielded in her appointed place.

So in political warfare, it is perfectly fitting that actual strife and battle should be apportioned to man, and that the influence of woman, radiating from the homes of our land, should inspire to lofty aims and purposes those who struggle for the right. I am thoroughly convinced that woman can in no better way than this usefully serve the cause of political betterment, and preserve her present immeasurable power of good. It is sane intelligence, and not sentimental delusion, that discovers between the relative duties and responsibilities of man and woman, as factors in the growth of civilization, a natural equilibrium, so nicely adjusted to the attributes and limitations of both that it cannot be disturbed without social confusion and peril. It is therefore not surprising that a multitude of good American men and women, who certainly are not lacking in solicitude for their country's welfare, are troubled lest this equilibrium should be jostled out of balance by the dissemination of notions which present a distorted view of the saving grace of womanhood as a constructive influence and a potent force in our homes, and in the moral activities of our nation. These good people believe that this saving grace cannot be protected and perpetuated in its ordained beauty and strength, except by protecting and perpetuating in their ordained loyalty and purity all the distinctive traits and attributes of woman's nature. They repudiate the idea that these things have been outrun by advance and progress and are no longer worth saving. On the contrary, their patriotic thoughtfulness and clear intelligence lead them to see that, now and for all time to come, the work and mission of women within the sphere to which God has adjusted them, must constitute the immutable and unchangeable foundations of all that human enlightenment can build. . . .

Nothing can be more palpable than that a safe regulation of our suffrage lies at the very foundation of American free institutions; and of course nothing more important than this can engage the attention of those who make our laws. Legislators should never neglect the dictates of chivalry in their treatment of woman; but this does not demand that a smirking appearance of acquiescence should conceal or smother a thoughtful lawmaker's intelligent disapproval of female suffrage. It is one of the chief charms of women that they are not especially amenable to argument; but that is not a reason why, when they demand the ballot as an inherent right, they should not be reminded that suffrage is a privilege which attaches neither to man nor to woman by nature. Nor could it be deemed discourteous if, when they claim the right to vote because women are taxed as owners of property, it is pointed out to them that they are not the only persons taxed as property-holders from whom the ballot is withheld, and that under present

conditions there is always a complete willingness to do every possible thing, by way of legislation, to secure and protect their
property rights. Our statute books are full of proof of this. . . .

I have sometimes wondered if the really good women who are
inclined to approve this doctrine of female suffrage are not delud-
ing themselves with purely sentimental views of the subject. Have
they not in some way allowed the idea to gain a place in their
minds that if the suffrage were accorded to women it would be
the pure, the honest, the intelligent and the patriotic of the sex
who would avail themselves of it? If they are drifting on the
smooth surface of such a pleasing conceit as this it behooves them
to take soundings and locate landmarks. They can perhaps thus
bring themselves to a realization of the fact that among women,
as is, unfortunately, the case now among men, it would not be
the best and most responsible that would most diligently use their
voting powers, and that, even if every woman in the land should
exercise the suffrage, the votes of the thoughtful and conscientious would almost certainly be largely outweighed by those of the
disreputable, the ignorant, the thoughtless, the purchased and the
coerced. It is not to the purpose to say that even with all this
the condition among women with the suffrage would be no worse
than it now is among men. We need something better for the
improvement of our suffrage, not an addition of the bad already
existing. Do respectable and public-spirited women who favor
female suffrage have a vague idea that all women endowed with
the franchise can be taught to exercise the privilege intelligently
and honestly? Who is to undertake this duty, and how? They may
rely upon it that the condition of civic fitness in which the suffrage finds the great mass of women will grow worse instead of
better. Vested with the power of suffrage equally with the best of
their sex, the unintelligent and characterless would be inclined to
resist the approach of those who assume with an air of superiority
to give them instruction in voting duty. Nor could such approach
be expected to end with mere resistance to teaching and influence.
We all know how much further women go than men in their social
rivalries and jealousies. Woman suffrage would give to the wives
and daughters of the poor a new opportunity to gratify their envy

and mistrust of the rich. Meantime these new voters would become either the purchased or cajoled victims of plausible political manipulators, or the intimidated and helpless voting vassals of imperious employers.

This phase of the suffrage question cannot better be presented than in the following words of another: "Women change politics less than politics change women.". . .

3

GENERAL DEFENSES
OF WOMAN SUFFRAGE

Alice Stone Blackwell, Losing Her Privilege (1890)

Alice Stone Blackwell (1857–1950), daughter of Lucy Stone and
Henry B. Blackwell, was co-editor of the *Woman's Journal* with
her father until his death and afterward sole editor until its de-
mise in 1917. A Phi Beta Kappa graduate of Boston University,
she was active in the National American Woman Suffrage Association, the Woman's Christian Temperance Union, and other
reform organizations. The following article is typical of many she
wrote to refute antisuffragist arguments. ["Losing Her Privilege,"
Woman's Journal, January 25, 1890.]

Prof. Goldwin Smith says:

That the sex has its privileges in America, no woman, it is presumed,
will deny. Do the woman's rights party expect to combine the prerogatives of both sexes, and have equality and privileges too? . . . Chivalry
depends on the acknowledged need of protection, and what is accorded
to a gentle helpmate would not be accorded to a rival. Man would
neither be inclined nor bound to treat with tenderness and forbearance
the being who was fighting and jostling him in all his walks of life,
wrangling with him in the law courts, wrestling with him on the
stump, manoeuvring against him in elections, haggling against him in

Wall Street, and perhaps encountering him on the race course and in the betting ring. But when woman has lost her privilege, what will she be but a weaker man?

If we were at present arguing the propriety of letting women practice law, make public speeches, take part in political canvassing, speculate in stocks, or bet at races, these remarks would be more to the point. But women already are as free before the law to do all these things as men are, and society does not seem to have been seriously overturned in consequence. Some of them, like public speaking, are perfectly fit for women to do; others, like betting, are not fit for anybody to do. But none of them have any immediate connection with voting.

What Prof. Smith means is that men would no longer show chivalry or tenderness to women if women were admitted to the suffrage. So Bishop Vincent is reported to have said that if women were allowed to vote, he should never again offer a lady his seat in a horse-car. But the Bishop had forgotten his logic. Why does he now offer a lady his seat? Is it because she cannot vote, or because she is presumably not so well able to stand as he is? A gentleman offers his seat to a lady, and, on the same principle, a young man offers his seat to an old man, although the old man can vote; and he does not think of offering it to a robust boy of eighteen, although the boy cannot vote any more than the lady. It is the consideration of physical strength for physical weakness, not the tribute of a voter to a non-voter. So far as the chivalry now shown to women has any rational basis, the same ground for it will continue to exist, and it will, doubtless, continue to be manifested by men of a chivalrous disposition. Men of the other sort are very apt to disregard it, in spite of the fact that women cannot vote. . . . It is a matter of education and custom more than anything else. The Mohammedan thinks women would cease to be respected if they walked the streets with faces unveiled. So they would in the East, where custom has caused it to be regarded as shocking. . . . Justice is better than chivalry, if we cannot have both; but the two are not at all incompatible. On the contrary, they help each other. "As all the vices play into one another's hands, so all the virtues stand shoulder to shoulder."

Carrie Chapman Catt, President's Annual Address (1902)

Carrie Chapman Catt (1859–1947), born in Wisconsin, began
her career as a schoolteacher and was superintendent of schools in
Mason City, Iowa. She was the organizing genius of the suffragist
movement, serving as president of the National American Woman
Suffrage Association from 1900 to 1902 and from 1915 to 1920.
The *President's Annual Address,* excerpted below, was delivered
before the thirty-fourth annual convention of the association in
Washington in February 1902 and was reprinted in pamphlet
form.

A campaigner in the recent New York municipal campaign
plead [*sic*] eloquently with the women to lend their aid. Said he:
"It is the proud duty of the women of this City to advise men
how to vote, since they have more time than men to intelligently
learn to comprehend the situation," and every Low follower
echoed: "True!" But, if women are competent to teach men how
to vote, why may they not vote themselves? . . .

The question of woman suffrage is a very simple one. The plea
is dignified, calm and logical. Yet, great as is the victory over conservatism which is represented in the accomplishment of man
suffrage, infinitely greater will be the attainment of woman suffrage. Man suffrage exists through the surrender of many a stronghold of ancient thought, deemed impregnable, yet these obstacles
were the veriest Don Quixote windmills compared with the opposition which has stood arrayed against woman suffrage.

Woman suffrage must meet precisely the same objections
which have been urged against man suffrage, but in addition, it
must combat sex-prejudice, the oldest, the most unreasoning, the
most stubborn of all human idiosyncracies [*sic*]. What *is* prejudice? An opinion, which is not based upon reason; a judgment,
without having heard the argument; a feeling, without being able
to trace from whence it came. And sex-prejudice is a pre-judgment
against the rights, liberties and opportunities of women. A belief,

without proof, in the incapacity of women to do that which they have never done. Sex-prejudice has been the chief hindrance in the rapid advance of the woman's rights movement to its present status, and it is still a stupendous obstacle to be overcome.

In the United States, at least, we need no longer argue woman's intellectual, moral and physical qualification for the ballot with the intelligent. The Reason of the best of our citizens has long been convinced. The justice of the argument has been admitted, but sex-prejudice is far from conquered.

When a great church official exclaims petulantly, that if women are no more modest in their demands men may be obliged to take to drowning female infants again; when a renowned United States Senator declares no human being can find an answer to the arguments for woman suffrage, but with all the force of his position and influence he will oppose it; when a popular woman novelist speaks of the advocates of the movement as the "shrieking sisterhood;" when a prominent politician says "to argue against woman suffrage is to repudiate the Declaration of Independence," yet he hopes it may never come, the question flies entirely outside the domain of reason, and retreats within the realm of sex-prejudice, where neither logic nor common sense can dislodge it. . . .

Sex-prejudice is the outgrowth of a theory practically universal throughout the world for many centuries past. It may be briefly stated as a belief that men were the units of the human race. They performed the real functions of the race; all the responsibilities and duties of working out the destiny of the race were theirs. Women were auxiliaries, or dependents, with no race responsibilities of their own. In the perpetuation of the race the contribution of the mother was negative and insignificant; that of the father vital and all-important. A favorite figure among writers for several centuries was the comparison of the father of the race to the seed, and the mother of the race to the soil. Man was considered the real creator of the race. Grant Allen states fairly the belief which dominated the thought of the world for many centuries when he said that women were simply "told off" for the express purpose of procreation, in the same manner as are drones in a hive of bees, and have no other place in society.

The world rarely inquires into the origin of a universal belief. It proceeds upon the theory that "whatever is, is right," and the very fact of the universality of any belief is accepted as a sufficient guarantee of its truth. Such a belief becomes a blind faith. Its defense is not reason, but feeling.

Add to a universal belief of this character, of which no one knows the origin, a supposed Divine authority for its existence, and it becomes well-nigh unmovable. . . .

. . . Four chief causes led to the subjection of women, each the logical deduction from the theory that men were the units of the race—obedience, ignorance, the denial of personal liberty, and the denial of right to property and wages. These forces united in cultivating a spirit of egotism and tyranny in men and weak dependence in women. . . . In fastening these disabilities upon women, the world acted logically when reasoning from the premise that man is the race and woman his dependent. The perpetual tutelage and subjection robbed women of all freedom of thought and action, and all incentive for growth, and they logically became the inane weaklings the world would have them, and their condition strengthened the universal belief in their incapacity. This world taught woman nothing skillful and then said her work was valueless. It permitted her no opinions and said she did not know how to think. It forbade her to speak in public, and said the sex had no orators. It denied her the schools, and said the sex had no genius. It robbed her of every vestige of responsibility, and then called her weak. It taught her that every pleasure must come as a favor from men, and when to gain it she decked herself in paint and fine feathers, as she had been taught to do, it called her vain.

This was the woman enshrined in literature. She was immortalized in song and story. Chivalry paid her fantastic compliments. As Diderot said: "when woman is the theme, the pen must be dipped in the rainbow, and the pages must be dried with a butterfly's wing." Surrounded by a halo of this kind of mysticism woman was encouraged to believe herself adored. This woman who was pretty, coquettish, affectionate, obedient, self effacive [*sic*], now gentle and meek, now furious and emotional, always ignorant, weak and silly, became the ideal woman of the world.

When at last the New Woman came, bearing the torch of truth, and with calm dignity asked a share in the world's education, opportunities and duties, it is no wonder these untrained weaklings should have shrunk away in horror. . . . Nor was it any wonder that man should arise to defend the woman of the past, whom he had learned to love and cherish. Her very weakness and dependence were dear to him and he loved to think of her as the tender clinging vine, while he was the strong and sturdy oak. He had worshiped her ideal through the age of chivalry as though she were a goddess, but he had governed her as though she were an idiot. Without the slightest comprehension of the inconsistency of his position, he believed this relation to be in accordance with God's command.

The fate of the woman question turns upon the truth or falsity of the premise from which the world has reasoned throughout the ages past. . . . Women are either inferior to men, or they are not.

Von Baer, a German scientist, pricked the bubble of the fallacy that "man is the race" in 1827 when he demonstrated that father and mother contribute equally to the physical, mental and moral characteristics of their children. This discovery was received reluctantly by scientists, but the fact is no longer questioned by those competent to judge. What a flood of light it throws upon the problem. . . .

If we find woman inferior to man we must find the reason not in her natural endowment, but in the environment which warped her growth. . . . It matters little, however, whether the woman of the past was contented or restless. The chief injury of her subjection did not come to her but to the race. No people can rise higher than its source and we now know that source is men and women, not men alone. The punishment of belittled motherhood comes unerringly to every people. There was once a time when China had free women, but their freedom was gradually stolen under the cover of the mandates of Confucius. China subjected its women more than any other people since she dwarfed their feet as well as their minds, and with the weight of this enslaved motherhood hanging like a millstone about its neck, the nation has stood still for hundreds of years. They say commerce, railroads and liberal ideas might yet save her from the final downfall which seems threatening. These would help, doubtless, but the one remedy which could bring back the breath of life, and start her climbing upward on the ladder of civilization once more would be freedom for the women who are the mothers of China.

If the punishment of the subjection of women is certain, the reward for liberality is equally sure. There are doubtless many reasons for the dominance of the Anglo-Saxon race, but none more important than the fact that the Anglo-Saxons have permitted to their women a larger individuality and independence than any other people. . . .

The whole aim of the woman movement has been to destroy the idea that obedience is necessary to women; to train women to such self-respect that they would not grant obedience and to train men to such comprehension of equity they would not exact it. . . . As John Stuart Mill said in speaking of the conditions which preceded the enfranchisement of men: "The noble has been gradually going down on the social ladder and the commoner has been gradually going up. Every half century has brought them nearer to each other;" so we may say, for the past hundred years, man as the dominant power in the world has been going down the ladder and woman has been climbing up. Every decade has brought them nearer together. The opposition to the enfranchisement of women is the last defense of the old theory that obedience is necessary for women, because man alone is the creator of the race.

The whole effort of the woman movement has been to destroy obedience of woman in the home. That end has been very generally attained, and the average civilized woman enjoys the right of individual liberty in the home of her father, her husband, and her son. The individual woman no longer obeys the individual man. She enjoys self-government in the home and in society. The question now is, shall all women as a body obey all men as a body? Shall the woman who enjoys the right of self-government in every other department of life be permitted the right of self-government in the State? It is no more right for all men to govern all women than it was for one man to govern one woman. It is no more right for men to govern women than it was for one man to govern other men. . . .

Finley Peter Dunne, Mr. Dooley on Woman's Suffrage (1909)

Finley Peter Dunne (1867–1936) was a journalist in Chicago and then New York and is famous for creating Mr. Dooley, whose dialogues with Hennessy in the latter's saloon provide caustic commentaries on American mores. ["Mr. Dooley on Woman's Suffrage," *The American Magazine*, LXVIII (June 1909), 198–200.]

"Well sir," said Mr. Dooley, "fr'm th' way this here female sufferage movement is sweepin' acrost th' counthry it won't be long befure I'll be seein' ye an' ye'er wife sthrollin' down th' sthreet to vote together."

"Niver," said Mr. Hennessy with great indignation. "It will niver come. A woman's place is in th' home darnin' her husband's childher. I mean—"

"I know what ye mean," said Mr. Dooley. "'Tis a favrite argymint iv mine whin I can't think iv annything to say. But ye can't help it, Hinnessy. Th' time is near at hand whin iliction day will mean no more to ye thin anny other day with th' fam'ly. Up to th' prisint moment it has been a festival marked: 'For gintlemen on'y.' It's been a day whin sthrong men cud go foorth, unhampered be th' prisince iv ladies, an' f'r th' honor iv their counthry bite each other. It was a day whin it was proper an' right f'r ye to slug ye'er best frind.

"But th' fair sect are goin' to break into this fine, manly spoort an' they'll change it. No more will ye leap fr'm ye'er bed on iliction mornin', put a brick in ye'er pocket an' go out to bounce ye'er impeeryal vote against th' walls iv inthrenched privilege. No more will ye spind th' happy mornin' hours meetin' ye'er frinds an' th' akeely happy avenin' hours receivin' none but inimies.

"No sir, in a few years, as soon as ye've had ye'er breakfast, ye'er fellow citizen who, as th' pote says, doubles ye'er expinses an' divides ye'er salary, will say to ye: 'Well, it's about time we wint down to th' polls an' cast my votes. An' I do wish ye'd tie ye'er necktie sthraight. Honorýa, bring me me new bonnet an' me Cashmere shawl an' get papa his stove pipe hat.' Thin ye'll be walked down th' sthreet, with a procission iv other married men in their best clothes an' their wanst a week shoes that hurt their feet. Th' sthreets will look like Easter Sundah. Ye'll meet ye'er frinds an' their wives comin' fr'm th' pollin' place an' talk with thim on th' corner.

" 'Good morning, Michael.'

" 'Ah, good morning, Cornelius.'

" 'A delightful morning is it not f'r th' exercise iv th' franchise.'

" 'Perfect! Howiver, I fear that such a morning may bring out a large republican vote.'

" 'I hope our frind Baumgarten will succeed in his candydacy.'

" 'I heartily agree with ye—he will make an excellent coroner, he's such good company.'

" 'Yes, indeed, a charming fellow f'r a Dutchman. Cud I prevail on ye an' ye'er lady to come an' have a tub iv ice cream sody with us?'

" 'Thank ye, Cornelius, we wud be delighted, but three is all I can hold. Shall I see ye at th' magic lanthern show to-night?'

"Th' pollin' place won't be in th' office iv a livry stable or a barber shop, but in a pleasant boodwar. As ye enter th' dure ye won't say to th' polisman on jooty: 'Good mornin', Pete; anny murdhers so far?'

"But wan iv th' judges will come forward an' bow an' say: 'Madam, can I show ye annything in ballots? This blue is wan iv our recent importations, but here is a tasty thought in ecru. F'r th' gintleman I'd ricommind something in dark brown to match th' socks. Will that be all? Th' last booth on th' right is unoccy-pied. Perhaps ye'er husband wud like to look at a copy iv th' *Ladies Home Journal* while ye'er preparin' th' ballots.'

"Ye needn't get mad about it, Hinnessy. Ye might as well face it. It's sure to come now that I see be th' pa-apers that female sufferage has been took up be ladies in our best s'ciety. It used to be diff'rent. Th' time was whin th' on'y female sufferigists that ye iver see were ladies, Gawd bless thim, that bought their millinery th' same place I buy mine, cut their hair short, an' discarded all iv their husband's names excipt what was useful f'r alimony.

"A fine lot iv rugged pathrites they were.

"I used to know wan iv thim—Docthor Arabella Miggs—as fine an old gintleman as ye iver see in a plug hat, a long coat an' bloomers. She had ivry argymint in favor iv female sufferage that ye iver heerd, an' years ago she made me as certain that women were entitled to a vote as that ye are entitled to my money.

"Ye are entitled to it if ye can get it. They ain't anny argymint against female sufferage that wudden't make me lible to arrest ivry time I'm seen near a pollin' place. But it isn't argymints or statistics that alters things in th' wurruld. Th' thick end iv a baseball bat will change a man's mind quicker an' more permanently thin anny discoorse.

"So th' first iv thim lady sufferigists had a hard time iv it, an' little boys used to go to their meetings to hoot at thim, an' they were took up in th' sthreet be polismen f'r pretindin' to look like gintlemen, an' th' pa-apers wud no more think iv printin' their speeches thin iv printin' a sermon in a church.

"Now, be hivens, 'tis diff'rent. 'Tis far diff'rent. I pick up th' pa-apers an' read:

" 'Gr-reat sufferage revival. Society queens take up th' cause. In th' magnificent L. Quince dhrawin' rooms iv Mrs. Percy Lumley's mansion in Mitchigan avnoo yesterdah afthernoon wan iv th' most successful sufferage teas iv th' season was held. Mrs. Lumley, who presided, was perfectly ravishing in a blue taffeta which set off her blonde beauty to perfection. She wore pearls an' carried a bunch iv American beauty roses. On th' platform with her were Mrs. Archibald Fluff, in green bombyzine with a pink coal scuttle hat. Mrs. Alfonso Vanboozen in a light yellow creation cut demi thrain an' manny other leaders iv th' smart set.

" 'A spirited debate was held over th' pint whether something shudden't be done to induce th' department stores to put in poll-ing places. Wan dhream iv beauty asked whether if it rained ilic-tion day wud th' iliction be held or postponed f'r betther weather. Th' chairman ruled that th' iliction wud have to go on rain or shine. "Iv coorse," says she, "in very bad weather we cud sind th' footman down with our votes. But we must not expict to gain this great reform without some sacrifice. (Applause.) In anny case th' tillyphone is always handy."

" 'A lady in th' aujeence wanted to know how old a lady wud have to be befure she cud vote. Says th' chairman: "To be effec-tive th' reform must be thorough. I am in favor iv makin' it legal f'r ivry woman to vote no matter how old she is an' I, therefore, wud put th' maximum age at a lib'ral figure, say thirty years. This gives all iv us a chance." (Cheers.) Afther th' meetin', a few voters dhropped in f'r an informal dance. Among those presint was.'

"An' there ye are. Ain't I again female sufferage? Iv coorse I am. Th' place f'r these spiled darlings is not in th' hurly burly iv life but in th' home, be th' fireside or above th' kitchen range. What do they know about th' vast machinery iv governmint? Ye an' I, Hinnessy, are gifted with a supeeryor intilligence in these matthers. Our opposition to a tariff is based on large pathriotic grounds. We have thought th' subjick out carefully, applyin' to it minds so sthrong that they cud crush a mountain an' so delicate that they cud pick up a sheet iv gold foil. We are in favor iv abol-ishin' th' tariff because it has thrown around this counthry a Chinese wall; because we are bribed be British goold fr'm th' Parsee merchant who riprisints th' Cobden Republican Marchin' Club iv London, England; because th' foreigner does or does not pay th' tax; because Sam'l J. Tilden was again th' tariff; because th' ultimate consumer must be proticted.

"Larkin on th' other hand, blessed with a republican intelleck since eighteen eighty four whin he become a protectionist because James G. Blaine was a fine man, annyway ye took him, is in favor iv a tariff on borax, curled hair, copra, steel ingots, an' art because cheap clothes makes a cheap man; because th' star spangled banner an long may it wag; because th' party that put down th' rebellyon an' stormed th' heights iv Lookout Mountain an' sthrewed th' bloody field iv Anteetam is th' same party (applause) that to-day is upholdin' th' tax on hides undher th' leadership iv th' incomp'rable hero Seerinio D. Payne. Often have I set here listenin' to ye an' Larkin discussin' this here question, wan moment thinkin' that I was as fine a pathrite as th' goose that saved Rome, be payin' more f'r me pants thin they were worth an' another moment fearin' I was a thraitor to th' flag f'r buyin' pants at all undher this accursed tariff. Both iv ye want to do what's best f'r th' counthry.

"But if ye put th' question up to th' ladies, if women undherstood th' tariff, which th' poor crathers don't, ye'd find they were against it f'r no higher reason thin that it made thim pay too much f'r th' childher's shoes an' stockin's. Can ye imagine annything baser thin that, to rejooce a great question like th' tariff down to a personal level, take all th' music an' pothry out iv it an' say: 'I'm again it, not because it has lowered th' morality iv ivrywan that it has binifitted, but because it's a shame that I have to pay eighty-six cints a pair f'r stockin's.'

"Women take a selfish view iv life. But what can ye expict fr'm a petted toy iv man's whim that has spent most iv her life thryin' to get four dollars worth iv merchandise f'r two dollars an' a half? Th' foolish, impractical little fluffy things! It wud be a shame to let thim hurl thimselves into th' coorse battles iv pollyticks. How cud ye explain to wan iv these ideelists wy we have th' Philippeens an' th' Sandwich Islands, an' why we keep up a navy to protict Denver, Colorado.

"We don't hear much about sufferage up our way in Ar-rchy road an' th' ladies that have got out their noblest hats in behalf iv th' cause complain that they can't stir up anny excitement among th' more numerous ladies that prefer to wear a shawl on their heads. Maybe th' reason is that these fair dhreamers haven't been able to figure out that a vote is goin' to do thim anny good. P'raps if ye asked ye'er wife about it she'd say:

" 'Well, ye've had ye'er vote f'r forty years. F'r forty years ye've governed this counthry be a freeman's ballot an' ye'er salary an' perquisites at th' mills still amounts to a dollar an' eighty-five

cints a day. If a vote hasn't done ye anny more good thin that I
don't think I can spare time fr'm me domestic jooties to use wan.
I will continue to look afther th' fam'ly, which is th' on'y capital
a poor man can accumylate to protict him fr'm poverty in his old
age. I'll stay at home an' see that th' boys an' girls are saved up
ontil they are old enough to wurruk f'r us. An' if ye want to amuse
ye'erself be votin' go on an' do it. Ye need recreation wanst in a
while, an' ye'er vote don't do anny wan no harm.' "

"I wudden't talk to me wife about votin' anny more thin she'd
talk to me about thrimmin' a hat," said Mr. Hennessy.

"Well," said Mr. Dooley, "if she gets a vote maybe she'll
thrim it to please ye. Annyhow it won't be a bad thing. What
this counthry needs is voters that knows something about
housekeeping."

Alice Duer Miller, Are Women People? (1915)

Alice Duer Miller (1874–1942), author, was the rhymester of
the feminist movement. She was a New York City–born graduate
of Barnard, class of 1899. The six pairs of antisuffragist "reasons"
in the fourth document are strictly accurate statements of commonly expressed opinions; only their matching is original with
Mrs. Miller. The six statements in the fifth document are also
completely accurate, the *reductio ad absurdum* consisting solely
in the substitution of "traveling on railway trains" for "voting."
[*Are Women People?: A Book of Rhymes for Suffrage Times*
(New York, 1915), pp. 13, 14–15, 40, 43, 46, 64.]

OUR IDEA OF NOTHING AT ALL

("I am opposed to woman suffrage, but I am not opposed to
woman."—*Anti-Suffrage speech of Mr.*[*Edwin Y.*] *Webb* [*Democratic congressman*] *of North Carolina.*)

> O women, have you heard the news
> Of charity and grace?
> Look, look, how joy and gratitude
> Are beaming in my face!

*For Mr. Webb is not opposed
To woman in her place!*

*O Mr. Webb, how kind you are
To let us live at all,
To let us light the kitchen range
And tidy up the hall;
To tolerate the female sex
In spite of Adam's fall.*

*O girls, suppose that Mr. Webb
Should alter his decree!
Suppose he were opposed to us—
Opposed to you and me.
What would be left for us to do—
Except to cease to be?*

LINES TO MR. BOWDLE OF OHIO

("The women of this smart capital are beautiful. Their beauty is disturbing to business; their feet are beautiful, their ankles are beautiful, but here I must pause."—Mr. *Bowdle's anti-suffrage speech in Congress, January 12, 1915.*)

*You, who despise the so-called fairer sex,
Be brave. There really isn't any reason
You should not, if you wish, oppose and vex
And scold us in, and even out of season;
But don't regard it as your bounden duty
To open with a tribute to our beauty.*

*Say, if you like that women have no sense,
No self-control, no power of concentration;
Say that hysterics is our one defence
Our virtue but an absence of temptation;
These I can bear, but, oh, I own it rankles
To hear you maundering on about our ankles.*

*Tell those old stories, which have now and then
Been from the Record thoughtfully deleted,
Repeat that favorite one about the hen,
Repeat the ones that cannot be repeated;
But in the midst of such enjoyments, smother
The impulse to extol your "sainted mother."*

[The following poem is not headed by a quotation. However, the one that precedes it has the following epigraph, which is equally appropriate to this poem: "The grant of suffrage to women is repugnant to instincts that strike their roots deep in the order of nature. It runs counter to human reason, it flouts the teachings of experience and the admonitions of common sense."—*New York Times, Feb. 7, 1915.*]

TO *The Times* EDITORIALS

Lovely Antiques, breathing in every line
The perfume of an age long passed away,
Wafting us back to 1829,
Museum pieces of a by-gone day,
You should not languish in the public press
Where modern thought might reach and do you harm,
And vulgar youth insult your hoariness,
Missing the flavor of your old world charm;
You should be locked, where rust cannot corrode
In some old rosewood cabinet, dimmed by age,
With silver-lustre, tortoise shell and Spode;
And all would cry, who read your yellowing page:
"Yes, that's the sort of thing that men believed
Before the First Reform Bill was conceived!"

OUR OWN TWELVE ANTI-SUFFRAGIST REASONS

1. Because no woman will leave her domestic duties to vote.
2. Because no woman who may vote will attend to her domestic duties.
3. Because it will make dissension between husband and wife.
4. Because every woman will vote as her husband tells her to.
5. Because bad women will corrupt politics.
6. Because bad politics will corrupt women.
7. Because women have no power of organization.
8. Because women will form a solid party and outvote men.
9. Because men and women are so different that they must stick to different duties.
10. Because men and women are so much alike that men, with one vote each, can represent their own views and ours too.

11. Because women cannot use force.

12. Because the militants did use force.

WHY WE OPPOSE WOMEN TRAVELLING ON RAILWAY TRAINS

1. Because travelling in trains is not a natural right.

2. Because our great-grandmothers never asked to travel in trains.

3. Because woman's place is the home, not the train.

4. Because it is unnecessary; there is no point reached by a train that cannot be reached on foot.

5. Because it will double the work of conductors, engineers and brakemen who are already overburdened.

6. Because men smoke and play cards in trains. Is there any reason to believe that women will behave better?

FEMINISM

"*Mother, what is a Feminist?*"
"*A Feminist, my daughter,*
Is any woman now who cares
To think about her own affairs
As men don't think she oughter."

4

THE "JUSTICE" ARGUMENT

Resolutions Passed at a Woman's Rights Convention (1851)

These resolutions, passed at the Second Worcester Convention, 1851, are typical expressions of the demand for the vote as a matter of right rather than as a reward for fitness or as a tactic to secure reforms. [*HWS* I, 825–26.]

1. *Resolved*, That while we would not undervalue other methods, the Right of Suffrage for Women is, in our opinion, the corner-stone of this enterprise, since we do not seek to protect woman, but rather to place her in a position to protect herself.

2. *Resolved*, That it will be woman's fault if, the ballot once in her hand, all the barbarous, demoralizing, and unequal laws relating to marriage and property, do not speedily vanish from the statute-book; and while we acknowledge that the hope of a share in the higher professions and profitable employments of society is one of the strongest motives to intellectual culture, we know, also, that an interest in political questions is an equally powerful stimulus; and we see, besides, that we do our best to insure education to an individual when we put the ballot into his hands; it being so clearly the interest of the community that one upon

whose decisions depend its welfare and safety, should both have free access to the best means of education, and be urged to make use of them.

3. *Resolved*, That we do not feel called upon to assert or establish the equality of the sexes, in an intellectual or any other point of view. It is enough for our argument that natural and political justice, and the axioms of English and American liberty, alike determine that rights and burdens—taxation and representation—should be co-extensive; hence women, as individual citizens, liable to punishment for acts which the laws call criminal, or to be taxed in their labor and property for the support of government, have a self-evident and indisputable right, identically the same right that men have, to a direct voice in the enactment of those laws and the formation of that government. . . .

6. *Resolved*, That, so far from denying the overwhelming social and civil influence of women, we are fully aware of its vast extent; aware, with Demosthenes, that "measures which the statesman has meditated a whole year may be overturned in a day by a woman"; and for this very reason we proclaim it the very highest expediency to endow her with full civil rights, since only then will she exercise this mighty influence under a just sense of her duty and responsibility; the history of all ages bearing witness, that the only safe course for nations is to add open responsibility wherever there already exists unobserved power.

7. *Resolved*, That we deny the right of any portion of the species to decide for another portion, or of any individual to decide for another individual what is and what is not their "proper sphere"; that the proper sphere for all human beings is the largest and highest to which they are able to attain; what this is, can not be ascertained without complete liberty of choice; woman, therefore, ought to choose for herself what sphere she will fill, what education she will seek, and what employment she will follow, and not be held bound to accept, in submission, the rights, the education, and the sphere which man thinks proper to allow her.

8. *Resolved*, That we hold these truths to be self-evident: That all men are created equal; that they are endowed by their

Creator with certain inalienable rights; that among these are life, liberty, and the pursuit of happiness; that, to secure these rights, governments are instituted among men, deriving their just powers from the consent of the governed; and we charge that man with gross dishonesty or ignorance, who shall contend that "men," in the memorable document from which we quote, does not stand for the human race; that "life, liberty, and the pursuit of happiness," are the "inalienable rights" of *half* only of the human species; and that, by "the governed," whose consent is affirmed to be the only source of just power, is meant that *half* of mankind only who, in relation to the other, have hitherto assumed the character of *governors*.

9. *Resolved*, That we see no weight in the argument that it is necessary to exclude women from civil life because domestic cares and political engagements are incompatible; since we do not see the fact to be so in the case of men; and because, if the incompatibility be real, it will take care of itself, neither men nor women needing any law to exclude them from an occupation when they have undertaken another incompatible with it. Second, we see nothing in the assertion that women, themselves, do not desire a change, since we assert that superstitious fears and dread of losing men's regard, smother all frank expression on this point; and further, if it be their real wish to avoid civil life, laws to keep them out of it are absurd, no legislator having ever yet thought it necessary to compel people by law to follow their own inclination.

10. *Resolved*, That it is as absurd to deny all women their civil rights because the cares of household and family take up all the time of some, as it would be to exclude the whole male sex from Congress, because some men are sailors, or soldiers in active service or merchants, whose business requires all their attention and energies.

Ernestine Rose, On Legal Discrimination (1851)

Ernestine Rose (1810–92) is chiefly remembered for her leadership in the campaign for the Married Women's Property Act, passed in New York in 1848. Mrs. Rose was exceptional among feminists, not only in that she was foreign-born and of Jewish background, but also in that she was a Freethinker and a follower of Robert Owen, the utopian socialist. The following speech, an example of the oratory for which she was also noted, was delivered at the same convention that passed the resolutions in the preceding document. [*HWS* I, 237–41.]

After having heard the letter read from our poor incarcerated sisters of France [a letter, written from prison, from two French socialist women hailing the convention that Mrs. Rose was addressing—*Ed.*], well might we exclaim, Alas, poor France! where is thy glory? Where the glory of the Revolution of 1848, in which shone forth the pure and magnanimous spirit of an oppressed nation struggling for Freedom? Where the fruits of that victory that gave to the world the motto, "Liberty, Equality, and Fraternity"? A motto destined to hurl the tyranny of kings and priests into the dust, and give freedom to the enslaved millions of the earth. Where, I again ask, is the result of those noble achievements, when woman, ay, one-half of the nation, is deprived of her rights? Has woman then been idle during the contest between "right and might"? Has she been wanting in ardor and enthusiasm? Or has she been recreant in hailing the motto of liberty floating on your banners as an omen of justice, peace, and freedom to man, that at the first step she takes practically to claim the recognition of her rights, she is rewarded with the doom of a martyr?

But right has not yet asserted her prerogative, for might rules the day; and as every good cause must have its martyrs, why should woman not be a martyr for her cause? But need we wonder that France, governed as she is by Russian and Austrian despotism, does not recognize the rights of humanity in the recognition of the rights of woman, when even here, in this far-famed land of freedom, under a Republic that has inscribed on its banner the great truth that "all men are created free and equal, and endowed with inalienable rights to life, liberty, and the pursuit of happiness"—a declaration borne, like the vision of hope, on wings of light to the remotest parts of the earth, an omen of freedom to the oppressed and down-trodden children of man—when, even here, in the very face of this eternal truth, woman, the mockingly so-called "better half" of man, has yet to plead for her rights, nay, for her life. For what is life without liberty, and what is liberty without equality of rights? And as for the pursuit of happiness, she is not allowed to choose any line of action that might promote it; she has only thankfully to accept what man in his magnanimity decides is best for her to do, and this is what he does not choose to do himself.

Is she then not included in that declaration? Answer, ye wise men of the nation, and answer truly; add not hypocrisy to oppression! Say that she is not created free and equal, and therefore (for the sequence follows on the premise) that she is not entitled to life, liberty, and the pursuit of happiness. But with all the audacity arising from an assumed superiority, you dare not so libel and insult humanity as to say, that she is not included in that declaration; and if she is, then what right has man, except that of might, to deprive woman of the rights and privileges he claims for himself? And why, in the name of reason and justice, why should she not have the same rights? Because she is woman? Humanity recognizes no sex; virtue recognizes no sex; mind recognizes no sex; life and death, pleasure and pain, happiness and misery, recognize no sex. Like man, woman comes involuntarily into existence; like him, she possesses physical and mental and moral powers, on the proper cultivation of which depends her happiness; like him she is subject to all the vicissitudes of life; like him she has to pay the penalty for disobeying nature's laws, and far greater penalties has she to suffer from ignorance of her more complicated nature; like him she enjoys or suffers with her country. Yet she is not recognized as his equal!

In the laws of the land she has no rights; in government she has no voice. And in spite of another principle, recognized in this Republic, namely, that "taxation without representation is tyranny," she is taxed to defray the expenses of that unholy, unrighteous custom called war, yet she has no power to give her vote against it. From the cradle to the grave she is subject to the power and control of man. Father, guardian, or husband, one conveys her like some piece of merchandise over to the other.

At marriage she loses her entire identity, and her being is said to have become merged in her husband. Has nature thus merged it? Has she ceased to exist and feel pleasure and pain? When she violates the laws of her being, does her husband pay the penalty? When she breaks the moral laws, does he suffer the punishment? When he supplies his wants, is it enough to satisfy her nature? And when at his nightly orgies, in the grog-shop and the oyster-cellar, or at the gaming-table, he squanders the means she helped, by her co-operation and economy, to accumulate, and she awakens to penury and destitution, will it supply the wants of her children to tell them that, owing to the superiority of man she had no redress by law, and that as her being was merged in his, so also ought theirs to be? What an inconsistency, that from the moment she enters that compact, in which she assumes the high responsibility of wife and mother, she ceases legally to exist, and becomes a purely submissive being. Blind submission in woman is considered a virtue, while submission to wrong is itself wrong, and resistance to wrong is virtue, alike in woman as in man.

But it will be said that the husband provides for the wife, or in other words, he feeds, clothes, and shelters her! I wish I had the power to make every one before me fully realize the degradation contained in that idea. Yes! he *keeps* her, and so he does a favorite horse; by law they are both considered his property. Both may, when the cruelty of the owner compels them to run away, be brought back by the strong arm of the law, and according to a still extant law of England, both may be led by the halter to the market-place and sold. This is humiliating indeed, but nevertheless true; and the sooner these things are known and understood, the better for humanity. It is no fancy sketch. I know that some endeavor to throw the mantle of romance over the subject, and treat woman like some ideal existence, not liable to the ills of life. Let those deal in fancy, that have nothing better to deal in; we have to do with sober, sad realities, with stubborn facts.

Again, I shall be told that the law presumes the husband to

be kind, affectionate, and ready to provide for and protect his wife. But what right, I ask, has the law to presume at all on the subject? What right has the law to intrust the interest and happiness of one being into the hands of another? And if the merging of the interest of one being into the other is a necessary consequence of marriage, why should the woman always remain on the losing side? Turn the tables. Let the identity and interest of the husband be merged in the wife. Think you she is not capable of as much justice, disinterested devotion, and abiding affection as he is? Oh, how grossly you misunderstand and wrong her nature! But we desire no such undue power over man; it would be as wrong in her to exercise it as it now is in him. All we claim is an equal legal and social position. We have nothing to do with individual man, be he good or bad, but with the laws that oppress woman. We know that bad and unjust laws must in the nature of things make man so too. If he is kind, affectionate, and consistent, it is because the kindlier feelings, instilled by a mother, kept warm by a sister, and cherished by a wife, will not allow him to carry out these barbarous laws against woman.

But the estimation she is generally held in, is as degrading as it is foolish. Man forgets that woman can not be degraded without its reacting on himself. The impress of her mind is stamped on him by nature, and the early education of the mother, which no after-training can entirely efface; and therefore, the estimation she is held in falls back with double force upon him. Yet, from the force of prejudice against her, he knows it not. Not long ago, I saw an account of two offenders, brought before a Justice of New York. One was charged with stealing a pair of boots, for which offense he was sentenced to six months' imprisonment; the other's crime was assault and battery upon his wife: he was let off with a reprimand from the judge! With my principles, I am entirely opposed to punishment, and hold, that to reform the erring and remove the causes of evil is much more efficient, as well as just, than to punish. But the judge showed us the comparative value which he set on these two kinds of *property*. But then you must remember that the boots were taken by a stranger, while the wife was insulted by her legal owner! Here it will be said, that such degrading cases are but few. For the sake of humanity, I hope they are. But as long as woman shall be oppressed by unequal laws, so long will she be degraded by man.

We have hardly an adequate idea how all-powerful law is in forming public opinion, in giving tone and character to the mass of society. To illustrate my point, look at that infamous detestable law, which was written in human blood, and signed and sealed with life and liberty, that eternal stain on the statute book of this country, the Fugitive Slave Law. Think you that before its passage, you could have found any in the free States—except a few politicians in the market—base enough to desire such a law? No! no! Even those who took no interest in the slave question, would have shrunk from so barbarous a thing. But no sooner was it passed, than the ignorant mass, the rabble of the self-styled Union Safety Committee, found out that we were a law-loving, law-abiding people! Such is the magic power of Law. Hence the necessity to guard against bad ones. Hence also the reason why we call on the nation to remove the legal shackles from woman, and it will have a beneficial effect on that still greater tyrant she has to contend with, Public Opinion.

Carry out the republican principle of universal suffrage, or strike it from your banners and substitute "Freedom and Power to one half of society, and Submission and Slavery to the other." Give woman the elective franchise. Let married women have the same right to property that their husbands have; for whatever the difference in their respective occupations, the duties of the wife are as indispensable and far more arduous than the husband's. Why then should the wife, at the death of her husband, not be his heir to the same extent that he is heir to her? In this inequality there is involved another wrong. When the wife dies, the husband is left in the undisturbed possession of all there is, and the children are left with him; no change is made, no stranger intrudes on his home and his affliction. But when the husband dies, the widow, at best receives but a mere pittance, while strangers assume authority denied to the wife. The sanctuary of affliction must be desecrated by executors; everything must be ransacked and assessed, lest she should steal something out of her own house; and to cap the climax, the children must be placed under guardians. When the husband dies poor, to be sure, no guardian is required, and the children are left for the mother to care and toil for, as best she may. But when anything is left for their maintenance, then it must be placed in the hands of strangers for safekeeping! The bringing-up and safety of the children are left with the mother, and safe they are in her hands. But a few hundred or thousand dollars can not be intrusted with her! . . .

According to a late act, the wife has a right to the property she brings at marriage, or receives in any way after marriage. Here is some provision for the favored few; but for the laboring many, there is none. The mass of the people commence life with no other capital than the union of heads, hearts, and hands. To the benefit of this best of capital, the wife has no right. If they are unsuccessful in married life, who suffers more the bitter consequences of poverty than the wife? But if successful, she can not call a dollar her own. The husband may will away every dollar of the personal property, and leave her destitute and penniless, and she has no redress by law. And even where real estate is left, she receives but a life-interest in a third part of it, and at her death, she can not leave it to any one belonging to her: it falls back even to the remotest of his relatives. This is law, but where is the justice of it? Well might we say that laws were made to prevent, not to promote, the ends of justice. . . .

Harriot K. Hunt, Tax Protest (1852)

Boston-born Harriot K. Hunt (1805–75) practiced medicine with her sister, although neither had any medical training. By 1835 they were successful enough to advertise as physicians. In 1847 and 1850 Harvard Medical School refused to admit Harriot, but in 1853 she received a medical degree from the Female Medical

College of Philadelphia. Starting in 1852, she sent an annual letter to the Boston authorities protesting her having to pay taxes while not allowed to vote. [*HWS* I, 259–60.]

To Frederick W. Tracy, Treasurer, and the Assessors, and other Authorities of the city of Boston, and the Citizens generally:

Harriot K. Hunt, physician, a native and permanent resident of the city of Boston, and for many years a taxpayer therein, in making payment of her city taxes for the coming year, begs leave to protest against the injustice and inequality of levying taxes upon women, and at the same time refusing them any voice or vote in the imposition and expenditure of the same. The only classes of male persons required to pay taxes, and not at the same time allowed the privilege of voting, are aliens and minors. The objection in the case of aliens is their supposed want of interest in our institutions and knowledge of them. The objection in the case of minors, is the want of sufficient understanding. These objections can not apply to women, natives of the city, all of whose property interests are here, and who have accumulated, by their own sagacity and industry, the very property on which they are taxed. But this is not all; the alien, by going through the forms of naturalization, the minor on coming of age, obtain the right of voting; and so long as they continue to pay a mere poll-tax of a dollar and a half, they may continue to exercise it, though so ignorant as not to be able to sign their names, or read the very votes they put into the ballot-boxes. Even drunkards, felons, idiots, and lunatics, if men, may still enjoy that right of voting to which no woman, however large the amount of taxes she pays, however respectable her character, or useful her life, can ever attain. Wherein, your remonstrant would inquire, is the justice, equality, or wisdom of this?

That the rights and interests of the female part of the community are sometimes forgotten or disregarded in consequence of their deprivation of political rights, is strikingly evinced, as appears to your remonstrant, in the organization and administration of the city public schools. Though there are open in this State and neighborhood, a great multitude of colleges and professional schools for the education of boys and young men, yet the city has very properly provided two High-Schools of its own, one Latin, the other English, in which the "male graduates" of the Grammar Schools may pursue their education still farther at the public expense. And why is not a like provision made for the girls? Why is their education stopped short, just as they have attained the age best fitted for progress, and the preliminary knowledge necessary to facilitate it, thus giving the advantage of superior culture to sex, not to mind?

The fact that our colleges and professional schools are closed against females, of which your remonstrant has had personal and painful experience; having been in the year 1847, after twelve years of medical practice in Boston, refused permission to attend the lectures of Harvard Medical College. That fact would seem to furnish an additional reason why the city should provide, at its own expense, those means of superior education which, by supplying our girls with occupation and objects of interest, would not only save them from lives of frivolity and emptiness, but which might open the way to many useful and lucrative pursuits, and so raise them above that degrading dependence, so fruitful a source of female misery.

Reserving a more full exposition of the subject to future occasions, your remonstrant, in paying her tax for the current year, begs leave to protest against the injustice and inequalities above pointed out.

This is respectfully submitted,

HARRIOT K. HUNT,
32 Garden Street, Boston, Mass.

Plaintiffs' Brief and Argument, *Minor vs. Happersett* (1872)

The case of *Minor vs. Happersett* grew out of an 1872 suit by Virginia L. Minor (1824–94) and her husband, Missouri feminists, for her right to vote. Although their brief cites several parts of the Constitution, it relies mainly on the Fourteenth Amendment, enacted in 1868, which for the first time defined United States citizenship. The Minors contended that suffrage was a right of citizenship. Suffragists hoped that a favorable decision would give women nationwide suffrage at once; the Supreme Court's opinion, handed down in 1875, made it clear that they would have to secure a separate amendment. [*HWS* II, 715–21, 723, 726–30, 732–33.]

VIRGINIA L. MINOR'S PETITION

IN THE CIRCUIT COURT OF ST. LOUIS COUNTY, DECEMBER TERM, 1872. *St. Louis County, ss.:* Virginia L. Minor and Francis Minor, her husband, Plaintiffs, *vs.* Reese Happersett, Defendant.

The plaintiff, Virginia L. Minor (with whom is joined her husband, Francis Minor, as required by the law of Missouri), states, that under the Constitution and law of Missouri, all persons wishing to vote at any election, must previously have been registered in the manner pointed out by law, this being a condition precedent to the exercise of the elective franchise.

That on the fifteenth day of October, 1872 (one of the days fixed by law for the registration of voters), and long prior thereto, she was a native-born, free white citizen of the United States, and of the State of Missouri, and on the day last mentioned she was over the age of twenty-one years.

That on said day, the plaintiff was a resident of the thirteenth election district of the city and county of St. Louis, in the State of Missouri, and had been so residing in said county and election district, for the entire period of twelve months and more, immediately preceding said fifteenth day of October, 1872, and for more than twenty years had been and is a tax-paying, law-abiding citizen of the county and State aforesaid.

That on said last mentioned day, the defendant, having been duly and legally appointed Registrar for said election district, and having accepted the said office of Registrar and entered upon the discharge of the duties thereof at the office of registration, . . .

it became and was then and there his duty to register all citizens, resident in said district as aforesaid, entitled to the elective franchise, who might apply to him for that purpose.

The plaintiff further states, that wishing to exercise her privilege as a citizen of the United States, and vote for Electors for President and Vice-President of the United States, and for a Representative in Congress, and for other officers, at the General Election held in November 1872: While said defendant was so acting as Registrar, on said 15th day of October, 1872, she appeared before him . . . and then and there offered to take and subscribe to the oath to support the Constitution of the United States and of the State of Missouri, as required by the registration law of said State, approved March 10, 1871, and respectfully applied to him to be registered as a lawful voter, which said defendant then and there refused to do. . . .

Defendant stated to plaintiff, that she was not entitled to be registered, or to vote, because she was not a "male" citizen, but a woman! That by the Constitution of Missouri, Art. II., Sec. 18, and by the aforesaid registration law of said State, approved March 10, 1871, it is provided and declared, that only "male citizens" of the United States, etc., are entitled or permitted to vote.

But the plaintiff protests against such decision, and she declares and maintains that said provisions of the Constitution and registration law of Missouri aforesaid, are in conflict with, and repugnant to the Constitution of the United States, which is paramount to State authority; and that they are especially in conflict with the following articles and clauses of said Constitution of the United States, to wit:

ART. I. SEC. 9—Which declares that no Bill of Attainder shall be passed.

ART. I. SEC. 10—No State shall pass any Bill of Attainder, or grant any title of nobility.

ART. IV. SEC. 2—The citizens of each State shall be entitled to all privileges and immunities of citizens in the several States.

ART. IV. SEC. 4—The United States shall guarantee to every State a republican form of government.

ART. VI.—This Constitution and the laws of the United States which shall be made in pursuance thereof, shall be the supreme law of the land, anything in the Constitutions or laws of any State to the contrary notwithstanding.

AMENDMENTS.

ART. V.—No person shall be . . . deprived of life, liberty, or property without due process of law.

ART. IX.—The enumeration in the Constitution of certain rights, shall not be construed to deny or disparage others retained by the people.

ART. XIV. SEC. 1—All persons born or naturalized in the United States, and subject to the jurisdiction thereof, are citizens of the United States and of the State wherein they reside. No State shall make or enforce any law which shall abridge the privileges or immunities of citizens of the United States. Nor shall any State deprive any person of life, liberty, or property, without due process of law; nor deny to any person within its jurisdiction, the equal protection of the laws.

The plaintiff states, that by reason of the wrongful act of the defendant as aforesaid, she has been damaged in the sum of ten thousand dollars, for which she prays judgment.

> JOHN M. KRUM,
> FRANCIS MINOR,　　　} *Atty's for Plffs.*
> JOHN B. HENDERSON,

. . . .

ARGUMENT AND BRIEF.—We think the chief difficulty in this case is one of fact rather than of law. The practice is against the plaintiff. The States, with one exception, which we shall notice hereafter more in detail, have uniformly claimed and exercised the right to act, as to the matter of suffrage, just as they pleased— to limit or extend it, as they saw proper. And this is the popular idea on the subject. Men accept it as a matter of fact, and take for granted it must be right. So in the days of African slavery, thousands believed it to be right—even a Divine institution. But this belief has passed away; and, in like manner, this doctrine of the right of the States to exercise unlimited and absolute control over the elective franchise of citizens of the United States, must and will give way to a truer and better understanding of the subject. The plaintiff's case is simply one of the means by which this end will ultimately be reached.

We claim, and presume it will not be disputed, that the elective franchise is a privilege of citizenship within the meaning of the Constitution of the United States. In order to get a clearer idea of the true meaning of this term citizenship, it may be well to recur for a moment to its first introduction and use in American law. . . . [There follows a history and discussion of the concept of "citizenship" in the United States.—*Ed.*]

In the new political sovereignty thus created, the feudal idea of dependence gave way to that of independence, and the people became their own sovereigns or rulers in the government of their own creation. Of this body politic, represented by the Constitution of the United States, all persons born or naturalized therein and subject to the jurisdiction thereof, are members; without distinction as to political rights or privileges, except that the head or chief of the new government must be native-born—and this exception the more strongly proves the rule. It is to this Constitution, therefore, we must look for the limitations, if any, that may be placed upon the political rights of the people or citizens of the United States. A limitation not found there, or authorized by that instrument, can not be legally exercised by any lesser or inferior jurisdiction.

But the subject of suffrage (or the qualifications of electors, as the Constitution terms it) is simply remitted to the States by the Constitution, to be regulated by them; not to limit or restrict the right of suffrage, but to carry the same fully into effect. It is impossible to believe that anything more than this was intended. In the first place, it would be inconsistent and at variance with the idea of the supremacy of the Federal government; and, next, if the absolute, ultimate, and unconditional control of the matter had been intended to be given to the States, it would have been so expressed. It would not have been left to doubt or implication. In so important a matter as suffrage, the chief of all political rights or privileges, by which, indeed, life, liberty, and all others are guarded and maintained, and without which they would be held completely at the mercy of others; we repeat, it is impossible to conceive that this was intended to be left wholly and entirely at the discretion of the States.

. . . There can be no division of citizenship, either of its rights or its duties. There can be no half-way citizenship. Woman, as a citizen of the United States, is entitled to all the benefits of that position, and liable to all its obligations, or to none. Only citizens are permitted to pre-empt land, obtain passports, etc., all of which woman can do; and, on the other hand, she is taxed (without her "consent") in further recognition of her citizenship; and yet, as to this chief privilege of all, she is forbidden to exercise it. We call upon the State to show its warrant for so doing— for inflicting upon the plaintiff and the class to which she belongs, the bar of perpetual disfranchisement, where no crime or offense is alleged or pretended, and without "due process of law."

We charge it as a "bill of attainder" of the most odious and oppressive character. The State can no more deprive a citizen of the United States of one privilege than of another, except by the "law of the land." There is no security for freedom if this be denied. To use the language of Mr. Madison, such a course "violates the vital principle of free government, that those who are to be bound by laws, ought to have a voice in making them." . . .

It is sometimes said this is one of the "reserved rights" of the States. But this can not be, for the simple reason that, as to the "privileges and immunities" of federal citizenship, they had no existence prior to the adoption of the Federal Constitution; how then could they be reserved?

As Mr. Justice Story says: "The States can exercise no powers whatsoever, which exclusively spring out of the existence of the National Government, which the Constitution does not delegate to them. . . . No State can say that it has reserved what it never possessed." . . .

We say, then, that the States may regulate, but they have no right to prohibit the franchise to citizens of the United States. They may prescribe the qualifications of the electors. They may require that they shall be of a certain age, be of sane mind, be free from crime, etc., because these are conditions for the good of the whole, and to which all citizens, sooner or later, may attain. But to single out a class of citizens and say to them, "Notwithstanding you possess all these qualifications, you shall never vote, or take part in your government," what is it but a bill of attainder? . . . [There follows a long "proof," supported by quotations from the Founding Fathers, that they intended the states to regulate but not define voting rights.—*Ed.*] Or, if a still further and later authority be desired, we have it in the language of Chief-Justice Taney, who says, in the Dred Scott case:

> In discussing this question we must not confound the rights of citizenship, which a State may confer within its own limits, and the rights of citizenship as a member of the Union. It does not by any means follow, because he has all the rights and privileges of a citizen of a State, that he must be a citizen of the United States. . . . But if he rank as a citizen of the State to which he belongs, within the meaning of the Constitution of the United States, then, whenever he goes into another State, the Constitution clothes him as to the rights of person, with all the privileges and immunities which belong to citizens of the State. And if persons of the African race are citizens of a State, and of the United States, they would be entitled to all of these privileges and immunities in every State, and the State could not restrict them; for they would hold these privileges and immunities under the paramount authority of the Federal government, and its courts would be bound to maintain and enforce them, the Constitution and laws of the State to the contrary notwithstanding. And if the States could limit or restrict them, or place the party in an inferior grade, this clause of the Constitution would be unmeaning, and could have no operation, and would give no rights to the citizen when in another State. He would have none but what the State itself chose to allow him. This is evidently not the construction or meaning of the clause in question. It guarantees rights to the citizen, and the State can not withhold them. . . .

Now, substitute in the above, for "persons of the African race," women, who are "citizens of the State and of the United States," and you have the key to the whole position. . . . [There follows a long discussion, with citations and quotations, to show that denial of the vote to women contravenes constitutional prohibitions of bills of attainder and denial of rights without due process, and an argument that suffrage is a privilege of citizenship.—*Ed.*]

A proper construction of Art. 1, Sec. 2, of the Constitution of the United States will further demonstrate the proposition we are endeavoring to uphold. That section is as follows:

ARTICLE 1, Section 2. The House of Representatives shall be composed of members chosen every second year by the people of the several States; and the electors in each State shall have the qualifications for electors of the most numerous branch of the State Legislature.

This section consists of two clauses, but in neither is there a word as to the sex of the elector. He, or she, must be one of the people, or "citizens," as they are designated in the Constitution, that is all.—(Story's Comms. §579.)

The "people" are to elect. This clause fixes the class of voters; the other clause is in subordination to that, and merely provides, that as touching qualifications, there shall be one and the same standard for the Federal and for the State elector. Both are mentioned and neither is or can be excluded by the other.

The right to vote is very different from the qualification necessary in a voter. A person may have the right to vote, and yet not possess the necessary qualifications for exercising it. In this case, the right to vote is derived from the Federal Constitution, which designates the class of persons who may exercise it, and provides that the Federal elector shall conform to the regulations of the State, so far as time, place, and manner of exercising it are concerned. But it is clear that under this authority the State has no right to lay down an arbitrary and impossible rule. As before stated by the Chief-Justice of Nevada: "To make the enjoyment of a right depend upon an impossible condition, is equivalent to an absolute denial of it under any condition."

In conclusion, we will consider, as briefly as possible, the points made by the Supreme Court of Missouri. We quote from the opinion:

The question presented then is, whether there is a conflict between the Constitution of the United States and the Constitution and laws of the State of Missouri on this subject. That the different States of the Union had a right, previous to the adoption of what is known as the XIV. Amendment to the Constitution of the United States, to limit the right to vote at election by their constitution and laws to the male sex, I think not at this day can be questioned.

Undoubtedly the practice in the different States, as we have before said, is against the claim made by the plaintiff, although, as we shall show, in the early days of the Republic this practice was by no means universal. But when the Court states that the right of the States to do this can not be questioned, it assumes the very point in controversy, and it fails to notice the distinction between "the rights of citizenship which a state may confer within its own limits, and the rights of citizenship as a member of the Union." (Chief-Justice Taney in Scott vs. Sanford, 19 Howard, 405.) . . .

In the one case he [the citizen] exercises the franchise under one jurisdiction or sovereignty, and in the other under a totally different one. In voting for Federal officers he exercises the freeman's right to take part in the government of his own creation, and he does this in contemplation of law, in his character or capacity of a citizen of the United States, and his right so to vote legally depends upon such status or character. Clearly, then, the right of a citizen of the United States to vote for Federal officers can only be exercised under the authority or sovereignty of the United States, not under some other authority or sovereignty, and consequently the citizen of the United States could not justly have been deprived of such right by the State, even before the adoption of the XIV. Amendment.

But whatever doubt there may have been as to this, we hold that the adoption of the XIV. Amendment put an end to it and placed the matter beyond controversy. The history of that Amendment shows that it was designed as a limitation on the powers of the States, in many important particulars, and its language is clear and unmistakable. "No State shall make or enforce any law which shall abridge the privileges and immunities of citizens of the United States." Of course all the citizens of the United States are by this protected in the enjoyment of their privileges and immunities. Among the privileges, that of voting is the highest and greatest. To an American citizen there can be none greater or more highly to be prized; and the preservation of this privilege to the citizens of the United States respectively is, by this Amendment, placed under the immediate supervision and care of the Government of the United States, who are thus charged with its fulfillment and guaranty.

By ratifying this Amendment the several States have relinquished and quit-claimed, so to speak, to the United States, all
claim or right, on their part, to "make or enforce any law which
shall abridge the privileges and immunities of citizens of the
United States." The State of Missouri, therefore, is estopped from
longer claiming this right to limit the franchise to "males," as a
State prerogative; and the Supreme Court of Missouri should have
so declared, and its failure to do so is error; because, by retaining
that word in the State Constitution and laws, not this plaintiff
only, but large numbers of other citizens of the United States are
"abridged" in the exercise of their "privileges and immunities as
citizens of the United States," by being deprived of their right or
privilege to vote for United States officers, as claimed by the plaintiff in her petition. Not only this, but we say further, that the
ratification of this amendment was, in intendment of law, a
solemn agreement, on the part of the States, that all existing legislation inconsistent therewith should be repealed, or considered
as repealed, and that none of like character should take place in
the future. The State of Missouri had acted upon this idea in
part, and its subsequent legislation, on the subject of the ballot,
has been as follows: The ratification of the XV. Amendment
(which we do not consider as having any direct bearing on the
point now being considered, inasmuch as this Amendment is
merely prohibitory—not conferring any right, but treating the ballot in the hands of the negro as an existing fact, and forbidding
his deprivation thereof). Next, amending the State Constitution
and registration law, by simply omitting the word "white" from
the clause "white male citizens."

This constitutes the entire legislation of the State of Missouri
on this subject since the adoption of the XIV. Amendment, and
this omission of the word "white" was designed to make the
State Constitution conform to the Amendment, so far as the negro
was concerned, leaving the women citizens of the United States
still under the ban of "involuntary servitude," in plain violation
of the Amendment.

So that, while the negro votes to-day in Missouri, there is not a
syllable of affirmative legislation by the State conferring the right

upon him. Whence, then, does he derive it? There is but one reply. The XIV. Amendment conferred upon the negro race in this country citizenship of the United States, and the ballot followed as an incident to that condition. Or, to use the more forcible language of this Court, in the Slaughter-house cases (16 Wall., 71), "the negro having, by the XIV. Amendment, been declared a citizen of the United States, is thus made a voter in every State of the Union." If this be true of the negro citizen of the United States, it is equally true of the woman citizen. And we invoke the interposition of this Court to effect, by its decree, that which the Supreme Court of Missouri should have done, and declare that this objectionable word must be omitted, or considered as omitted from the Constitution and registration law of said State. . . .

We proceed with our quotation from the opinion:

In this changed state of affairs, it was thought by those who originated and adopted this Amendment, that it was absolutely necessary that these emancipated people should have the elective franchise, in order to enable them to protect themselves against unfriendly legislation, in which they could take no part; that unless these people had the right to vote, and thus protect themselves against oppression, their freedom from slavery would be a mockery, and their condition but little improved. It was to remedy this that the XIV. Amendment to the Constitution was adopted. It was to compel the former slave States to give these freedmen the right of suffrage, and to give them all of the rights of other citizens of the respective States, and thus make them equal with other citizens before the law.

It would be impossible for us to give any better reason for woman's need of the ballot than the court has here given for that of the negro, except that woman's condition is even more helpless than his. . . .

We again quote from the opinion:

It was only intended to give the freedmen the same rights that were secured to all other classes of citizens in the State, and that if the other male inhabitants of the State over the age of twenty-one years enjoyed the right of suffrage, so should the males among the freedmen over the age of twenty-one years enjoy the same right; it was not intended that females, or persons under the age of twenty-one years, should have the right of suffrage conferred on them.

In reply to this, we might content ourselves with saying that it is mere assertion, and can hardly be dignified as argument; but we answer, that if the XIV. Amendment does not secure the ballot to woman, neither does it to the negro; for it does not in terms confer the ballot upon any one. As we have already shown, it is the altered condition of citizenship that secures to the negro this right; but this plaintiff might well reply, I was born to that condition, and yet am denied its privileges. . . .

Although the point is not alluded to by the Supreme Court of Missouri, yet, as we desire to meet every possible objection, we think this a proper place to notice an argument sometimes put forward, based upon the XV. Amendment. . . . As this Amendment says, that the right of citizens of the United States to vote shall not be denied or abridged by the United States, or by any State, on account of race, color, or previous condition of servitude, it is claimed by some that it may be abridged on other grounds. But . . . the IX. Amendment to the Constitution effectually puts an end to the application of this principle by declaring that the enumeration in the Constitution of certain rights shall not be construed to deny or disparage others retained by the people. . . .

We ask the court to consider what it is to be disfranchised; not this plaintiff only, but an entire class of people, utterly deprived of all voice in the government under which they live! We say it is to her, and to them, a Despotism, and not a Republic. What matters it that the tyranny be of many instead of one? Society shudders at the thought of putting a fraudulent ballot into the ballot-box! What is the difference between putting a fraudulent ballot in, and keeping a lawful ballot out? Her disfranchised condition is a badge of servitude. . . .

Either we must give up the principles announced in the Declaration of Independence, that governments derive their just powers from the consent of the governed; and are formed by the people to protect their rights, not to withhold them; or we must acknowledge the truth contended for by the plaintiff, that citizenship carries with it every incident to every citizen alike. . . .

The first amendment to the Constitution declares that Congress shall make no law abridging freedom of speech or of the press, thus incorporating into the organic law of this country absolute freedom of thought or opinion. We presume it will not be doubted that the States are equally bound with Congress by this prohibition, not only because, as Chief-Justice Taney says, "the Constitution of the United States, and every article and clause in it, is a part of the law of every State in the Union, and is the paramount law" (Prigg *vs.* The Comm., 16 Peters R., 628), but because, in the very nature of things, freedom of speech or of thought can not be divided. It is a personal attribute, and once secured is forever secured. To vote is but one form or method of expressing this freedom of speech. Speech is a declaration of thought. A vote is the expression of the will, preference, or choice. Suffrage is one definition of the word, while the verb is defined, to choose by suffrage, to elect, to express or signify the mind, will, or preference, either *viva voce*, or by ballot. We claim then that the right to vote, or express one's wish at the polls, is embraced in the spirit, if not the letter, of the First Amendment, and every citizen is entitled to the protection it affords. It is the merest mockery to say to this plaintiff, you may write, print, publish, or speak your thoughts upon every occasion, except at the polls. There your lips shall be sealed. It is impossible that this can be American law!

Again, it is the opinion of some that suffrage is somehow lodged in the government, whence it is dispensed, or conferred upon the citizen, thus completely reversing the actual fact. Suffrage is never conferred by government upon the citizen. He holds it by a higher title. In this country government is the source of power, not of rights. These are vested in the individual—are personal and inalienable. Society can only acquire the authority to regulate these rights, or declare them forfeited, for cause. . . .

But this clause of the Missouri law further violates the XIII. Amendment, which declares that neither slavery nor involuntary servitude shall exist in the United States, except for crime, etc. . . . We say that this Missouri law violates this amendment, inasmuch as it places the plaintiff in a disfranchised condition, which is none other than a condition of servitude—of "involuntary servitude,"

because, although a citizen in the fullest acceptation of the term
—a member of this body politic—one of the "people"—she has
never consented to this law; has never been permitted to express
either consent or dissent, nor given any opportunity to express her
opinion thereon, in the manner pointed out by law, while at the
same time she is taxed, and her property taken to pay the very
men who sat in judgment upon and condemned her!

Finally—Such is the nature of this privilege—so individual—
so purely personal is its character, that its indefinite extension de-
tracts not in the slightest degree from those who already enjoy it,
and by an affirmation of the plaintiff's claim all womanhood
would be elevated into that condition of self-respect that perfect
freedom alone can give.

Susan B. Anthony's Constitutional Argument (1873)

In 1872 Susan B. Anthony and other women voted for President
in Rochester, New York, and were indicted. She was eventually
convicted but refused to pay the fine imposed, and no effort was
ever made to collect it. The following is the speech Miss Anthony
delivered in fifty districts in two counties in upstate New York
before her trial in June 1873. [Ida Husted Harper, *The Life and
Work of Susan B. Anthony*, II (Indianapolis, 1898), 977–87.]

Friends and Fellow-Citizens:—I stand before you under indict-
ment for the alleged crime of having voted at the last presidential
election, without having a lawful right to vote. It shall be my
work this evening to prove to you that in thus doing, I not only
committed no crime, but instead simply exercised my citizen's
right, guaranteed to me and all United States citizens by the
National Constitution beyond the power of any State to deny.

Our democratic-republican government is based on the idea of
the natural right of every individual member thereof to a voice
and a vote in making and executing the laws. We assert the prov-

ince of government to be to secure the people in the enjoyment of their inalienable rights. We throw to the winds the old dogma that government can give rights. No one denies that before governments were organized each individual possessed the right to protect his own life, liberty and property. When 100 or 1,000,000 people enter into a free government, they do not barter away their natural rights; they simply pledge themselves to protect each other in the enjoyment of them through prescribed judicial and legislative tribunals. They agree to abandon the methods of brute force in the adjustment of their differences and adopt those of civilization. Nor can you find a word in any of the grand documents left us by the fathers which assumes for government the power to create or to confer rights. The Declaration of Independence, the United States Constitution, the constitutions of the several States and the organic laws of the Territories, all alike propose to *protect* the people in the exercise of their God-given rights. Not one of them pretends to bestow rights.

All men are created equal, and endowed by their Creator with certain inalienable rights. Among these are life, liberty and the pursuit of happiness. To secure these, governments are instituted among men, deriving their just powers from the consent of the governed.

Here is no shadow of government authority over rights, or exclusion of any class from their full and equal enjoyment. Here is pronounced the right of all men, and "consequently," as the Quaker preacher said, "of all women," to a voice in the government. And here, in this first paragraph of the Declaration, is the assertion of the natural right of all to the ballot; for how can "the consent of the governed" be given, if the right to vote be denied? Again:

Whenever any form of government becomes destructive of these ends, it is the right of the people to alter or abolish it, and to institute a new government, laying its foundations on such principles, and organizing its powers in such form, as to them shall seem most likely to effect their safety and happiness.

Surely the right of the whole people to vote is here clearly implied; for however destructive to their happiness this government might become, a disfranchised class could neither alter nor abolish it, nor institute a new one, except by the old brute force method of insurrection and rebellion. One-half of the people of this nation today are utterly powerless to blot from the statute books an unjust law, or to write there a new and just one. The women, dissatisfied as they are with this form of government, that enforces taxation without representation—that compels them to obey laws to which they never have given their consent—that imprisons and hangs them without a trial by a jury of their peers—that robs them, in marriage, of the custody of their own persons, wages and children—are this half of the people who are left wholly at the mercy of the other half, in direct violation of the spirit and letter of the declarations of the framers of this government, every one of which was based on the immutable principle of equal rights to all. By these declarations, kings, popes, priests, aristocrats, all were alike dethroned and placed on a common level, politically, with the lowliest born subject or serf. By them, too, men, as such, were deprived of their divine right to rule and placed on a political level with women. By the practice of these declarations all class and caste distinctions would be abolished, and slave, serf, plebeian, wife, woman, all alike rise from their subject position to the broader platform of equality.

The preamble of the Federal Constitution says:

We, the people of the United States, in order to form a more perfect union, establish justice, insure domestic tranquillity, provide for the common defence, promote the general welfare and secure the blessings of liberty to ourselves and our posterity, do ordain and establish this Constitution for the United States of America.

It was we, the people, not we, the white male citizens, nor we, the male citizens; but we, the whole people, who formed this Union. We formed it not to give the blessings of liberty but to secure them; not to the half of ourselves and the half of our posterity, but to the whole people—women as well as men. It is downright mockery to talk to women of their enjoyment of the blessings of liberty while they are denied the only means of securing them provided by this democratic-republican government—the ballot.

The early journals of Congress show that, when the committee reported to that body the original articles of confederation, the very first one which became the subject of discussion was that respecting equality of suffrage. Article IV said:

The better to secure and perpetuate mutual friendship and intercourse between the people of the different States of this Union, the free inhabitants of each of the States (paupers, vagabonds and fugitives from justice excepted) shall be entitled to all the privileges and immunities of the free citizens of the several States.

Thus, at the very beginning, did the fathers see the necessity of the universal application of the great principle of equal rights to all, in order to produce the desired result—a harmonious union and a homogeneous people. . . .

[Miss Anthony here quotes Luther Martin and James Madison to the same effect.—Ed.]

These assertions by the framers of the United States Constitution of the equal and natural right of all the people to a voice in the government, have been affirmed and reaffirmed by the leading statesmen of the nation throughout the entire history of our government. Thaddeus Stevens, of Pennsylvania, said in 1866: "I have made up my mind that the elective franchise is one of the inalienable rights meant to be secured by the Declaration of Independence." B. Gratz Brown, of Missouri, in the three days' discussion in the United States Senate in 1866, on Senator Cowan's motion to strike "male" from the District of Columbia suffrage bill, said:

Mr. President, I say here on the floor of the American Senate, I stand for universal suffrage; and as a matter of fundamental principle, do not recognize the right of society to limit it on any ground of race or sex. I will go farther and say that I recognize the right of franchise as being intrinsically a natural right. I do not believe that society is authorized to impose any limitations upon it that do not spring out of the necessities of the social state itself. Sir, I have been shocked, in the course of this debate, to hear senators declare this right only a conventional and political arrangement, a privilege yielded to you and me and others; not a right in any sense, only a concession! Mr. President, I do not hold my liberties by any such tenure. On the contrary, I believe that whenever you establish that doctrine, whenever you crystallize that idea in the public mind of this country, you ring the death-knell of American liberties.

Charles Sumner, in his brave protests against the Fourteenth and Fifteenth Amendments, insisted that so soon as by the Thirteenth Amendment the slaves became free men, the original powers of the United States Constitution guaranteed to them equal rights—the right to vote and to be voted for. In closing one of his great speeches he said:

I do not hesitate to say that when the slaves of our country became "citizens" they took their place in the body politic as a component part of the "people," entitled to equal rights and under the protection of these two guardian principles: First, that all just governments stand on the consent of the governed; and second, that taxation without representation is tyranny; and these rights it is the duty of Congress to guarantee as essential to the idea of a republic.

. . . The clauses of the United States Constitution cited by our opponents as giving power to the States to disfranchise any classes of citizens they please, are contained in Sections 2 and 4, Article I. The second says:

The House of Representatives shall be composed of members chosen every second year by the people of the several States; and the electors in each State shall have the qualifications requisite for electors of the most numerous branch of the State legislature.

This can not be construed into a concession to the States of the power to destroy the right to become an elector, but simply to prescribe what shall be the qualifications, such as competency of intellect, maturity of age, length of residence, that shall be deemed necessary to enable them to make an intelligent choice of candidates. If, as our opponents assert, it is the duty of the United States to protect citizens in the several States against higher or different qualifications for electors for representatives in Congress than for members of the Assembly, then it must be equally imperative for the national government to interfere with the States, and forbid them from arbitrarily cutting off the right of one-half the people to become electors altogether. . . . Surely, to regulate can not be to annihilate; to qualify can not be wholly to deprive. To this principle every true Democrat and Republican said amen, when applied to black men by Senator Sumner in his great speeches from 1865 to 1869 for equal rights to all; and when, in 1871, I asked that senator to declare the power of the United States Constitution to protect women in their right to vote—as he had done for black men—he handed me a copy of all his speeches during that reconstruction period, and said:

Put "sex" where I have "race" or "color," and you have here the best and strongest argument I can make for woman. There is not a doubt but women have the constitutional right to vote, and I will never vote for a Sixteenth Amendment to guarantee it to them. I voted for both the Fourteenth and Fifteenth under protest; would never have done it but for the pressing emergency of that hour; would have insisted that the power of the original Constitution to protect all citizens in the equal enjoyment of their rights should have been vindicated through the courts. But the newly-made freedmen had neither the intelligence, wealth nor time to await that slow process. Women do possess all these in an eminent degree, and I insist that they shall appeal to the courts, and through them establish the powers of our American magna charta to protect every citizen of the republic.

But, friends, when in accordance with Senator Sumner's counsel I went to the ballot-box, last November, and exercised my citizen's right to vote, the courts did not wait for me to appeal to them— they appealed to me, and indicted me on the charge of having voted illegally. Putting sex where he did color, Senator Sumner would have said:

Qualifications can not be in their nature permanent or insurmountable. Sex can not be a qualification any more than size, race, color or previous condition of servitude. A permanent or insurmountable qualification is equivalent to a deprivation of the suffrage. In other words, it is the tyranny of taxation without representation, against which our Revolutionary mothers, as well as fathers, rebelled.

For any State to make sex a qualification, which must ever result in the disfranchisement of one entire half of the people, is to pass a bill of attainder, an ex post facto law, and is therefore a violation of the supreme law of the land. By it the blessings of liberty are forever withheld from women and their female posterity. For them, this government has no just powers derived from the consent of the governed. For them this government is not a democracy; it is not a republic. It is the most odious aristocracy ever established on the face of the globe. An oligarchy of wealth, where the rich govern the poor; an oligarchy of learning, where the educated govern the ignorant; or even an oligarchy of race, where the Saxon rules the African, might be endured; but this oligarchy of sex which makes father, brothers, husband, sons, the oligarchs over the mother and sisters, the wife and daughters of every household; which ordains all men sovereigns, all women subjects—carries discord and rebellion into every home of the nation. . . . The moment you deprive a person of his right to a voice in the government, you degrade him from the status of a citizen of the republic to that of a subject. It matters very little to him whether his monarch be an individual tyrant, as is the Czar of Russia, or a 15,000,000 headed monster, as here in the United States; he is a powerless subject, serf or slave; not in any sense a free and independent citizen. . . .

Though the words persons, people, inhabitants, electors, citizens, are all used indiscriminately in the national and State constitutions, there was always a conflict of opinion, prior to the war, as to whether they were synonymous terms, but whatever room there was for doubt, under the old regime, the adoption of the Fourteenth Amendment settled that question forever in its first sentence:

All persons born or naturalized in the United States, and subject to the jurisdiction thereof, are citizens of the United States, and of the State wherein they reside.

The second settles the equal status of all citizens:

No State shall make or enforce any law which shall abridge the privileges or immunities of citizens of the United States; nor shall any State deprive any person of life, liberty or property without due process of law, or deny to any person within its jurisdiction the equal protection of the laws.

The only question left to be settled now is: Are women persons? I scarcely believe any of our opponents will have the hardihood to say they are not. Being persons, then, women are citizens, and no State has a right to make any new law, or to enforce any old law, which shall abridge their privileges or immunities. Hence, every discrimination against women in the constitutions and laws of the several States is today null and void, precisely as is every one against negroes.

Is the right to vote one of the privileges or immunities of citizens? I think the disfranchised ex-rebels and ex-State prisoners all will agree that it is not only one of them, but the one without which all the others are nothing. Seek first the kingdom of the ballot and all things else shall be added, is the political injunction.

Webster, Worcester and Bouvier all define citizen to be a person, in the United States, entitled to vote and hold office. Prior to the adoption of the Thirteenth Amendment, by which slavery was forever abolished and black men transformed from property to persons, the judicial opinions of the country had always been in harmony with this definition: In order to be a citizen one must be a voter. Associate-Justice Washington, in defining the privileges and immunities of the citizen, more than fifty years ago, said: "They include all such privileges as are fundamental in their nature; and among them is the right to exercise the elective franchise, and to hold office." Even the Dred Scott decision, pronounced by the Abolitionists and Republicans infamous because it virtually declared "black men had no rights white men were bound to respect," gave this true and logical conclusion, that to be one of the people was to be a citizen and a voter. . . . What right in this country has the Irishman the day after he receives his naturalization papers that he did not possess the day before, save the right to vote and hold office? The Chinamen now crowding our Pacific coast are in precisely the same position. What privilege or immunity has California or Oregon the right to deny them, save that of the ballot? Clearly, then, if the Fourteenth Amendment was not to secure to black men their right to vote it did nothing for them, since they possessed everything else before. But if it was intended to prohibit the States from denying or abridging their right to vote, then it did the same for all persons, white women included, born or naturalized in the

United States; for the amendment does not say that all male persons of African descent, but that all persons are citizens.

The second section is simply a threat to punish the States by reducing their representation on the floor of Congress, should they disfranchise any of their male citizens, and can not be construed into a sanction to disfranchise female citizens, nor does it in any wise weaken or invalidate the universal guarantee of the first section.

However much the doctors of the law may disagree as to whether people and citizens, in the original Constitution, were one and the same, or whether the privileges and immunities in the Fourteenth Amendment include the right of suffrage, the question of the citizen's right to vote is forever settled by the Fifteenth Amendment. "The right of citizens of the United States to vote shall not be denied or abridged by the United States, or by any State, on account of race, color or previous condition of servitude." How can the State deny or abridge the right of the citizen, if the citizen does not possess it? There is no escape from the conclusion that to vote is the citizen's right, and the specifications of race, color or previous condition of servitude can in no way impair the force of that emphatic assertion that the citizen's right to vote shall not be denied or abridged.

The political strategy of the second section of the Fourteenth Amendment failing to coerce the rebel States into enfranchising their negroes, and the necessities of the Republican party demanding their votes throughout the South to ensure the re-election of Grant in 1872, that party was compelled to place this positive prohibition of the Fifteenth Amendment upon the United States and all the States thereof.

If once we establish the false principle that United States citizenship does not carry with it the right to vote in every State in this Union, there is no end to the petty tricks and cunning devices which will be attempted to exclude one and another class of citizens from the right of suffrage. It will not always be the men combining to disfranchise all women; native born men combining to abridge the rights of all naturalized citizens, as in Rhode Island. It will not always be the rich and educated who may combine to cut off the poor and ignorant; but we may live to see the hard-working, uncultivated day laborers, foreign and native born, learning the power of the ballot and their vast majority of numbers, combine and amend State constitutions so as to disfranchise the Vanderbilts, the Stewarts, the Conklings and the Fentons. It is a poor rule that won't work more ways than one. Establish this precedent, admit the State's right to deny suffrage, and there is no limit to the confusion, discord, and disruption that may await us. There is and can be but one safe principle of government—equal rights to all. Discrimination against any class on account of color, race, nativity, sex, property, culture, can but embitter and disaffect that class, and thereby endanger the safety of the whole people. Clearly, then, the national government not only must define the rights of citizens, but must stretch out its powerful hand and protect them in every State in this Union. . . .

5

THE "EXPEDIENCY" ARGUMENT. I: RACISM AND XENOPHOBIA ENLISTED IN THE CAUSE OF WOMAN SUFFRAGE

Henry B. Blackwell, What the South Can Do (1867)

One of the principal arguments used by suffragists might be termed the "statistical" argument: that since there were in the South more white women than blacks of both sexes, woman suffrage would insure white supremacy. The following is the first major statement of this argument. [Henry B. Blackwell, "What the South Can Do: How the Southern States Can Make Themselves Masters of the Situation" (1867), in *HWS* II, 929–31.]

To the Legislatures of the Southern States:—I write to you as the intellectual leaders of the Southern people—men who should be able and willing to transcend the prejudices of section —to suggest the only ground of settlement between North and South which, in my judgment, can be successfully adopted.

Let me state the political situation. The radical principles of the North are immovably fixed upon negro suffrage as a condition of Southern State reconstruction. The proposed Constitutional Amendment is not regarded as a finality. It satisfies nobody, not even its authors. In the minds of the Northern people the negroes are now associated with the idea of loyalty to the Union. They are considered citizens. They are respected as "our allies." It is believed in the North that a majority of the white people of the South are at heart the enemies of the Union. The advocates of negro suffrage daily grow stronger and more numerous.

On the other hand, a majority of the Southern white population are inflexibly opposed to negro suffrage in any form, universal or qualified, and are prepared to resist its introduction by every means in their power. In alliance with the President and the Northern Democracy, they protest against any and all terms of reconstruction, demand unconditional readmission, and await in gloomy silence the Republican initiative.

This absolute and growing antagonism can only end, if continued, in one of two results, either in a renewal of civil war, or in a concession by the South of political equality to the negro. But in the case of war, the South can not possibly succeed. The North is to-day far stronger in men and money, in farms and factories, than she was in 1860. She is now trained to war, conscious of overwhelming strength, flushed with victory, and respected, as never before, by the nations of Europe. Moreover, she is much more united in political sentiment. Do not again deceive yourselves. If you should resort to arms, the North would be practically unanimous. The President would instantly be impeached and a radical successor appointed. The South has lost social unity with the loss of slavery. She can not fight better than before. And the braver her action, the more terrible would be her fate.

Gentlemen, these are the facts—not theories. Wise men try to see things as they are, uncolored by opinion or preference. The interest of both North and South, since they must live together, is peace, harmony, and real fraternity. No adjustment can fully succeed unless it is acceptable to both sections. Therefore the statesman and patriot must find a common ground as a basis of permanent reconciliation.

Now the radicalism of the North is actual, organic, and progressive. Recognize the fact. But if "governments derive their just powers from the consent of the governed"—if "taxation without representation is tyranny"—and "on these two commandments hang all the (Republican) law and the prophets"—then these propositions are as applicable to women as to negroes. "Consistency is a jewel." The principle is so broad that, if you accept it in its entirety, you can afford to lead—not follow.

The population of the late slave States is about 12,000,000; 8,000,000 white, 4,000,000 black. The radicals demand suffrage for the black men on the ground named above. Very good. Say to them, as Mr. Cowan said to the advocates of negro male suffrage in the District, "Apply your principle! Give the suffrage to all men and women of mature age and sound mind, and we will accept it as the basis of State and National reconstruction."

Consider the result from the Southern standpoint. Your 4,000,-000 of Southern white women will counterbalance your 4,000,000 of negro men and women, and thus the political supremacy of your white race will remain unchanged.

Think well of this. It is a calculation of the relative political influences of white women and of negroes which perhaps your people have not yet considered. Let us make the statement in figures. Estimating one male voter to every five persons, your present vote is:

White males	1,600,000
Add white females	1,600,000
Total white voters	3,200,000
Negro males	800,000
Negro females	800,000
Total negro voters	1,600,000

Suppose all the negroes vote one way and all the whites the

other, your white majority would be 1,600,000—equal to your
present total vote. Thus you would control your own State legislation. Meanwhile, your influence in the councils of the nation
will be greater than ever before, because your emancipated slaves
will be counted in the basis of representation, instead of as formerly, in the ratio of five for three. In the light of the history of
your Confederacy, can any Southerner fear to trust the women of
the South with the ballot?

But the propriety of your making the proposal lies deeper than
any consideration of sectional expediency. If you must try the
Republican experiment, try it fully and fairly. Since you are compelled to union with the North, remove every seed of future controversy. If you are to share the future government of your States
with a race you deem naturally and hopelessly inferior, avert the
social chaos, which seems to you so imminent, by utilizing the
intelligence and patriotism of the wives and daughters of the
South. Plant yourselves upon the logical Northern principle. Then
no new demands can ever be made upon you. No future inroads
of fanaticism can renew sectional discord.

The effect upon the North would be to revolutionize political
parties. "Justice satisfies everybody." The negro, thus protected
against oppression by possessing the ballot, would cease to be the
prominent object of philanthropic interest. Northern distrust,
disarmed by Southern magnanimity, would give place to the live-
liest sentiments of confidence and regard. The great political
desideratum would be attained. The negro question would be
forever removed from the political arena. National parties would
again crystallize upon legitimate questions of National interest—
questions of tariff, finance, and foreign relations. The disastrous
conflict between Federal and State jurisdictions would cease.
North and South, no longer hammer and anvil, would forget and
forgive the past. School-houses and churches would be our fortifi-
cations and intrenchments. Capital and population would flow,
like the Mississippi, toward the Gulf. The black race would gravi-
tate by the law of nature toward the tropics. The memory and
spirit of Washington would be cherished; and every deed of
genuine gallantry and humanity would be treasured as the common
glory of the republic.

Do you say that Northern Republicans would not accept such a proposition? They can not avoid it. The matter is in your own hands.

In New Jersey (then a slave State) from 1776 to 1807, a period of thirty-one years, women and negroes voted on precisely the same footing as white men. No catastrophe, social or political, ensued. The following is an extract from the New Jersey election law of 1797:

"Sec. 9. Every voter shall openly and in full view deliver his or her ballot, which shall be a single written ticket containing the names of the person, or persons, for whom he or she votes," etc.

Your Southern Legislatures can extend suffrage on equal terms to "all inhabitants," as the New Jersey State Convention did in 1776. Then let the Republicans in Congress refuse to admit your Senators and Representatives, if they dare. If so, they will go under. Upon that issue fairly made up, the men of positive convictions would rally round the new and consistent Democratic party. The very element which has destroyed slavery would side with the victorious South, and "out of the nettle danger you would pluck the flower safety."

Respectfully yours, HENRY B. BLACKWELL.
NEW YORK, January 15, 1867.

Olympia Brown, On the Foreign Menace (1889)

Olympia Brown (1835–1926) became a Universalist minister in 1862. She had a parish in Weymouth, Massachusetts, but in 1878 moved to Wisconsin, and it was as a resident of that state that she delivered this speech at the 1889 convention of the National American Woman Suffrage Association. [HWS IV, 148–49.]

FOREIGN RULE

["After pointing out the glory of a country which offered a home to all, and expressing a belief in universal suffrage," write the editors of the HWS, "she continued:"]

In Wisconsin we have by the census of 1880 a population of

910,072 native-born, 405,425 foreign-born. Our last vote cast was 149,463 American, 189,469 foreign; thus you see nearly 1,000,000 native-born people are out-voted and out-governed by less than half their number of foreigners. Is that fair to Americans? Is it just to American men? Will they not, under this influence, in a little while be driven to the wall and obliged to step down and out? When the members of our Legislatures are the greater part foreigners, when they sit in the office of mayor and in all the offices of our city, and rule us with a rod of iron, it is time that American men should inquire if we have any rights that foreigners are bound to respect. . . .

The last census shows, I think, that there are in the United States three times as many American-born women as the whole foreign population, men and women together, so that the votes of women will eventually be the only means of overcoming this foreign influence and maintaining our free institutions. There is no possible safety for our free school, our free church or our republican government, unless women are given the suffrage and that right speedily. . . . The question in every political caucus, in every political convention, is not what great principles shall we announce, but what kind of a document can we draw up that will please the foreigners? . . .

When we remember that the first foot to touch Plymouth Rock was a woman's—that in the first settlement of this country women endured trials and privations and stood bravely at the post of duty, even fighting in the ranks that we might have a republic—and that in our great Western world women came at an early day to make the wilderness blossom as the rose, and rocked their babies' cradles in the log cabins when the Indians' war-whoop was heard on the prairies and the wolves howled around their doors—when we remember that in the last war thousands of women in the Northwest bravely took upon themselves the work of the households and the fields that their husbands and sons might fight the battles of liberty—when we recollect all this, and then are told that loyal women, pioneer women, the descendants of the Pilgrim Fathers, are not even to ask for the right of suffrage lest the Scandinavians should be offended, it is time to rise in indignation and ask, Whose country is this? Who made it? Who have periled their lives for it?

Our American women are property holders and pay large taxes; but the foreigner who has lived only one year in the State, and ten days in the precinct, who does not own a foot of land, may vote away their property in the form of taxes in the most reckless manner, regardless of their interests and their rights. Women are well-educated; they are graduating from our colleges; they are reading and thinking and writing; and yet they are the political inferiors of all the riff-raff of Europe that is poured upon our shores. It is unbearable. There is no language that can express the enormous injustice done to women. . . .

We are in danger in this country of Catholic domination, not because the Catholics are more numerous than we are, but because the Catholic church is represented at the polls and the Protestant church is not. The foreigners are Catholic—the greater portion of them; the foreigners are men—the greater part of them, and members of the Catholic church, and they work for it and vote for it. The Protestant church is composed of women. Men for the most part do not belong to it; they do not care much for it except as something to interest the women of their household. The consequence is the Protestant church is comparatively unrepresented at the ballot-box. . . .

I urge upon you, women, that you put suffrage first and foremost, before every other consideration upon earth. Make it a religious duty and work for the enfranchisement of your sex, which means the growth and development of noble characters in your children; for you can not educate your children well surrounded by men and women who hold false doctrines of society, of politics, of morals. . . .

Resolutions Adopted at a Convention (1893)

These resolutions, unanimously adopted at the 1893 convention of the National American Woman Suffrage Association, are thoroughly typical of the period between Reconstruction and about 1910. The first applies Henry B. Blackwell's "statistical" argument to the North as well as to the South. [*HWS* IV, 216n.]

Resolved, That without expressing any opinion on the proper qualifications for voting, we call attention to the significant facts that in every State there are more women who can read and write than the whole number of illiterate male voters; more white women who can read and write than all negro voters; more American women who can read and write than all foreign voters; so that the enfranchisement of such women would settle the vexed question of rule by illiteracy, whether of home-grown or foreign-born production.

Resolved, That as all experience proves that the rights of the laboring man are best preserved in governments where he has possession of the ballot, we therefore demand on behalf of the laboring woman the same powerful instrument, that she may herself protect her own interests; and we urge all organized bodies of working women, whether in the field of philanthropy, education, trade, manufacture or general industry, to join our association in the endeavor to make woman legally and politically a free agent, as the best means for furthering any and every line of woman's work.

Resolved, That in all States possessing School Suffrage for women, suffragists are advised to organize in each representative district thereof, for the purpose of training and stimulating women voters to exercise regularly this right, using it as a preparatory school for the coming work of full-grown citizenship with an unlimited ballot. We also advise that women everywhere work for the election of an equal number of women and men upon school boards, that the State in taking upon itself the education of children may provide them with as many official mothers as fathers.

WHEREAS, Many forms of woman suffrage may be granted by State Legislatures without change in existing constitutions; therefore,

Resolved, That the suffragists in every State should petition for

Municipal, School and Presidential Suffrage by statute, and take every practicable step toward securing such legislation.

Resolved, That we urge all women to enter protest, at the time of paying taxes, at being compelled to submit to taxation without representation.

Carrie Chapman Catt, Danger to Our Government (1894)

Carrie Chapman Catt made this speech at a suffrage meeting in Iowa in a year of militant nationwide strike activity, before she became a national suffragist leader. [*Woman's Journal*, December 15, 1894.]

This Government is menaced with great danger, and that danger cannot be averted by the triumph of the party of protection, nor by that of free trade, nor by the triumph of single tax or of free silver. That danger lies in the votes possessed by the males in the slums of the cities, and the ignorant foreign vote which was sought to be bought up by each party, to make political success. It made no difference whether that vote was usually found with one party or not (except that one has more respect for an open bid than for a disguised one), the corrupting influence was just the same. In the mining districts the danger has already reached this point—miners are supplied with arms, watching with greedy eyes for the moment when they can get in their deadly work of despoiling the wealth of the country. The hoodlums of Chicago gave us a forecast of their intent to reproduce the horrors of the Old World when their numbers are sufficiently increased, and every ship load of foreigners brings them nearer to their object. These men hold the government of the large cities in the hollow of their hands. There is but one way to avert the danger—cut off the vote of the slums and give to woman, who is bound to suffer all, and more than man can, of the evils his legislation has brought upon the nation, the power of protecting herself that man has secured for himself—the ballot. Put the ballot in the hands of every person of sound mind in the nation. If that would make the vote too cumbersome, cut it off at the bottom, the vote of the slums. For several years past the proportion of men to women immigrating to this country has been increasing and has reached that of seven to one. In the five years preceding and including 1890, 1,020,032 men of voting age came to this country. And as in fourteen States an immigrant may vote, according to the laws of some States, in one year, or, in some, six months (as in Kansas), or in four months (as in Wisconsin), or in three months (as in Michigan), we can get some idea of their influence with the Government. Not only is the native-born American jeopardized in life and property, but the citizens of foreign birth who desire good government. It will be readily seen that granting the vote to woman and cutting off the vote of the slums, if it could not be otherwise controlled, would result at once in good to the nation. And those good men who fear that evil would result to woman by depositing her opinion where it will be counted, who yet, like Dr. Parkhurst, call upon woman to face the dangers of walking day after day upon the streets frequented by the men who have built up Tammany, to use their influence upon voters to tear it down, when a little piece of paper deposited in a ballot-box, which would take but a small part of one day, surrounded by no greater danger, would do the work far more effectually. This shows how tenacious of power men are when once possessing it, even when they mean to use that power for good as they see it.

Belle Kearney, The South and Woman Suffrage (1903)

In the 1890's a suffragist movement gradually developed in the South. Although the maintenance of white supremacy was not the southern suffragists' primary motivation, its desirability was something they all took for granted and some of them spotlighted in their propaganda. As suffragism's abolitionist origins receded into the past, the southern women found the northern leaders more and more sympathetic to their point of view. The following speech, by Mississippi suffragist Belle Kearney (1863–1939), at the 1903 convention of the National American Woman Suffrage Association in New Orleans, can be considered a signal of this growing understanding. ["The South and Woman Suffrage," *Woman's Journal*, April 4, 1903.]

[The first part of the speech, omitted here, traces the history of slavery in the colonies and the United States.—*Ed.*]

. . . By degrees, slavery became the bone of contention in politics. In course of time it would probably have been abolished by the Southerners themselves, if they had been left to work out their own destiny and that of the black man in bonds, but a conflict of ideas gathered to a storm-center between the Puritan of the North and the Cavalier of the South, and the institution was wiped out in blood. . . .

The world is scarcely beginning to realize the enormity of the situation that faces the South in its grapple with the race question which was thrust upon it at the close of the Civil War, when 4,500,000 ex-slaves, illiterate and semi-barbarous, were enfranchised. Such a situation has no parallel in history. In forging a path out of the darkness, there were no precedents to lead the way. All that has been and is being accomplished is pioneer statecraft. The South has struggled under its death-weight for nearly forty years, bravely and magnanimously.

The Southern States are making a desperate effort to maintain the political supremacy of Anglo-Saxonism by amendments to their constitutions limiting the right to vote by a property and educational qualification. If the United States government had been wise enough to enact such a law when the negro was first enfranchised, it would have saved years of bloodshed in the South, and such experiences of suffering and horror among the white people here as no other were ever subjected to in an enlightened nation.

The present suffrage laws in the different Southern States can be only temporary measures for protection. Those who are wise enough to look beneath the surface will be compelled to realize the fact that they act as a stimulus to the black man to acquire both education and property, but no incentive is given to the poor whites; for it is understood, in a general way, that any man whose skin is fair enough to let the blue veins show through, may be allowed the right of franchise.

The industrial education that the negro is receiving at Tuskegee and other schools is only fitting him for power, and when the black man becomes necessary to a community by reason of his skill and acquired wealth, and the poor white man, embittered by his poverty and humiliated by his inferiority, finds no place for himself or his children, then will come the grapple between the races.

To avoid this unspeakable culmination, the enfranchisement of women will have to be effected, and an educational and property qualification for the ballot be made to apply, without discrimination, to both sexes and to both races. It will spur the poor white to keep up with the march of progression [sic], and enable him to hold his own. The class that is not willing to measure its strength with that of an inferior is not fit to survive.

The enfranchisement of women would insure immediate and durable white supremacy, honestly attained; for, upon unquestionable authority, it is stated that "in every Southern State but one, there are more educated women than all the illiterate voters, white and black, native and foreign, combined." As you probably know, of all the women in the South who can read and write, ten out of every eleven are white. When it comes to the proportion of property between the races, that of the white outweighs that of the black immeasurably. The South is slow to grasp the great fact that the enfranchisement of women would settle the race question in politics.

The civilization of the North is threatened by the influx of foreigners with their imported customs; by the greed of monopolistic wealth, and the unrest among the working classes; by the strength of the liquor traffic, and by encroachments upon religious belief.

Some day the North will be compelled to look to the South for redemption from these evils, on account of the purity of its Anglo-Saxon blood, the simplicity of its social and economic structure, the great advance in prohibitory law, and the maintenance of the sanctity of its faith, which has been kept inviolate. Just as surely as the North will be forced to turn to the South for the nation's salvation, just so surely will the South be compelled to look to its Anglo-Saxon women as the medium through which to retain the supremacy of the white race over the African. . . .

Anglo-Saxonism is the standard of the ages to come. It is, above all else, the granite foundation of the South. Upon that its civilization will mount; upon that it will stand unshaken. . . .

Thank God the black man was freed! I wish for him all possible happiness and all possible progress, but not in encroachments upon the holy of holies of the Anglo-Saxon race. . . .

6

THE "EXPEDIENCY" ARGUMENT. II: OTHER FORMS

Anna Garlin Spencer, Duty to the Women of Our New Possessions (1899)

Once suffragists began to demand the vote not solely as a matter of right but also on the ground that they could effect specific reforms with it, their propaganda instantly reflected all current issues. In 1899 the headlines featured annexation of Hawaii and occupation of the Philippines, and, in the same year, the Reverend Anna Garlin Spencer, of Rhode Island, spoke on the "Duty to the Women of Our New Possessions" at the convention of the National American Woman Suffrage Association. [*HWS* IV, 328–34.]

. . . Bebel says, "Woman was the first human being to taste of bondage." True, and her bondage has been long and bitter; but the subjection of woman to man in the family bond was a vast step upward from the preceding condition. It gave woman release from the terrible labor-burdens of savage life; it gave her time and strength to develop beauty of person and refinement of taste and manners. It gave her the teaching capacity, for it put all the younger child-life into her exclusive care, with some leisure at command to devote to its mental and moral, as well as physical, well-being. It led to a closer relationship between man and woman than the world had known before, and thus gave each the advantage of the other's qualities. And always and everywhere the subjection of woman to man has had a mitigation and softening of hardships unknown to other forms of slavery, by reason of the power of human affection as it has worked through sex-attraction. As soon, however, as the slavery of woman to man was outgrown and obsolete it became (as was African slavery in a professedly democratic country like our own) "the sum of all villainies." And to-day there is no inconsistency so great, and therefore no condition so hurtful and outrageous, as the subjection of women to men in a civilization which like ours assumes to rest upon foundations of justice and equality of human rights. . . .

To-day these considerations (especially the failure fully to apply the doctrine of equality of human rights to women, even in the most advanced centers of modern civilization) have an especial and most fateful significance in relation to the women of the more backward races as they are brought into contact with our modern civilization. I said the peoples with whom we are now being brought as a nation into vital relationship may be still in the matriarchate. If they are not, most of them are certainly in some transition stage from that to the father-rule. Not all peoples have had to pass through the entire subjection of women to men which marked our ancestral advance. The more persistent tribal relationship and collective family life have sometimes softened the process of social growth which was so harsh for women under the old Roman law and the later English common law. It may be that the dusky races of Africa and of the islands of the sea, as well as our Aryan cousins of India, may pass more easily through the stages of attachment of man's responsibility to the family life than we, with our tough fiber of character, were able to do. If so, in the name of justice they should have the chance!

But if we, who have not yet "writ large" in law and political rights that respect for woman which all our education, industry, religion, art, home life and social culture express; if we, who are still inconsistent and not yet out of the transition stage from the father-rule to the equal reign of both sexes; if we lay violent hands upon these backward peoples and give them only our law and our political rights as they relate to women, we shall do horrible injustice to the savage women, and through them to the whole process of social growth for their people. When we tried to divide "in severalty" the lands of the American Indian, we did violence to all his own sense of justice and co-operative feeling when we failed to recognize the women of the tribes in the distribution. We then and there gave the Indian the worst of the white man's relationship to his wife, and failed utterly, as in the nature of the case we must have done, to give him the best of the white man's relation to his wife.

When in India, as Mrs. Garrett Fawcett has so finely shown, we introduce the technicalities of the English law of marriage to bind an unwilling wife to her husband, we give the Hindoo the slavery of the Anglo-Saxon wife, but we do not give him that spirit of Anglo-Saxon marriage and home-life which has made that slavery often scarcely felt, and never an unmixed evil. If, to-day, in the Hawaiian Islands or in Cuba we fail to recognize the native women, who still hold something of the primitive prestige of womanhood, fail to recognize them as entitled to a translation, under new laws and conditions, of the old dignity of position, we shall not only do them an injustice, but we shall forcibly give the Hawaiian and Cuban men lessons in the wrong side and not the right side of our domestic relations. Above all, if in the Philippines we abruptly and with force of arms establish the authority of the husband over the wife, by recognizing men only as property-owners, as signers of treaties, as industrial rulers and as domestic law-givers, we shall introduce every outrage and injustice of women's subjection to men, without giving these people one iota of the sense of family responsibility, of protection of and respect for woman, and of deep and self-sacrificing devotion to childhood's needs, which mark the Anglo-Saxon man.

In a word, if we introduce one particle of our belated and illogical political and legal subjection of women to men into any savage or half-civilized community, we shall spoil the domestic virtues that community already possesses, and we shall not (because we can not so abruptly and violently) inoculate them with the virtues of civilized domestic life. Nature will not be cheated. We can not escape, nor can we roughly and swiftly help others to escape, the discipline of ages of natural growth.

This all means that we need another Commission to go to all the lands in which our flag now claims a new power of oversight and control—a Commission other than that so recently sent to the Philippines—to see what may be done to bring order to that distracted group of islands. We need a Commission which shall study domestic rather than political conditions, and which shall look for the under-currents of social growth rather than the more showy political movements. We should have on that Commission two archaeologists, a man and a woman. . . .

[A discussion followed the Reverend Mrs. Spencer's paper. The participants whose remarks are excerpted below are Helen Philleo Jenkins, of Michigan, Octavia W. Bates, of Michigan, Henry B. Blackwell, of Massachusetts, and Susan B. Anthony, of New York.—*Ed.*]

Mrs. JENKINS: . . . Whatever power in government may be given to the men of our new possessions in selecting their rulers, let the same privilege be accorded the women. It may be said that the women are ignorant, and need yet to be held in subjection—that they are unfit to have a voice in the new order of things. Let us not be deceived. Probably the women are no more ignorant and stupid than the masses of men in these newly acquired regions—excepting always the few men whom circumstances have developed. The ignorant mother can guide her child quite as safely as its ignorant father. Men and women in all nations and tribes are pretty nearly on a level as to common sense and forethought for the future good of the family. Indeed, the interests of the home, protection of the children, and the morals and behavior of the community make the standard of even unlettered women one notch higher than that of their ignorant husbands. Let us of this nation hesitate before we establish a sex supremacy that it may take long centuries to overcome. . . .

Thousands of dollars are expended on a military commission; it is sent to investigate the commercial possibilities, the financial opportunities, in remote lands; but the army, the commerce, the finance are not all there is of a nation. There are more vital interests—there is something which lies at the very base of the nation, without which it could not exist—the homes, the women and the children. It is the social conditions that need special consideration in our country's dealings with these new lands.

Miss BATES: . . . In the presence of the events which have transpired during the past year, and in all the discussions pertaining to the new peoples who have suddenly become our protégés, seldom if ever does one hear a word about the women, who, all will admit, are a most important factor in the civilization—or the lack of it—which we have taken under our control.

We women are here at this time to do our best to awaken the public conscience to a realizing sense of the state of affairs. We are the result of what the religion, the education of the nineteenth century, and the liberty which it has granted to women have made us. We are ready and willing and competent to befriend our less favored sisters beyond the seas, and to extend to them the benefits we enjoy, so far as they are able to receive them; but—the tragedy of it—in a certain sense we are utterly helpless to reach them and to give them what they, unconsciously to themselves, so grievously need. There is no place for the thought of the women of this land in the plans of the nation for the study of these questions.

No matter how much our speaker may think and write and publish on this subject—aye, and women like her—no matter how wise the conclusions they reach, is it at all likely that their voices will be listened to in the din and blare and clash of warring political parties, or respected in legislative halls? Or is it probable that the advocates of territorial expansion will pause a moment to ponder on the woman side of that question? We, to-day, are discussing this subject without even the shadow of a hope of putting our convictions into practice. Is it any wonder that women at large are dead to the importance of this matter? . . .

I am in favor of pushing the question to the utmost—not that I have any hope that such a Commission will be appointed, but because it furnishes a most valuable argument for extending the suffrage to women: first, in order that, by its possession, they may have an uncontested, legally-defined right of serving on such commissions; and, second, because of the opportunity it offers for proving to the world the necessity of commissions like this for settling questions and conditions of which women form a central and integral part. Of course if we possessed the suffrage, we should have no necessity for a discussion like the present. Everything we are saying would seem like truisms then, instead of being contested point by point, as it is to-day. . . .

Mr. BLACKWELL: . . . In those islands are peoples ranging from absolute savagery to mediaeval civilization, from fighters with blow-guns and bows and arrows to fighters with Mauser rifles and modern artillery. Laws and institutions suited to the needs of one tribe are unsuited to those of another. Side by side are Catholicism, Mohammedanism and heathenism. Their amusements vary from cannibalism to cock-fighting. Their social status ranges from barbarous promiscuity to Moslem polygamy and thence to Hindoo monogamy. But everywhere exist masculine domination and feminine subjection, under varied forms of political despotism, tempered with Protestant liberalism in the case of Hawaii. To establish over all these diverse social conditions the rigid principles of the English common law, which prevail largely in our jurisprudence, will perpetuate and intensify the tyranny of husband over wife, of father over offspring.

We see the consequences already in the British West Indies, where negro women generally prefer to live outside of legal marriage because as wives they find themselves subjected to practical serfdom. In Jamaica 75 per cent. of the births are illegitimate for this reason. When I visited Haiti, I was told to my great surprise that the homes and small farms were usually owned by the women. Expressing my admiration of this chivalrous recognition of

women's right to the homestead, I was informed that there was
no such sentiment. It was solely because the men were so lazy and
unreliable that the perpetuity of the race was endangered. The
fathers of the children were here to-day and away to-morrow. They
spent their time in loafing, drinking, gambling and plotting "revolutions." The women, anchored by the love for their children,
lived in the little huts on their small plantations, raising yams and
bananas, and if the men became too drunken and abusive the
women ordered them to leave. Among those people, in a tropical
climate, with land to squat upon, most of the work is done by
the women. Let no one imagine that the so-called "matriarchate"
of early ages was an ideal condition of society. It was based primarily upon the industrial and moral irresponsibility of men.

In our new possessions, side by side with these primitive conditions, we have great bodies of Chinese and Hindoo coolies, who
represent ancient and fossilized types of civilized society, patient,
economical, industrious, monogamous and exclusive in their family
relations. The trouble is that where Western civilization interferes
with Oriental abuses it does not go far enough. When in India the
British government prohibited the custom of burning widows on
the funeral pyre of their deceased husbands, widows became the
slaves of their husband's relatives, and were actually believed to be
responsible for his death and were ill-treated accordingly. When
infanticide was forbidden and peace maintained, population multiplied until famine became chronic. The only salvation for the
women of our new possessions lies in a legal recognition of their
personal, industrial, social and political equality. If, as seems too
probable, their rights shall be simply ignored in the reconstruction,
women will suffer all the disabilities of the law, without the practical alleviations afforded by an enlightened public opinion. Such
women, even more than those of our own States, will need the
ballot as a means of self-protection. . . .

Miss Anthony: I have been overflowing with wrath ever since
the proposal was made to engraft our half-barbaric form of government on Hawaii and our other new possessions. I have been studying how to save, not them, but ourselves from the disgrace. This is
the first time the United States has ever tried to foist upon a new

people the exclusively masculine form of government. Our business should be to give this people the highest form which has been attained by us. When our State governments were originally formed, there was no example of woman suffrage anywhere, but now we have a great deal of it, and everywhere it has done good. The principle is constantly spreading. . . .

We are told it will be of no use for us to ask this measure of justice—that the ballot be given to the women of our new possessions upon the same terms as to the men—because we shall not get it. It is not our business whether we are going to get it; our business is to make the demand. Suppose during these fifty years we had asked only for what we thought we could secure, where should we be now? Ask for the whole loaf and take what you can get.

Florence Kelley, Three Addresses (1898, 1903, and 1905)

Around the turn of the century, suffragists paid increasing attention to the exploitation of women in factories. One of the principal propagandists in this field was Florence Kelley (1859–1932), daughter of a member of Congress. After graduation from Cornell she practiced law in Illinois and was an agent for the U.S. Department of Labor. She married a fellow socialist, Dr. Lazare Wischnewetzky, whom she later divorced, receiving custody of their three children. In 1893 Governor Altgeld appointed her the first woman Chief Inspector of Factories in Illinois. Later she moved to New York, to become secretary of the National Consumers' League. Between 1905 and 1909 Mrs. Kelley, as she was known, was a vice-president of the National American Woman Suffrage Association. The following excerpts are from three typical speeches, the first delivered at the 1898 convention of the Association, the second at the annual meeting of the Massachusetts Woman Suffrage Association in 1903, and the third at the 1905 convention of the NAWSA [*HWS* IV, 311–13; *Woman's Journal*, November 7, 1903, July 22, 1905.]

WORKING WOMAN'S NEED OF THE BALLOT

No one needs all the powers of the fullest citizenship more urgently than the wage-earning woman, and from two different
points of view—that of actual money wages and that of her wider
needs as a human being and a member of the community.

The wages paid any body of working people are determined by
many influences, chief among which is the position of the particular body of workers in question. Thus the printers, by their
intelligence, their powerful organization, their solidarity and united
action, keep up their wages in spite of the invasion of their domain
by new and improved machinery. On the other hand, the garment-
workers, the sweaters' victims, poor, unorganized, unintelligent,
despised, remain forever on the verge of pauperism, irrespective of
their endless toil. If, now, by some untoward fate the printers
should suddenly find themselves disfranchised, placed in a position
in which their members were politically inferior to the members
of other trades, no effort of their own short of complete enfranchisement could restore to them that prestige, that good standing in the esteem of their fellow-craftsmen and the public at large
which they now enjoy, and which contributes materially in support of their demand for high wages.

In the garment trades, on the other hand, the presence of a
body of the disfranchised, of the weak and young, undoubtedly
contributes to the economic weakness of these trades. Custom,
habit, tradition, the regard of the public, both employing and
employed, for the people who do certain kinds of labor, contribute
to determine the price of that labor, and no disfranchised class of
workers can permanently hold its own in competition with enfranchised rivals. But this works both ways. It is fatal for any
body of workers to have forever hanging from the fringes of its
skirts other bodies on a level just below its own; for that means
continual pressure downward, additional difficulty to be overcome
in the struggle to maintain reasonable rates of wages. Hence,
within the space of two generations there has been a complete
revolution in the attitude of the trades-unions toward the women
working in their trades. Whereas forty years ago women might
have knocked in vain at the doors of the most enlightened trade-

union, to-day the Federation of Labor keeps in the field paid organizers whose duty it is to enlist in the unions as many women as possible. The workingmen have perceived that women are in the field of industry to stay; and they see, too, that there can not be two standards of work and wages for any trade without constant menace to the higher standard. Hence their effort to place the women upon the same industrial level with themselves in order that all may pull together in the effort to maintain reasonable conditions of life.

But this same menace holds with regard to the vote. The lack of the ballot places the wage-earning woman upon a level of irresponsibility compared with her enfranchised fellow workingman. By impairing her standing in the community the general rating of her value as a human being, and consequently as a worker, is lowered. In order to be rated as good as a good man in the field of her earnings, she must show herself better than he. She must be more steady, or more trustworthy, or more skilled, or more cheap in order to have the same chance of employment. Thus, while women are accused of lowering wages, might they not justly reply that it is only by conceding something from the pay which they would gladly claim, that they can hold their own in the market, so long as they labor under the disadvantage of disfranchisement? . . .

Finally, the very fact that women now form about one-fifth of the employes in manufacture and commerce in this country has opened a vast field of industrial legislation directly affecting women as wage-earners. The courts in some of the States, notably in Illinois, are taking the position that women can not be treated as a class apart and legislated for by themselves, as has been done in the factory laws of England and on the continent of Europe, but must abide by that universal freedom of contract which characterizes labor in the United States. This renders the situation of the working woman absolutely anomalous. On the one hand, she is cut off from the protection awarded to her sisters abroad; on the other, she has no such power to defend her interests at the polls, as is the heritage of her brothers at home. This position is untenable, and there can be no pause in the agitation for full political power and responsibility until these are granted to all the women of the nation.

FLORENCE KELLEY ON WORKING GIRLS

I was asked to speak here to-day, perhaps, because I have been living for years among working people, and have been brought into close touch with the younger and more defenceless working women. I am sick of hearing of the establishment of model boarding-houses to give them a little better quarters at night, and improved lunch-rooms for their noon-day meal, and refuges and asylums for those who yield to the temptations and hardships of their life. Much better results would be got by giving to all women the right to make the lives of working girls more comfortable all along the line, and by giving these young women the right to a voice in their own affairs, which the more thoughtful of them are learning earnestly to desire. . . .

To the wives and daughters of working men, it is a great loss of self-respect, and of respect from the men of their families, that they are at a disadvantage politically. It is a bitter moment for many a working woman when her son casts his first vote. Then he respects her opinion even less than before. The working man's wife needs the vote for her protection even more than does the competing girl. She has no voice as to a strike or a boycott, and she is much less considered after she marries and leaves the Union than she was before.

These women as a rule will not originate, but they will fight well under leaders. There is a great source of strength, which could be utilized for the suffrage movement and other reforms, in the sober and temperate wives of drinking men; and there is an amount of suffrage sentiment among them which only those know who have been brought much in contact with the wives of working men.

THE YOUNG BREADWINNERS' NEED OF WOMEN'S ENFRANCHISEMENT

. . . To-night while we sleep, several thousand little girls will be working in textile mills, all the night through, in the deafening noise of the spindles and looms spinning and weaving cotton and woolen, silks and ribbons for us to buy. . . . If the mothers and the teachers in Georgia could vote, would the Georgia Legislature have refused at every session for the last three years to stop the work in the mills of children under twelve years of age?

Would the New Jersey Legislature have passed that shameful repeal bill enabling girls fourteen years to work all night, if the mothers in New Jersey were enfranchised? Until the mothers in the great industrial States are enfranchised, we shall none of us be able to free our consciences from participation in this great evil. No one in this room to-night can feel free from such participation. The children make our shoes in the shoe factories; they knit our stockings, our knitted underwear in the knitting factories. They spin and weave our cotton underwear in the cotton mills. Children braid straw for our hats, they spin and weave the silk and velvet wherewith we trim our hats. They stamp buckles and metal ornaments of all kinds, as well as pins and hat-pins. Under the sweating system, tiny children make artificial flowers and neckwear for us to buy. They carry bundles of garments from the factories to the tenements, little beasts of burden, robbed of school life that they may work for us.

We do not wish this. We prefer to have our work done by men and women. But we are almost powerless. Not wholly powerless, however, are citizens who enjoy the right of petition. For myself, I shall use this power in every possible way until the right to the ballot is granted, and then I shall continue to use both.

What can we do to free our consciences? There is one line of action by which we can do much. We can enlist the workingmen on behalf of our enfranchisement just in proportion as we strive with them to free the children. No labor organization in this country ever fails to respond to an appeal for help in the freeing of the children.

For the sake of the children, for the Republic in which these children will vote after we are dead, and for the sake of our cause, we should enlist the workingmen voters, with us, in this task of freeing the children from toil.

Jessie Ashley, Relation of Suffragism to Working-Class Women
(1911)

Jessie Ashley (?–1919), like Florence Kelley, was exceptional
among suffragist leaders in that she was a socialist. She was born
in New York City to a wealthy family, and received LL.B. and
LL.M. degrees from New York University in 1902 and 1903. She
practiced law in New York and taught the woman's law class in
NYU Law School while active in the Socialist Party and the
Women's Trade Union League. In 1911, while treasurer of the
National American Woman Suffrage Association, she wrote a series of "National Headquarters Letters" in the *Woman's Journal*.
The two reproduced here, from the April 22 and June 24 issues,
evoked protests from more conservative members of the
organization.

Recently a large suffrage organization in New York passed resolutions endorsing trade unionism and expressing sympathy with
the efforts of the working class to improve their condition.

This step would seem to be a recognition of the fact that the
woman suffrage movement has heretofore been a middle class
movement, and, further, that to succeed the movement must be
extended to include the working class. It would seem to be a direct
proffer of co-operation, a wise tit-for-tat sort of policy, made necessary by the persistent indifference of the working class toward
equal suffrage. This is a fact that must be faced. In this country
suffragists have failed to reach the working people. They have
succeeded in getting resolutions passed endorsing woman suffrage
by many large labor organizations; they have succeeded in getting
leading men closely in touch with labor to make ringing suffrage
speeches. But the laboring class as a class remains not only indifferent but suspicious.

An incident during the impressive march of the workers after
the Triangle fire pointed out this attitude. A girl from among the

marching crowd ran out to join the writer, calling her by name. After marching for a few moments she spoke of the protest meeting held by the College [Equal Suffrage] League a few nights before, and said expressively: "I thought you suffragists weren't any good, but if you are that sort, I'll change my mind." She voiced the feeling of the majority of working girls; and yet some suffragists had tried to persuade the College League not to hold the protest meeting because it would "hurt suffrage by mixing it up with outside interests."

We are thus confronted by two points of view. One, that suffrage is a clear-cut issue, and must be kept quite apart from all other questions; it consists of a single demand: "Give to women the right to vote." Let there be as many arguments for this as you please, but let there be no arguments for anything else until the ballot is in the hands of women—then they may do what they will. This is the time-honored, theoretical point of view. It was at first academic, it is now practical and political, but it remains in essence the same.

The other point of view is of more recent growth, and has been forced upon suffragists by the complete failure of middle-class arguments and middle-class activities to rouse the working class to any enthusiasm for the suffrage struggle. It would seem that there must be something wrong in a method that fails to enlist the sympathy of the very women who need the ballot most. Therefore suffragists have begun to recognize not only that the working class man will eventually decide the question of giving the ballot to women, but that to him the question is squarely: "Will woman suffrage help the working class?"

What, then, these suffragists ask, are we doing to reach the working woman? Is it true that in the main suffragists fail to feel the red blood of humanity pulsing through them? Is it not true that they have an ever-present consciousness of what the middle-class "average person" will think about this question or that? Is not "expediency" the guiding star of suffrage conduct, and is not the dread of "mixing suffrage up" with outside issues merely a narrow view of what the suffrage movement really stands for? A failure to realize that the extension of the right of suffrage follows in the wake of the extension of industry, an extension of democracy, but forced by economic conditions?

What are the arguments that the working girl hears when she stops to listen to an impassioned soap-box orator from the suffrage ranks? "Taxation without representation is tyranny." She shrugs —she doesn't know she pays taxes. "The right to vote is the natural, inherent, inalienable right of every adult human being." She turns away. She knows that as a matter of fact she has no right to vote, and she doesn't care. But before she is out of ear-shot comes the plea, "Women must have the ballot in order to protect their homes, to protect their children." She hurries on her way. She has no home nor any children, and she knows she could not do much to protect either on wages of three dollars a week. So the disappointed orator wonders what is wrong.

In reality, suffragists come to the working class as outsiders. They do not show any knowledge whatsoever of working class interests. And, aside from futile argument, what do they do? Do they ever come forward with vigorous backing of purely working class legislation? Has there been a single protest from suffragists anywhere against the Mexican situation? Have suffragists ever shown themselves ready to support legislation that would help the workers, but would at the same time wipe out their own dividends? Have they taken pains to point out to working women the trend of our court decisions? Has there been any organized effort whatsoever to ascertain the working class point of view and meet it?

Suffragists can reach moneyed interests by middle-class arguments; they can reach professional interests by middle-class arguments; they can even, to a certain extent, reach labor leaders. But the working class as a class will stand aside until they are taught from within and in terms that appeal to them why they should demand the ballot for women. There are already many busy teaching them this, but they are not sent by suffragist organizations.

Many readers of The Woman's Journal may dissent from the line of argument attempted in this letter, but probably all will agree that The Woman's Journal is today the greatest single purely suffragist influence in the suffragist movement in our country, and that it is bound to extend its influence until the vote is won. It therefore behooves The Journal to express clearly the great world-wide sweep of the movement for the freedom of women. It stands committed to full adult suffrage, and if our national policy can be as broad and farseeing and as fearlessly uncompromising toward the interests of working women, it will have rendered a service to our country as a whole that cannot be overestimated.

[Miss Ashley opens the second article with a quotation from a newspaper concerning a recent suffragist parade; the paper contrasted the marching ladies to those women seen daily on a subway train at six o'clock on their way home from work.—*Ed.*]

. . . Is this not strangely illuminating? The baldness of the contrast between those subway girls and the handsome parading ladies is like a lightning flash clearing for a moment the whole dim subject. For it is those "handsome ladies," and they alone, who have begun to see that women must stand and think and work together, and they, alas, are not the ones whose need to do so is the greatest.

For the most part the handsome ladies are well satisfied with their personal lot, but they want the vote as a matter of justice, while the fluttering, jammed-in subway girls are terribly blind to the whole question of class oppression and of sex oppression. Only the women of the working class are really oppressed, but it is not only the working class woman to whom injustice is done. Women of the leisure class need freedom, too. All women, of whatever class, must become conscious of their position in the world; all must be made to stand erect and become self-reliant, free human beings. . . .

Is there a common camp from which we can all march to demand the ballot? We who believe in the power and the destiny of the working class know that no possible common ground exists when the exercise of the ballot is an issue; the working man, jammed like the girls into the subway trains, should not vote as does the owner of the subway train, nor should the fluttering girls vote as would the handsome ladies. Upon this point there can be no room for doubt.

But is it impossible for all women to work together to uproot an injustice common to all? Is there no way to bring this about? Surely there should be. We must be rid of mere ladylikeness, we must succeed in making the oppressed class of women the most urgent in the demand for what we all must have. When we have brought this about, we women shall be irresistibly strong. But, while we lack enthusiasm and the consecration that can be derived only from the knowledge of great wrongs, we shall continue to show a certain amount of weakness; and great wrongs are not suffered by the handsome ladies as a class, but they are suffered by the working class as a whole. If the working girls ever become really alive to their situation, they will throw themselves into the fight for the ballot in overwhelming numbers, and on that day the suffrage movement will be swept forward by the forces that command progress.

Jane Addams, On Woman Suffrage (1915 and 1906)

Jane Addams (1860–1935), one of the most eminent women in American history, is not ordinarily thought of as a suffragist; yet she was first vice-president of the National American Woman Suffrage Association between 1911 and 1913. But Hull-House, which she founded in 1889, was the center of her life. The following are two of her statements in favor of suffrage. ["Why Women Should Vote," in Frances M. Björkman and Annie G. Porritt, eds., *Woman Suffrage: History, Arguments and Results* (New York, 1915), pp. 131–33; and "Jane Addams Declares Ballot for Women Made Necessary by Changed Conditions," Chicago Sunday *Record-Herald*, April 1, 1906 (clipping in Jane Addams Papers, Friends Historical Library, Swarthmore College).]

. . . [M]any women to-day are failing to discharge their duties

to their own households properly simply because they do not per-
ceive that as society grows more complicated it is necessary that
woman shall extend her sense of responsibility to many things
outside of her own home if she would continue to preserve the
home in its entirety. One could illustrate in many ways. A
woman's simplest duty, one would say, is to keep her house clean
and wholesome and to feed her children properly. Yet if she lives
in a tenement house, as so many of my neighbors do, she cannot
fulfill these simple obligations by her own efforts because she is
utterly dependent upon the city administration for the conditions
which render decent living possible. Her basement will not be
dry, her stairways will not be fireproof, her house will not be provided with sufficient windows to give light and air, nor will it be
equipped with sanitary plumbing, unless the Public Works Department sends inspectors who constantly insist that these elementary decencies be provided. Women who live in the country
sweep their own dooryards and may either feed the refuse of the
table to a flock of chickens or allow it innocently to decay in the
open air and sunshine. In a crowded city quarter, however, if the
street is not cleaned by the city authorities no amount of private
sweeping will keep the tenement free from grime; if the garbage
is not properly collected and destroyed a tenement house mother
may see her children sicken and die of diseases from which she
alone is powerless to shield them, although her tenderness and
devotion are unbounded. She cannot even secure untainted meat
for her household, she cannot provide fresh fruit, unless the meat
has been inspected by city officials, and the decayed fruit, which
is so often placed upon sale in the tenement districts, has been
destroyed in the interests of public health. In short, if woman
would keep on with her old business of caring for her house and
rearing her children she will have to have some conscience in regard to public affairs lying quite outside of her immediate household. The individual conscience and devotion are no longer
effective.

Chicago one spring had a spreading contagion of scarlet fever
just at the time that the school nurses had been discontinued because business men had pronounced them too expensive. If the

women who sent their children to the schools had been sufficiently public-spirited and had been provided with an implement through which to express that public spirit they would have insisted that the schools be supplied with nurses in order that their own children might be protected from contagion. In other words, if women would effectively continue their old avocations they must take part in the slow upbuilding of that code of legislation which is alone sufficient to protect the home from the dangers incident to modern life. . . .

. . . Insanitary housing, poisonous sewage, contaminated water, infant mortality, the spread of contagion, adulterated food, impure milk, smoke-laden air, ill-ventilated factories, dangerous occupations, juvenile crime, unwholesome crowding, prostitution and drunkenness are the enemies which the modern cities must face and overcome would they survive. Logically, its electorate should be made up of those who can bear a valiant part in this arduous contest, those who in the past have at least attempted to care for children, to clean houses, to prepare foods, to isolate the family from moral dangers, those who have traditionally taken care of that side of life which inevitably becomes the subject of municipal consideration and control as soon as the population is congested. To test the elector's fitness to deal with this situation by his ability to bear arms is absurd. These problems must be solved, if they are solved at all, not from the military point of view, not even from the industrial point of view, but from a third which is rapidly developing in all the great cities of the world—the human welfare point of view. . . . The statement is sometimes made that the franchise for women would be valuable only so far as the educated women exercised it. This statement totally disregards the fact that those matters in which woman's judgment is most needed are far too primitive and basic to be largely influenced by what we call education. . . .

Six Predictions of the Results of Women's Enfranchisement
(1852, 1891, 1898, 1903, and 1914)

Sometimes suffragists made rather large predictions about what women would do with their new power once they had the vote. Here are six such prophecies. The first is a song, "A Hundred Years Hence," written by Frances Dana Gage in 1852. Mrs. Gage (1808–84), born in Ohio of New England stock, was the mother of eight children. She traveled through many states from 1849 to 1855 lecturing on women's rights. In 1853 the family moved to St. Louis, where they were ostracized for their abolitionist sympathies. The song was sung by the Hutchinson Family Singers at a woman-suffrage convention in 1876. It is printed in *HWS* III, 38n–39n. The second item is an unsigned "Editorial Note" from the *Woman's Journal*, August 1, 1891. The third is from Henry B. Blackwell, "The War with Spain," *ibid.*, April 16, 1898. The fourth is from Alice Stone Blackwell, "The Lady or the Tiger?" *ibid.*, November 14, 1903. The fifth is from Alice Stone Blackwell, "War in Europe," *ibid.*, August 8, 1914. The sixth is a statement by Carrie Chapman Catt as reported in the *New York Times*, August 6, 1914.

> *One hundred years hence, what a change will be made,*
> *In politics, morals, religion and trade,*
> *In statesmen who wrangle or ride on the fence,*
> *These things will be altered* a hundred years hence.
>
> *Our laws then will be uncompulsory rules,*
> *Our prisons converted to national schools,*
> *The pleasure of sinning 'tis all a pretense,*
> *And the people will find it so,* a hundred years hence.
>
> *Lying, cheating and fraud will be laid on the shelf,*
> *Men will neither get drunk nor be bound up in self,*
> *But all live together, good neighbors and friends,*
> *Just as* Christian folks *ought to,* a hundred years hence.

Then woman, man's partner, man's equal shall stand
While beauty and harmony govern the land,
To think for oneself will be no offense,
The world will be thinking a hundred years hence.

Oppression and war will be heard of no more,
Nor the blood of a slave leave his print on our shore,
Conventions will then be a useless expense,
For we'll all go free-suffrage a hundred years hence.

Instead of speech-making to satisfy wrong,
All will join the glad chorus to sing Freedom's song;
And if the Millen[n]ium is not a pretense,
We'll all be good brothers a hundred years hence.

During the past week several Boston newspapers have given great prominence to the details of a brutal prize fight, accompanying these with appreciative editorial comments. The streets were vocal with the shrill cries of the newsboys,—"All about the prize fight!" If women were voters and had a voice in legislation, this brutal business would be promptly suppressed.

. . . *The Woman's Journal* has hitherto refrained from discussing the question of forcible intervention to terminate the horrors of civil war and enforced wholesale starvation of innocent noncombatants in Cuba. It has refrained, because women, as yet, are not recognized as having any responsibility in the matter, and because there is no way of making their opinions respected. It has repeatedly, but briefly, called attention to the monstrous injustice of deciding the question of war or peace without consulting the women, who constitute one-half of the citizens of the nation, and who are equally interested with the men.

For himself, the present writer believes that if women were voters there would have been no war; that even now war would be averted, and Cuba freed without further bloodshed. . . .

. . . If women had had the ballot, Tammany would not have returned to power in New York. . . .

The sudden outbreak of war in Europe has filled thoughtful men and women all over the world with horror. With no sufficient cause, in a quarrel which does not really concern them, thousands of men will be led to butcher other thousands against whom they have no grievance, whose faces they have never seen until they are brought together to kill each other. . . .

Duels between individuals are now recognized as a relic of barbarism. These gigantic duels between nations are equally foolish and a hundred-fold more barbarous. Let us do our utmost to hasten the day when the wishes of the mothers shall have their due weight in public affairs, knowing that by so doing we hasten the day when wars shall be no more.

. . . [Carrie Chapman] Catt said she felt that if the women had had the vote in all the countries now at war the conflict would have been prevented.

"Women would have been conservative," she said yesterday. "They have sense, and they know that it may not be possible for one nation to keep the peace while the others are armed and at war, but internationally, they might do it. War falls on the women most heavily, and more so now than ever before. This war should be a good argument for suffrage. It shows that men, as I have always believed, are as hysterical as women, only they show it in a different way. Women weep and men fight."

IV

UNFINISHED
BUSINESS

WITH THE ENACTMENT of the Nineteenth Amendment in 1920, the single issue on which most feminists could agree disappeared. Since then there has been no significant feminist movement as such. There have been separate organizations to promote the interests of women as scholars, women as mothers, women as unionists, and so on, and a small and ineffective National Woman's Party. But the activities of these organizations have rarely been reported even in the women's pages of the newspapers. In this post–1920 period the documents most appropriately labeled feminist have been largely the work of individuals expressing their own views rather than writing in behalf of a movement, and the question they most often deal with is once again: What is woman's "sphere"?

Other factors besides the enactment of the suffrage amendment contributed to the ebb of feminism: in the 1920's the acceptability of increased social freedom for girls; in the 1930's the economic crisis of such overwhelming urgency as to discredit, for many people, any "special" group's demand for more rights; during World War II the entrance of women into occupations formerly the exclusive preserve of men; the postwar "back-to-the-home" movement among young women; and, throughout this nearly fifty-year period, psychologists' sanction of the old distinction between the "spheres." All these factors dampened any potential feminism as either unnecessary or unnatural.

A surprising feature of recent writings on the relation of public policy to woman's status is the relative superficiality of proposals in the President's Report *and other such documents. That is not to say that the elimination of remaining discriminations in state and federal law is not desirable. Rather, such discriminations barely touch the lives of most women; few are even aware they exist. Far more important is the substantial remaining inequality in private hiring and promotion and even more in thought and custom. The sources of the inequality have turned out to be less tangible—and less curable by legislation—than most feminists thought.*

It is this intangibility that makes for diffuseness and contradiction in recent writing on the subject. As long as disfranchisement could be blamed, feminists could write pointed and persuasive arguments for the vote. But what is the ultimate cause of the undiminished popularity of wife and mother-in-law jokes by stand-up comedians, or the preference of many college men for girls who are not their intellectual equals? One article in the following section defines the problem in terms of the unending and mind-emptying housework that occupies most women's lives; whereas Betty Friedan's Feminine Mystique *deplores the cult of domesticity willingly embraced by young women. The woman's-rights movement is one among many to demonstrate that articulating a grievance is far simpler than prescribing its cure—which is why a section entitled "Unfinished Business" can include a document written eighty years ago.*

I

PUBLIC POLICY

The Equal-Rights Amendment: Senate Hearing (1931)

The following document is an excerpt from remarks by witnesses before a Senate committee hearing on the proposed Equal-Rights Amendment, which read: "Men and women shall have equal rights throughout the United States and every place subject to its jurisdiction. Congress shall have power to enforce this article by appropriate legislation." This amendment, in various forms, was introduced repeatedly in Congress; its strongest supporter was the National Woman's Party and its strongest opponents spokesmen for women workers. [*Equal Rights*. Hearing before a Subcommittee of the Committee on the Judiciary, United States Senate, 71st Congress, 3d session, on S.J. Res. 52, a Joint Resolution Proposing an Amendment to the Constitution of the United States Relative to Equal Rights for Men and Women. January 6, 1931 (Washington, 1931), pp. 5, 7–8, 10–13, 16, 32–34, 36–37, 45, 66–67.]

[Statement of Burnita Shelton Matthews, chairman, lawyers' council of the National Woman's Party:]

There are many discriminations in the laws against women. The discriminations show the need for the proposed equal rights amendment.

The woman, even in the home—that place so often designated as her "appropriate sphere"—does not share equally in the husband's authority. The father is the sole natural guardian of minor children in Alabama and Georgia. Michigan, New York, and Massachusetts are among the States where the father alone is usually entitled to the services and earnings of a minor child. In Iowa and Montana the right to recover damages for loss of a child's services and earnings in case of injury to the child belongs primarily to the father.

The Louisiana Code provides that a child owes both parents obedience, "honor and respect," but in case of difference between the parents, "the authority of the father prevails.". . . In Arkansas and West Virginia, when a person dies, leaving a father and mother but no will and no descendants, the property of the decedent goes to the father to the exclusion of the mother. . . . [Many more examples given.]

The double standard of morals is recognized in practically all States. In Maryland a man may divorce his wife for being unchaste before marriage, but a divorce is not available to a woman on that ground. In Minnesota a husband whose wife is guilty of infidelity may collect damages from her paramour. On the other hand, no wife whose husband is guilty of infidelity may claim compensation from his paramour.

Under the laws of Tennessee a woman divorced for adultery and living with the adulterer is rendered incapable of disposing of any of her lands, but no such incapacity is imposed upon a man guilty of similar conduct. . . . [Many more examples given.]

Despite the adoption of the woman suffrage amendment to the National Constitution, the political rights of women are not equal to those of men.

Women are sometimes excluded from high public offices. . . . [Gives examples.]

Night work is open to men but closed to women in certain employments in 16 States. . . . Women workers are displaced by men as a result of minimum wage laws setting a standard below which their wages may not fall, but not regulating men's wages. . . .

Another method by which the industrial opportunities of women have been restricted is the limiting of the occupation[s] which women may enter. For instance, a law passed in Ohio in 1919 and still in force bars women from sixteen or more occupations.

The Woman's Party believes that labor legislation should be based on the occupation, not the sex of the worker. In that way women will not be placed at a disadvantage in competing with men for employment. . . .

Throughout the country, at the present time, efforts are being made to solve the unemployment situation by throwing women out of work. The wool manufacturers, due to the pressure of the organized employees in the wool industry, consisting mostly of men, have ruled that women be excluded from night work in the wool manufacturing establishments, beginning with the first of March, 1931.

The Textile Institute has urged that women be excluded from night work in the textile establishments, and so after the first of March women are barred from night work, and that includes not only married women but single women as well who are dependent upon their jobs for their bread and butter.

As women go more and more into new occupations, competition becomes more keen, and efforts are made to have women come under further special restrictions in order that they may be rendered ineffective as competitors.

In the State of California, a few years ago, a bill was introduced providing that the 8-hour law in that State be extended to women physicians, women in real-estate offices, women in banks, women insurance agents; in fact, women in almost every activity under the sun in California. This was backed by the labor groups but was opposed by the women themselves who fortunately secured its defeat. . . .

[Statement of Anita Pollitzer, Vice Chairman, National Woman's Party:]

Mr. Chairman, our point is that in no respect should the rights of women be left to the whims of individuals, legislatures or organizations, but, just as men are citizens of this land, knowing that all their rights, privileges, and duties are guaranteed them by law, so we feel that they should be established for women.

To those of us who, ever since we have been adults, have

worked for suffrage, equal rights seems a very logical sequence [sequel?—*Ed.*] to the suffrage amendment. It seems so right that we really resent having to come to ask for our rights. We are not asking for any special rights. We are not asking for anything but the same opportunity to be human beings in this land of ours. Now, we have injected nothing into this equal rights movement that apparently has not been there from time immemorial. The leaders of men from the very earliest days have spoken in terms of equality.

. . . It has taken more than 10 years in New York State to try to get the first dent made in jury service. It will take ten times six years and more to get these infinitesimal laws removed from the statute books of the State. It is not only these laws that confront us. There will be crises affecting the lives of women always, as long as we allow our laws and our customs, and in the minds of men and women, this accepted and expected rule that there will be a difference in their treatment. . . .

[Statement of Rose Schneiderman, President, National Women's Trade Union League, New York:]

For the purpose of this hearing, I represent the 12 national organizations opposed to the equal rights amendment.

We are not against equality when we say we oppose the amendment, because most of the 12 organizations are working very diligently to bring about equality among men and women, the widest kind of equality, but we are opposed to this measure because we feel that it is an unwise measure, and that it would create a great deal of trouble everywhere; we would have a great deal of litigation as to what was equality in particular instances and so on, and we feel that equality can better be brought about by removing specific restrictions through specific laws. . . .

Our experience has shown us, especially in the industrial field, that this amendment would work havoc.

The National Women's Trade Union League, which I have the honor to represent, has for 27 years worked in the industrial field trying to organize, to educate, to bring about leadership among women, and we feel that the laws that have been built up through those 27 years would be wiped off the statute books with the enactment of this amendment. . . .

We hear a lot about girls and women having the right to work when and at what they will, and so on and so forth. As a matter of fact, we know that industry is so organized to-day that it is impossible for any woman to stand up and say, "I will work now. I prefer to work from midnight to 6 or 8 o'clock in the morning rather than work from 8 in the morning to 5 o'clock in the afternoon." We know that industry is become more and more mechanized; that employers are realizing the cost of overhead; that work must be done in specified hours, at specified times; and no factory, no employer, will run his power because I decide that I want to stay home during the day and therefore I will work during the night. We know also that with the mechanization of industry work has become less skilled. We know also that mechanization has brought about more speed.

We are absolutely committed to trade-unionism as the only way real equality can ever be attained, but nevertheless we know that the great majority of women in industry are outside of the trade-union movement. . . . The great bulk of our girls, the great bulk of women in industry, are between the ages of 16 and 25. Women still look upon marriage and home and children as their career. They have not found a career in industry because there is none. You can not find a career in sewing on buttons or in testing bulbs or in canning peaches or anything of that kind. There is no career in that; and, whether rightly or wrongly, girls still look upon marriage as their right and their vocation. Because of this the plea for organization is not always responded to at the time and in the way that we would like to see it.

That is why we need laws in the States. The previous speakers here seem to feel that the best thing to bring about is competition between men and women. One of the speakers has said, "We are not concerned with men. We are concerned with our own class." Well, when that question comes to the working people, our answer is that we are concerned about both men and women, because we can not separate ourselves from our men folks. They are the men we are to marry. They are our fathers, brothers, and sweethearts, and we can not say that we prefer unlimited competition in the family, so to speak, because we know what competition does to workers. We are interested in eliminating competition because only then will the men and women in the working class be able to attain any kind of equality, and we say that protective labor laws go toward that step of bringing the women's standard up a little toward the standards of men.

For instance, the dressmakers of New York City have a 40-hour week. They enjoy the blessings of organization, but if we had no labor laws in the State of New York, a manufacturer could move up to Mount Vernon or Poughkeepsie and work women there 60 or 72 hours a week. The men in New York City who make dresses would very quickly come to the organized women there and say, "Now, see here, so and so is working 60 hours a week. I can't give you a 40-hour week. I am sorry." Then a great strike would take place and lots of employers would move out to Poughkeepsie and work the longer hours, and we would have quite a time bringing about better conditions. But in New York State the difference between the union standard of a 40-hour week and the legal standard of a 48-hour week for women is not as great as it would be if unlimited hours were permitted for employers to work, and the result is that the State law makes it easier to enforce the union standard.

Now, there is a great deal of talk of home responsibilities and the need for women to be able to work any hours and under any conditions to meet those responsibilities. There is no doubt that women have home responsibilities. . . . However, we must not forget that men have responsibilities, too. I do not feel that we can enter into a war between men and women, especially where working men and women are concerned. . . . What we want to do is bring women up to men's level rather than remove all safeguards that would tear that level down. . . .

The ladies who are here advocating this amendment, I am afraid, have the grandiose idea of bringing about through the stroke of a pen this marvelous thing called equality. We know that equality is not brought about that way. Equality has to happen first within yourself. You have to regard yourself as a human being, and that can not be done by passing a law. That has to be a process of education and a process of growth, and it can only happen through the programs that these 12 organizations represented here to-day are pursuing. It can not be done quickly. . . .

[Statement of Frieda Miller, Director of the Bureau of Women and Children, New York State Department of Labor:]

. . . [I]t seems to me that the women's party proposal is an outmoded method of procedure. It is the laissez faire idea that our economists stressed and worked on a hundred and odd years ago. On the other hand, this group of organizations, which is working for specific measures of improvement, is very much more in the current of modern industrial and economic thought which recognizes that planning and controlled conditions in industry are necessary for this tremendously complex organization under which all of us must live our lives to-day. . . .

. . . We feel that the workers' part in the job must be planned, controlled, and organized. The legislation which we have backed and which we expect to continue to support is part of such a planned industry, in which the women who work shall not be driven beyond limits which are good for them and good for the system of which they form a part. In other words, we regard this work as standard setting, as making rules out of our experience which industry shall have to follow in order to maintain the usefulness and health and social well-being of these participants. . . .

Let me just give you specifically the type of thing that our laws require, the special rules governing the employment of women. There is a provision in the labor law requiring seats for women wherever it is possible for them to be used in their employment. Separate washrooms and toilets are required for women. That is a differential law which I suppose the equal rights amendment would do away with. Dressing and emergency rooms are required for women. . . .

The minimum age for employment in certain dangerous occupations is set by law. Prohibition of work for a specified period after childbirth is established by law. In these separate rules we have set standards for women apart from men. There are, of course, many of the great basic standards of industry which apply equally to both; that is, standards of fire protection, standards of lighting and cleanliness, and guarding of machinery which are set for everybody to whom they apply. No one questions those general standards, and we believe that the special standards for women are usually aimed toward bringing up the conditions of women to those already enjoyed by men in industry. We do recognize that occasionally in setting those standards individuals have lost a job which they had previously had, but we have never been able to find such an extensive holocaust as has been pictured here this morning. . . .

[Statement of Mrs. William J. Carson, Philadelphia Chairman of the Committee on the Legal Status of Women of the National League of Women Voters:]

In conclusion the legislative committee including the 12 organizations is opposed to the so-called equal-rights amendment for the following reasons, in addition to those involving special legislation for women in industry:

(1) That it is unnecessary since undesirable discriminations not only can be removed without a Federal amendment but are being continually so removed.

(2) That it is undesirable to interfere with the State-right principle of our Federal form of government by giving Congress power to legislate in a field that in some respects is still in a laboratory, experimental stage in many of the States.

(3) That it is undesirable to make every case involving a differentiation between men and women a Federal question that can ultimately be settled only by the Supreme Court.

(4) That no definition of "equal rights" is contained in the amendment and that this would result in confusion and uncertainty as between State jurisdiction and within the confines of individual States; that this confusion would involve lengthy litigation and much unnecessary hardship.

(5) That we need freedom from such rigid interference as would in all probability result from such an amendment to work out slowly and soundly the best solution of a good many problems

affecting the relationships of men and women. The League of Women Voters believes in the enactment of measures which, in view of the actual biological, social, and occupational differences between men and women, tend to secure for women a true equality. We are not seeking a mathematical equality to be always measured and balanced, making sure that neither men nor women have one thing more or less than the other. This rigid, mathematical sort of equality we believe to be implicit in this amendment which we are opposing. The end we are seeking by careful study of each differentiation and by definite legislation drafted on the basis of such study—the end we are seeking is not equality in the sense of identity but justice and human happiness and opportunities for the most useful development of citizens of the country regardless of sex—an end to which equality is only a means. . . .

[Further statement of Burnita Shelton Matthews:]
. . . [I]t is not the effort of the Woman's Party at all to wipe out protective legislation but to try to see that the legislation is extended to both and that no handicap is placed on women.

One speaker has said that women can not stand up and say when they will work. Of course they can't. The laws in many States determine that for them but not for men. She speaks also of the prevention of work before and after childbirth. Well, no woman is going to work just before and after childbirth unless she has to. What is the use of saying she can't work when no provision is made for taking care of her during this period in case she is in need?

The attorney from Philadelphia stated that there are no discriminations against women in State constitutions except those with regard to jury service and public office. There are also discriminations pertaining to homesteads and other property rights, as for example, in Georgia and South Carolina. I don't see why we should be so extremely afraid of the word "equality." We have it in a great many State constitutions. Moreover, we have "equal" protection guaranteed in the fourteenth amendment to the Federal Constitution.

American Women: Report of the President's Commission (1965)

The *President's Report*, as the volume is usually called, has two main sections: the report of the President's commission on women's status, and the commission's report on its committees' reports. The following excerpt is from the second of those sections, and from the chapter headed "Civil and Political Rights." [Margaret Mead and Frances Balgley Kaplan, eds., *American Women: The Report of the President's Commission on the Status of Women and Other Publications of the Commission* (New York, 1965), pp. 147–57. The footnotes, marked in the original by asterisks, daggers, and other such signs, have been numbered.]

Although women in the United States are more equitably treated now than they have ever been, discriminations against them based on sex still remain in both law and practice. Reports of the Commission and its Committees document a wide variety of examples of inequitable treatment. Indeed, there would hardly have been need for a Commission on the Status of Women had the belief prevailed that women's rights were fully recognized. Those concerned with the status of women have long held that it would be easier to identify and eradicate many kinds of discrimination if broad recognition of the principle of women's equality were embodied in the law. While this objective is widely accepted, disagreement has existed on the best means to attain it, with the greatest controversy centering around the pros and cons of an equal-rights amendment to the United States Constitution.

CONSTITUTIONAL RECOGNITION OF THE EQUALITY OF WOMEN

THE EQUAL-RIGHTS AMENDMENT. The proposed equal-rights amendment to the United States Constitution provides in part: "Equality of rights under the law shall not be denied or abridged by the United States or by any State on account of sex."

This or a similar proposal has been introduced in each Congress since 1923 and has repeatedly been reported on favorably by the Senate Judiciary Committee. The Senate approved the proposed amendment in 1950 and in 1953, but added the "Hayden rider" to it on the floor. The rider provides that the amendment "shall not be construed to impair any rights, benefits, or exemptions now or hereafter conferred by law upon persons of the female sex." Supporters of the equal-rights amendment generally oppose the "Hayden rider" because they believe that it is under the guise of special "rights," "benefits," and exemptions that women have been denied opportunities that are available to men and that such exceptions contradict or nullify the principle of legal equality. Most supporters of the amendment think its passage is necessary because they believe that the Fifth and Fourteenth Amendments, as interpreted by the courts, do not afford women protection against discriminatory legal treatment.[1] Those who oppose the amendment are fearful that it would threaten protective benefits that women have acquired over the years. They further believe that such a broad constitutional declaration is not a satisfactory way of dealing with a host of complex and varied provisions ranging from laws governing family relations to those relating to women in industry.

The equal-rights amendment apparently is not intended to require identical legal treatment of the sexes. The Report of the Senate Judiciary Committee in 1962 [2] indicated that the amendment probably would render unconstitutional laws restricting the legal capacity of married women, those dealing with jury service that treat women differently than men, and restrictive work laws applying only to women. The Senate Report stated further that the amendment would not affect laws granting maternity benefits or criminal laws governing sexual offenses, nor would it require equal treatment of men and women for purposes of military service any more than all men are treated equal for purposes of

---

[1] "A Brief in Favor of an Equal Rights Amendment," prepared for the Committee on Civil and Political Rights by Judge Libby Sacher and Joyce Capps, on behalf of the National Federation of Business and Professional Women's Clubs (1963), is available for study in the offices of the Women's Bureau.

[2] Senate Report 2192, 87th Congress, 2nd Session.

military duty, but women apparently would be equally subject to military conscription. With respect to alimony and support, the Report indicated that under the amendment alimony laws probably could not favor women solely because of their sex, but a divorce decree could award support to a mother if she was granted custody of the children.

It would, of course, ultimately be a matter for the courts to determine when equality of rights under the laws has been denied or abridged on account of sex, just as it is for the courts now to determine when due process of the law or equal protection under the laws is denied women under the Fifth or Fourteenth Amendments.

Litigation under the Fourteenth Amendment. The Commission and the Committee studied these arguments, and others,[3] and concluded that the Fifth and Fourteenth Amendments *do* embody the principle of equality for women, but that clarification by judicial interpretation is urgently needed.

The opinion of members of the Committee and the Commission were strongly influenced by a document prepared at the request of the Committee by one of its members, Miss Pauli Murray.[4]

Miss Murray's comprehensive legal memorandum analyzed court opinions and separate opinions expressing concurrence and dissent, in cases involving sex distinctions based on the Fourteenth Amendment. She noted that great changes have occurred in women's activities and interests and in society's attitude toward them since these decisions were handed down. She concluded that

[3] In addition to the brief prepared by the National Federation of Business and Professional Women's Clubs already noted, the Committee received the varying views of other organizations on this question. Opinions were presented by the American Association of University Women, American Civil Liberties Union, American Federation of Labor and Congress of Industrial Organizations, American Medical Women's Association, American Nurses' Association, League of Women Voters of the United States, National Association of Women Lawyers, National Council of Catholic Women, National Council of Jewish Women, and National Woman's Party.

[4] "A Proposal to Reexamine the Applicability of the Fourteenth Amendment to State Laws and Practices Which Discriminate on the Basis of Sex Per Se," (1962) by Pauli Murray, Senior Fellow, Law School, Yale University, is available for study in the offices of the Women's Bureau.

the Supreme Court, if presented with an appropriate test case, would today interpret the Fourteenth Amendment as prohibiting unreasonable discrimination based on sex.

In the past, the courts have consistently upheld laws providing different treatment for women than for men, usually on the basis of the state's special interest in protecting the health and welfare of women. In its opinions on cases alleging discrimination on account of sex brought under the Fourteenth Amendment, the Supreme Court has never held that a law classifying persons on the basis of sex is unreasonable and therefore unconstitutional.

The Fourteenth Amendment to the United States Constitution provides in part: "No State shall make or enforce any law which shall abridge the privileges or immunities of citizens of the United States; nor shall any State deprive any person of life, liberty, or property, without due process of law; nor deny to any person within its jurisdiction the equal protection of the laws."

In the nineteenth century, the Supreme Court held that the Fourteenth Amendment did not confer upon women the right to vote or the right to practice law within a state. As has been noted, in a series of cases decided between 1908 and 1937, the Court upheld various state labor laws that were applicable to women but not to men. In 1948 it held that a state law forbidding the licensing of females (with certain exceptions) as bartenders did not violate the Fourteenth Amendment. And as recently as 1961, it upheld a Florida law providing that no female be taken for jury service unless she registers with the clerk of the court her desire to serve.

The language of the Fourteenth Amendment appears sufficiently broad to reach all arbitrary class discriminations and would therefore seem to cover discrimination based on sex.

In one case, the Supreme Court stated:

"Throughout our history differences in race and color have defined easily identifiable groups which have at times required the aid of the courts in securing equal treatment under the laws. But community prejudices are not static, and from time to time other differences from the community norm may define other groups which need the same protection. Whether such a group exists within a community is a question of fact. Where the existence of a distinct class is demonstrated, and it is further shown that the laws, as written or as applied, single out that class for different treatment not based on some reasonable classification, the guarantees of the Constitution have been violated. The Fourteenth Amendment is not directed solely against discrimination due to a 'two-class theory'—that is, based upon differences between 'white' and Negro." [5]

In very recent decisions on cases concerning school desegregation (1954, 1955),[6] the extension of the concept of state action (1961, 1963),[7] reapportionment of state legislatures (1962),[8] and the right of persons under arrest to have counsel (1963)[9] the Supreme Court has enunciated principles illustrating the capacity of the Constitution to reflect modern concepts of the importance of human values and individual rights.

"The genius of the American Constitution is its capacity through judicial interpretation for growth and adaptation to changing conditions and human values," Miss Murray wrote. ". . . It must be recalled that the earlier decisions on women's rights reflected the prevailing attitudes of a parochial society in which human rights had neither gained recognition as a universal concept nor received the comprehensive analysis which they are being given today. Archaic notions expressed in some of those cases would hardly be countenanced by an enlightened court of the nineteen-sixties. The more important precedents were established nearly fifty years ago before the worldwide technological, social, and political revolution which has followed two World Wars had made its impact upon American society and institutions."

The Supreme Court has not reviewed the constitutionality of some of the discriminatory legal provisions noted in the Commis-

---

[5] Hernandez v. Texas, 347 U.S. 475, 478 (1954).

[6] Brown v. Board of Education, 347 U.S. 483 (1954), 349 U.S. 294 (1955).

[7] Burton v. Wilmington Parking Authority, 365 U.S. 715 (1961); Peterson v. City of Greenville, 373 U.S. 244 (1963); Lombard v. State of Louisiana, 373 U.S. 267 (1963).

[8] Baker v. Carr, 369 U.S. 186 (1962).

[9] Gideon v. Wainwright, 372 U.S. 335 (1963).

sion Report. Examples of state laws that the Committee thought should be subjected to judicial scrutiny include provisions totally excluding women from jury service, domiciliary rules that operate to restrict a married woman's right to vote, and provisions restricting married women but not married men in the right to contract. In addition, there are undoubtedly instances of official practices that discriminate against women; as, for example, discrimination in public employment. It should be noted that the equal-employment opportunity provisions of the Civil Rights Act of 1964 will not apply to public employment.

Members of the Committee and Commission were unanimous in their hope that, in a properly presented case, the Supreme Court would give full effect to the principle of equality of rights for men and women, thereby clarifying and establishing this principle in federal constitutional doctrine.

JURY SERVICE

Women are still ineligible to serve on state juries in Alabama, Mississippi, and South Carolina. Twenty-six states and the District of Columbia permit women to claim exemptions not available to men. . . . The Commission's desire to equalize jury service for men and women would, if implemented, require changes in all states except the 21 that permit women to serve on juries on the same basis as men. The removal of sex distinctions in state laws in regard to jury service would not mean that women having the care of small children would be forced out of the home; it would mean only that eligibility for an exemption and excuse from jury service would be the same for either sex. Indeed, some states now permit members of both sexes to claim exemption for child care.

PERSONAL AND PROPERTY RIGHTS

The Committee's survey of married women's personal and property rights disclosed many instances in which the law sanctions their inequitable treatment. In suggesting remedies, the Commission balanced a desire to find and eliminate discrimination with

an equivalent interest in encouraging women to assume appropriate responsibility. Both the Commission and the Committee
were influenced by recent developments in matrimonial property
systems around the world reported in the 1958 United Nations
Report on the Legal Status of Married Women.[10] These systems
reflect widespread recognition of married women as independent
persons before the law, and recognize the economic partnership
involved in marriage and the financial contribution of the wife
who works only in the home.

The material that follows documents the Commission's recommendations in this area and is adapted from the Report of the
Committee on Civil and Political Rights.

OWNERSHIP AND CONTROL OF PROPERTY. In 42 states and the
District of Columbia, earnings and property acquired during marriage are owned separately by the spouses; in 8 states, all in the
West or Southwest, earnings and most property acquired by either
spouse during marriage are owned in common. Thus there are
two basic types of matrimonial property systems in the United
States.

The systems of the separate-property states derive from the English common law. The common-law concepts of matrimonial
property evolved from the needs of an agricultural, feudal society
in which the husband was regarded as the head of the family and
the guardian of his wife. A woman was considered as having lost
her personal entity upon marriage, a fiction that furnished the
basis for close to total legal disability of a married woman.

Common-law rules have been modified by statute in most
states, so that today a wife generally has full capacity to own and
control her separate property. Traces of the old common-law
system may be seen in 3 states—Alabama, Florida, and Indiana—
which still require the joinder[11] of the husband in the conveyance
of the wife's property.

The 8 community-property states—Arizona, California, Idaho,
Louisiana, New Mexico, Nevada, Texas, and Washington—
adopted the French or Spanish civil-law concept of community

[10] "Legal Status of Married Women," United Nations Publication ST/SOA/35.
[11] The joining of two or more causes of action in the same declaration.

property. In general, under this system, whatever is acquired by the efforts of the husband or the wife during marriage constitutes part of a common fund. Management and control, however, generally rests in the husband. Either the husband or wife, or both, may also have "separate property," such as that belonging to either at the time of marriage or that acquired through gift, inheritance, or in exchange for other separate property. Most of these states subsequently adopted the common law as the law of decision where the statutes failed to cover a particular situation.

In all states, a wife is able to control her separate personal property independently of her husband. The last exception, the Texas law requiring a husband to join in the transfer of his wife's stocks and bonds, was repealed during the 1963 legislative session.

All states, in varying degrees, have modified by statute some of the outmoded disabilities of married women, but some inequities remain even in the operation of state matrimonial-property systems. For example, in the separate-property states, a wife has no legal rights to any part of her husband's earnings or property during the existence of the marriage, aside from a right to be properly supported. Hence, if she does not have earnings or property of her own, she is completely dependent upon his largesse for anything above and beyond the money she needs for support. On the other hand, under community-property systems, a wife has an interest in the commonly owned property, but a husband generally has exclusive authority to manage and control that property.

CIVIL CAPACITY. Under the common law brought to the United States from England, a married woman was virtually a legal nonentity. In addition to the prohibitions on owning or controlling property, she could not enter into contracts, sue or be sued in her own name, engage in business in her own name, act as surety [12] or fiduciary (trustee), receive her own earnings, or dispose of her property by will.

Beginning in the middle of the nineteenth century, various states adopted the married women's property acts, which were

[12] A person who has made himself responsible for another and who remains primarily liable for such things as the payment of a debt, settlement of a claim; one who makes himself responsible for the appearance of another in court on a specified date.

designed to remove the legal disabilities imposed on women upon marriage. The provisions of these statutes, and also the judicial interpretation of these laws, vary considerably from state to state.

Although today all of the states have removed most of the common-law disabilities of married women, some remnants of past centuries still remain. In some states, a married woman does not have legal capacity to become a surety or guarantor.[13] A number of states limit her right to sue or be sued in her own name. Earnings under the community-property system belong to the common fund. While some of the community-property states permit a wife to receive and control her own earnings within the communal-property concept they generally qualify her right to do so. For example, in California she has control of her earnings only until such time as they are commingled with the community property. In Nevada and Idaho she has absolute control only if she is living separate and apart from her husband. In Texas, as part of the community property, a wife's earnings are subject to the control of her husband.

A few states still restrict the right of a wife to engage in a separate business. These states have enacted "free dealer" or "sole trader" statutes that require some type of formal procedure before a wife may engage in an independent business. For example, 4 states—California, Florida, Nevada, and Pennsylvania—require court approval, and in Massachusetts a married woman and her husband must file a certificate with the city or town clerk in order to prevent the personal property of her business from being liable for her husband's debts.

INHERITANCE RIGHTS. Under the influence of feudalism, the English common law developed rules by which land descended to the lineal offspring, males being preferred to females. Neither spouse was the heir to the other spouse's lands. The estates of dower [14] and courtesy [15] provided a wife and husband respectively

---

[13] One who contracts to be answerable for the performance of another's obligations or promises.

[14] "Dower" represented that portion of a deceased husband's real estate, usually a third, in which the widow had a legal lifetime interest.

[16] "Courtesy" represented the life interest of tenure a man had in the landed estate of his deceased wife in case she had borne him children capable of inheriting.

with an interest in the other's real property. Thus, dower became the chief support of a widow.

Today in nearly all states a widow has a statutory share in her husband's property, both real and personal, of which he cannot deprive her by will. In some states the statutory share is in addition to dower, in some it is in lieu of dower, and in some she can elect which to take. State laws generally provide a husband with a similar share in his wife's property.

The disposition of community property follows a different pattern. In Arizona, California, Idaho, Louisiana, Nevada, and Washington, the surviving spouse takes ½ of the community property while the other half is subject to the testamentary disposition of the decedent. In the absence of a will, the second half may go to the surviving spouse as well, or to the children or to both. In Texas, the surviving spouse takes title to the entire community property if there are no surviving children and to ½ if the deceased spouse is survived by any children or their descendants. In New Mexico, upon the wife's death, the entire community property may vest in the husband, whereas upon the husband's death, the wife's right to obtain the entire property is subject to the husband's right to dispose by will of his half of it.

The statutory shares as provided by state law generally apply only to property owned at the time of death. Although the estate of dower prevents a husband from disposing of real property without his wife's consent during their marriage, there is usually no like safeguard against improper alienation of personal property. State inheritance laws give some protection against improper alienation of property to a surviving spouse, but generally do not provide similar safeguards to protect the surviving minor children.

DOMICILE. A person's domicile or legal residence is important because it may determine many personal rights and obligations. For example, the place of domicile determines in which state the right to vote may be exercised, where an individual may run for public office, where one may be called for jury service, where a divorce may be filed, where personal property and income taxes may be levied, where the assets of a decedent will be administered, where one may receive welfare benefits, and where one may be eligible for admission to state hospitals and other state institutions.

A person's domicile generally is the place which he intends to be his permanent home. However, this rule does not normally apply to married women; the common-law rule with respect to the domicile of a married woman is that her domicile, by automatic operation of law, is her husband's, without regard to her intent or actual residence. This rule, if not modified, can restrict the basic rights of a married woman, particularly if she is not living in the same state as her husband. A married woman in such circumstances may be barred from voting, running for public office, and sitting on a jury, because she lacks the required domicile. Further, because state tax laws vary, a wife's personal property located with her in one jurisdiction may be taxed by a state with a higher rate if such a state happens to be her husband's domicile.

In a special study of state law on domicile, the Women's Bureau of the United States Department of Labor found that most of the law on the subject has been established by court decision. Since case law is subject to some interpretation, classification is difficult. However, on the basis of this study, it appears that today there are only 4 states—Arkansas, Delaware, Hawaii, and New Hampshire—recognizing a married woman's right to acquire her own domicile, independently of her husband, for all purposes, without limitation. Forty-two states and the District of Columbia permit a married woman to acquire an independent domicile for all purposes if she is living apart from her husband for cause; of these, only 18 permit a married woman to acquire an independent domicile if she is separated from her husband by mutual agreement or if her husband acquiesces to the separation. All states permit a married woman to establish a separate domicile for purposes of instituting divorce proceedings. However, in addition to Arkansas, Delaware, Hawaii, and New Hampshire, only 15 states permit, without limitation, a married woman to acquire her own domicile for the purpose of voting: 6 for the purpose of election to public office, 5 for the purpose of jury service, 7 for the purpose of taxation, and 5 for the purpose of probate. . . .

RESPONSIBILITY FOR FAMILY SUPPORT. In dealing with problems of family law occurring during or at the dissolution of a marriage, the Commission and the Committee emphasized women's responsibilities as well as rights in the partnership.

The husband generally has primary legal responsibility for family support. However, in most states, a wife has secondary liability, and in more than half the states, the wife is liable for the support of her husband if he is in need and unable to support himself.

Whether or not a wife works outside the home is a matter to be decided within each family. When it is decided that a wife should take outside employment, it is reasonable that her income as well as her husband's be used to help support the children. On the other hand, when a family decides that it is necessary or desirable for the wife to work only in the home and the wife has no independent income, the husband must necessarily bear the full responsibility for family support.

As a practical matter, a dispute as to which party should pay how much of the family expenses does not arise in a normal family situation. It is only when agreement cannot be reached or when the marriage is disrupted that problems regarding family support obligations arise. It is for those situations that the law must provide standards and means for enforcing those standards.

Neither the Commission nor the Committee intended the recommendation regarding woman's responsibility to support herself and her children to be used to pressure women to leave their homemaking functions for paid employment. Neither group expressed any opinion on whether a wife should be responsible for the support of her husband when he is capable of supporting himself.

GUARDIANSHIP OF CHILDREN. Under the old common law, the father was considered the natural guardian of his minor child and, as such, had the care, custody, and control, and the responsibility of the education of the child. Today, this rule has been abrogated by statute and court decision in the majority of states, which provide that natural guardianship of a minor child is vested jointly in both parents.

However, 6 states—Alaska, Georgia, Louisiana, North Carolina, Oklahoma, and Texas—still provide by statute that the father is the preferred natural guardian of a minor child.

HOMESTEAD LAWS. Most states have enacted some type of homestead law to prevent the family home from being sold to satisfy debts. Such statutes usually specify the size of the homestead and include a monetary limitation: in some states, the monetary value of the homestead exemption is unrealistically low. In North Carolina and Ohio, for example, the homestead exemption is limited to $1,000, and in Michigan, to $2,500. In addition, some state laws appear to be too restrictive concerning the persons who may claim the homestead exemption. For example, in West Virginia, where only a husband or parent residing in the state or the infant children of deceased or insane parents may claim the homestead exemption, the law offers no protection to a childless widow.

This Committee recommendation on the Homestead Laws and another, which proposed study of the need for fair-employment legislation (which is discussed in the chapter on employment), were the Committee's only suggestions that the Commission did not endorse. The Commission believed that the problem involved in the Homestead Laws affected too few women to warrant a formal recommendation.

2

GLANCES TOWARD THE FUTURE

Frances E. Willard, How to Win: A Book for Girls (1888)

Frances E. Willard (1839–98) was president of the Evanston (Illinois) College for Ladies between 1871 and 1874 but found her true vocation when she joined the temperance movement. She served the Woman's Christian Temperance Union as president from 1879 until her death. In addition she was a suffragist, and, at the end of her life, a socialist. In this tract she confidently predicts several developments that she considers necessary for true equality of the sexes; some of her predictions have not yet come true. [*How to Win: A Book for Girls* (5th ed., New York, 1888), pp. 48–57.]

No doubt my readers have asked ere this the inevitable question: "Why does that seem natural and fitting for a young woman to do and to aspire to now which would have been no less improper than impossible a hundred years ago?" Sweet friends, it is because *the ideal of woman's place in the world is changing in the average mind.* For as the artist's idea precedes his picture, so the ideal woman must be transformed before the actual one can be. In an age of brute force, the warrior galloping away to his adven-

tures waved his mailed hand to the lady fair who was enclosed for
safe keeping in a grim castle with moat and drawbridge. But to-
day, when spirit force grows regnant, a woman can circumnavigate
the globe alone, without danger of an uncivil word, much less of
violence. . . . In brief, the barriers that have hedged women into
one pathway and men into another, altogether different, are growing thin, as physical strength plays a less determining part in our
life drama. All through the vegetable and animal kingdoms the
fact of sex does not widely differentiate the broader fact of life,
its environment and its pursuits. Hence, the immense separate-
ness which sex is called in to explain when we reach the plane of
humanity, is to be accounted for largely on artificial grounds. In
Eden it did not exist, nor in the original plan of creation, as stated
in these just and fatherly words: "And God said, 'Let us make
man in our own image, after our own likeness. Let them have
dominion.'. . . So God created man in His own image, in the
image of God created he him, male and female created he them,
and God blessed them, and said unto them, '. . . replenish the
earth and subdue it . . . and have dominion over every living
thing.' " After the fall came the curse, which may have been no
part of the original design, and from which the Gospel's triumph
is releasing us, for there is "neither male nor female in Christ
Jesus." Who knows but that the origin of evil was contempo-
raneous with man's assertion of supremacy over one who was
meant to be his equal comrade? . . .

    . . . Half the world's wisdom, more than half its purity, and
nearly all its gentleness, are to-day to be set down on woman's
credit side. Weighted with the alcohol and tobacco habits, Brother
Jonathan will have to make better time than he is doing now, if
he keeps step with Sister Deborah across the threshold of the
twentieth century. For the law of survival of the fittest will inevitably choose that member of the firm who is cleanliest, most
wholesome, most accordant with God's laws of nature and of
grace, to survive. To the blindness or fatuity which renders him
oblivious of the fact that the coming woman is already well-nigh
here, our current writer of the W. D. Howells and Henry James
school owes the dreary monotony of his "society novel." Not more

"conventional" was the style of art known as "Byzantine," which repeated with barren iteration its placid and colorless "type," than are the pages of this dreary pair, whose books will put a period to the literary sentence of their age. The "American novel" will not be written until the American woman, a type now to be found in Michigan, Boston, Cornell, and other universities, shall have taken her place, twentieth-century product that she is, beside the best survivals of young men in similar institutions, and wrought out the Home, the Church, the State that are to be. . . .

What will the new ideal of woman *not* be? Well, for example, she will never be written down in the hotel register by her husband after this fashion: "John Smith and Wife." He would as soon think of her writing, "Mrs. John Smith and Husband." Why does it not occur to any one to designate him thus? Simply because he is so much more than that. He is the leading force in the affairs of the Church; he helps decide who shall be pastor. (So will she.) He is, perhaps, the village physician, or merchant (so she will be, perhaps—indeed, they are oftentimes in partnership, nowadays, and I have found their home a blessed one.) He is the village editor. (Very likely she will be his associate.) He is a voter. (She would be, beyond a peradventure.) For the same reason you will never read of her marriage that "the minister pronounced them MAN and *wife*," for that functionary would have been just as likely to pronounce them "husband and woman," a form of expression into which the regulation reporter will be likely to fall one of these days, it being, really, not one whit more idiotic than the time-worn phrase, "man and wife." The ideal woman of the future will never be designated as "the *Widow* Jones," because she will be so much more than that—"a provider" for her children, "a power" in the Church, "a felt force" in the State. . . .

The ideal woman will play Beatrice to man's Dante in the Inferno of his passions. She will give him the clew out of materialism's Labyrinth. She will be civilization's Una, taming the Lion of disease and misery. The State shall no longer go limping on one foot through the years, but shall march off with steps firm and equipoised. The keen eye and deft hand of the housekeeper shall help to make its every-day walks wholesome; the skill in detail, trustworthiness in finance, motherliness in sympathy, so long extolled in private life, shall exalt public station. Indeed, if I were asked the mission of the ideal woman, I would reply: IT IS TO MAKE THE WHOLE WORLD HOMELIKE. . . . A true woman carries home with her everywhere. . . . But "home's not merely four square walls."

Some people once thought it was, and they thought, also, that you might as well throw down its Lares and Penates as to carry away its weaving-loom and spinning-wheel. But it survived this spoliation; and when women ceased to pick their own geese and do their own dyeing, it still serenely smiled. The sewing-machine took away much of its occupation; the French and Chinese laundries have intruded upon its domain; indeed the next generation will no doubt turn the cook-stove out of doors, and the housekeeper, standing at the telephone, will order better cooked meals than almost any one has nowadays, sent from scientific caterers by pneumatic tubes, and the débris thereof returned to a general cleaning-up establishment; while houses will be heated, as they are now lighted and supplied with water, from general reservoirs.

Women are fortunate in belonging to the less tainted half of the race. Dr. Benjamin Ward Richardson tells us that but for this conserving fact it would deteriorate to the point of failure. A bright old lady said, after viewing a brewery, distillery, and tobacco factory: "Ain't I thankful that the women folks hain't got all that stuff to chew and smoke and swallow down!" It behooves us to offset force of muscle by force of heart, that what our strong brothers have done to subdue the material world for us, who are not their equals in physical strength, may be offset by what we shall achieve for them in bringing in the reign of "Sweeter manners, purer laws." For the world is slowly making the immense discovery that not what woman *does*, but what she *is*, makes home a possible creation. It is the Lord's ark, and does not need steadying; it will survive the wreck of systems and the crash of theories, for the home is but the efflorescence of woman's nature under the nurture of Christ's Gospel. She came into the college and elevated it, into literature and hallowed it, into the business world and ennobled it. She will come into government and purify it, into politics and cleanse its Stygian pool, for woman will make homelike every place on this round earth. Any custom, or traffic, or party on which a woman cannot look with favor is irrevocably doomed. Its welcome of her presence and her power is to be the final test of its fitness to survive. . . .

No greater good can come to the manhood of the world than is prophesied in the increasing community of thought and works between it and the world's womanhood. The growing individuality, independence, and prestige of the gentler sex steadily require from the stronger a higher standard of character and purer habits of life. This blessed consummation, so devoutly to be wished, is hastened, dear girlish hearts, by every prayer you offer, by every hymn you sing, by every loving errand of your willing feet and gentle hands. You are the true friends of tempted manhood, bewildered youth, and every little child. The steadfast faith and loyal, patient work you are to do, in the white fields of reform, will be the mightiest factor in woman's contribution to the solution of this Republic's greatest problem, and will have their final significance in the thought and purpose, not that the world shall come into the home, but that the home, embodied and impersonated in its womanhood, shall go forth into the world.

I have no fears for the women of America. They will never content themselves remaining stationary in methods or in policy, much less sound a retreat in their splendid warfare against the saloon in law and in politics. . . .

Thorstein Veblen, Theory of the Leisure Class (1899)

Thorstein Veblen, like Frances Willard eleven years earlier, here makes a still unfulfilled prediction. [*Theory of the Leisure Class*, pp. 229–34.]

It has been well and repeatedly said by popular writers and speakers who reflect the common sense of intelligent people on questions of social structure and function that the position of woman in any community is the most striking index of the level of culture attained by the community. This remark is perhaps truer as regards the stage of economic development than as regards development in any other respect. At the same time the position assigned to the woman in the accepted scheme of life, in any community or under any culture, is in a very great degree an expression of traditions which have been shaped by the circumstances of an earlier phase of development, and which have been but partially adapted to the existing economic circumstances, or to the existing exigencies of temperament and habits of mind by which the women living under this modern economic situation are actuated. . . .

The several phases of the "woman question" have brought out in intelligible form the extent to which the life of women in modern society, and in the polite circles especially, is regulated by a body of common sense formulated under the economic circumstances of an earlier phase of development. It is still felt that woman's life, in its civil, economic, and social bearing, is essentially and normally a vicarious life, the merit or demerit of which is, in the nature of things, to be imputed to some other individual who stands in some relation of ownership or tutelage to the woman. So, for instance, any action on the part of a woman which traverses an injunction of the accepted schedule of proprieties is felt to reflect immediately upon the honor of the man whose woman she is. There may of course be some sense of incongruity in the mind of any one passing an opinion of this kind on the woman's frailty or perversity; but the common-sense judgment of the community in such matters is, after all, delivered without much hesitation, and few men would question the legitimacy of their sense of an outraged tutelage in any case that might arise. On the other hand, relatively little discredit attaches to a woman through the evil deeds of the man with whom her life is associated.

The good and beautiful scheme of life, then—that is to say the scheme to which we are habituated—assigns to the woman a "sphere" ancillary to the activity of the man; and it is felt that any departure from the traditions of her assigned round of duties is unwomanly. If the question is as to civil rights or the suffrage, our common sense in the matter—that is to say the logical deliverance of our general scheme of life upon the point in question —says that the woman should be represented in the body politic and before the law, not immediately in her own person, but through the mediation of the head of the household to which she belongs. It is unfeminine in her to aspire to a self-directing, self-centered life; and our common sense tells us that her direct participation in the affairs of the community, civil or industrial, is a menace to that social order which expresses our habits of thought as they have been formed under the guidance of the traditions of the pecuniary culture. . . . Women have a very alert sense of what the scheme of proprieties requires, and while it is true that many of them are ill at ease under the details which the code imposes, there are few who do not recognize that the existing moral order, of necessity and by the divine right of prescription, places the woman in a position ancillary to the man. In the last analysis, according to her own sense of what is good and beautiful, the woman's life is, and in theory must be, an expression of the man's life at the second remove.

But in spite of this pervading sense of what is the good and natural place for the woman, there is also perceptible an incipient development of sentiment to the effect that this whole arrangement of tutelage and vicarious life and imputation of merit and demerit is somehow a mistake. Or, at least, that even if it may be a natural growth and a good arrangement in its time and place, and in spite of its patent aesthetic value, still it does not adequately serve the more everyday ends of life in a modern industrial community. Even that large and substantial body of well-bred, upper and middle-class women to whose dispassionate, matronly sense of the traditional proprieties this relation of status commends itself as fundamentally and eternally right—even these, whose attitude is conservative, commonly find some slight discrepancy in detail between things as they are and things as they should be in this respect. But that less manageable body of modern women who, by force of youth, education, or temperament, are in some degree out of touch with the traditions of status received from the barbarian culture, and in whom there is, perhaps, an undue reversion to the impulse of self-expression and workmanship—these are touched with a sense of grievance too vivid to leave them at rest.

In this "New-Woman" movement—as these blind and incoherent efforts to rehabilitate the woman's pre-glacial standing have been named—there are at least two elements discernible, both of which are of an economic character. These two elements or motives are expressed by the double watchword, "Emancipation" and "Work." Each of these words is recognized to stand for something in the way of a wide-spread sense of grievance. The prevalence of the sentiment is recognized even by people who do not see that there is any real ground for a grievance in the situation as it stands today. It is among the women of the well-to-do classes, in the communities which are farthest advanced in industrial development, that this sense of a grievance to be redressed is most alive and finds most frequent expression. That is to say, in other words, there is a demand, more or less serious, for emancipation from all relation of status, tutelage, or vicarious life; and the revulsion asserts itself especially among the class of women upon whom the scheme of life handed down from the regime of status imposes with least mitigation a vicarious life, and in those communities whose economic development has departed farthest from the circumstances to which this traditional scheme is adapted. The demand comes from that portion of womankind which is excluded by the canons of good repute from all effectual work, and which is closely reserved for a life of leisure and conspicuous consumption.

More than one critic of this new-woman movement has misapprehended its motive. The case of the American "new woman" has lately been summed up with some warmth by a popular observer of social phenomena: "She is petted by her husband, the most devoted and hard-working of husbands in the world. . . . She is the superior of her husband in education, and in almost every respect. She is surrounded by the most numerous and delicate attentions. Yet she is not satisfied. . . . The Anglo-Saxon 'new woman' is the most ridiculous production of modern times, and destined to be the most ghastly failure of the century." Apart from the depreciation—perhaps well placed—which is contained in this presentment, it adds nothing but obscurity to the woman question. The grievance of the new woman is made up of those things which this typical characterization of the movement urges as reasons why she should be content. She is petted, and is permitted, or even required, to consume largely and conspicuously—vicariously for her husband or other natural guardian. She is exempted, or debarred, from vulgarly useful employment—in order to perform leisure vicariously for the good repute of her natural (pecuniary) guardian. These offices are the conventional marks of the un-free, at the same time that they are incompatible with the human impulse to purposeful activity. But the woman is endowed with her share—which there is reason to believe is more than an even share—of the instinct of workmanship, to which futility of life or of expenditure is obnoxious. She must unfold her life activity in response to the direct, unmediated stimuli of the economic environment with which she is in contact. The impulse is perhaps stronger upon the woman than upon the man to live her own life in her own way and to enter the industrial process of the community at something nearer than the second remove.

So long as the woman's place is consistently that of a drudge, she is, in the average of cases, fairly contented with her lot. She not only has something tangible and purposeful to do, but she has also no time or thought to spare for a rebellious assertion of such human propensity to self-direction as she has inherited. And after the stage of universal female drudgery is passed, and a vicarious leisure without strenuous application becomes the accredited employment of the women of the well-to-do classes, the prescriptive force of the canon of pecuniary decency, which requires the observance of ceremonial futility on their part, will long preserve high-minded women from any sentimental leaning to self-direction and a "sphere of usefulness." This is especially true during the earlier phases of the pecuniary culture, while the leisure of the leisure class is still in great measure a predatory activity, an active assertion of mastery in which there is enough of tangible purpose of an invidious kind to admit of its being taken seriously as an employment to which one may without shame put one's hand. This condition of things has obviously lasted well down into the present in some communities. It continues to hold to a different extent for different individuals, varying with the vividness of the sense of status and with the feebleness of the impulse to workmanship with which the individual is endowed. But where the economic structure of the community has so far outgrown the scheme of life based on status that the relation of personal subservience is no longer felt to be the sole "natural" human relation; there the ancient habit of purposeful activity will begin to assert itself in the less conformable individuals against the more recent, relatively superficial, relatively ephemeral habits and views which the predatory and the pecuniary culture have contributed to our scheme of life. . . .

In a sense, then, the new-woman movement marks a reversion to a more generic type of human character, or to a less differentiated expression of human nature. It is a type of human nature which is to be characterized as proto-anthropoid, and, as regards the substance if not the form of its dominant traits, it belongs to a cultural stage that may be classed as possibly sub-human. The particular movement or evolutional feature in question of course shares this characterization with the rest of the later social development, in so far as this social development shows evidence of a reversion to the spiritual attitude that characterizes the earlier, undifferentiated stage of economic revolution. Such evidence of a general tendency to reversion from the dominance of the invidious interest is not entirely wanting, although it is neither plentiful nor unquestionably convincing. The general decay of the sense of status in modern industrial communities goes some way as evidence in this direction; and the perceptible return to a disapproval of futility in human life, and a disapproval of such activities as serve only the individual gain at the cost of the collectivity or at the cost of other social groups, is evidence to a like effect. There is a perceptible tendency to deprecate the infliction of pain, as well as to discredit all marauding enterprises, even where these expressions of the invidious interest do not tangibly work to the material detriment of the community or of the individual who passes an opinion on them. It may even be said that in the modern industrial communities the average, dispassionate sense of men says that the ideal character is a character which makes for peace, good-will, and economic efficiency, rather than for a life of self-seeking, force, fraud, and mastery.

Charlotte Perkins Gilman, Are Women Human Beings? (1912)

Charlotte Perkins Gilman here reiterates her favorite argument that the common humanity of men and women is far more important than their sex difference and will inevitably erase artificial barriers to women's engaging in "human" activities. The "major error" she complains of still colors many discussions of the woman question. ["Are Women Human Beings? A Consideration of the Major Error in the Discussion of Woman Suffrage," *Harper's Weekly*, May 25, 1912, p. 11.]

. . . As social evolution has never waited for the complete enlightenment of mankind, we find the enfranchisement of women going on in all civilized countries; but since the opposition to it is strong enough to cause years of delay and a continuous outlay of organized effort, it seems worth while to point out the main error actuating that opposition.

It may seem difficult to select a major error among such a self-contradictory confusion; but under all these miscellaneous reiterated objections one governing conviction continually obtrudes itself. It colors all the utterances of the Organization Opposed to the Extension of Suffrage to Women. It exclusively dominates the grave opinions of pathologists. It is the animus of all the books written against "the woman's movement." It is the painfully visible actuating impulse of the ill-considered objections of "the man in the street," and also of the similar expressions of "the woman in the home." And . . . it is the feeling animating a leading editorial in the New York *Times,* and a peculiarly typical "Letter from the People" in that paper, called forth by the recent impressive parade of our suffragists.

This error is due to a certain arrested development of thought. It consists in seeing in women only feminine characteristics; and, conversely, seeing in all the complex functions of civilization only masculine characteristics.

Under this conception it is held, quite naturally, that women need to do nothing more than fulfil[l] their "womanly duties," *i.e.*, to be wives, mothers, and houseworkers; that for them to desire any other activities in life is to be unwomanly, unnatural, to become some sort of pervert or monster. They are spoken of as "de-natured women," as "epicene," as "unsexed," as "seeking to become men." Miss Ida Tarbell in a recent magazine article describes women's professional and industrial advance as "Making a Man of Herself."

Otto Weininger, in his much-discussed book, *Sex and Character*, elaborated a theory of mixed inheritance, showing that some women inherited a proportion of masculine characteristics and some men inherited a proportion of feminine characteristics, thus explaining the undeniable phenomenon of their having many characteristics in common.

The late Mr. Grant Allen expressed this world-view in clear scientific phrase when he said that women were not only "not the human race—they were not even half the human race, but a sub-species set apart for purposes of reproduction merely."

The still later Mr. H. B. Marriott-Watson has put it with even more exquisite precision, saying of the American woman, "Her constitutional restlessness has caused her to abdicate those functions which alone excuse or explain her existence."

Now comes Sir Almoth Wright, M.D., in a three-column letter to the London *Times*. . . . Speaking as one long conversant with many female invalids, he rashly generalizes from his personal experience of morbid phenomena, and says, "No doctor can ever lose sight of the fact that the mind of woman is always threatened with danger from the reverberations of her physiological emergencies."

He sees, in the advance of women into wider social relations, only the perverse action of suppressed, embittered, or atrophied femininity. He sees in them, of course, nothing but femininity: that which he considers normal and admires, or which he considers abnormal and condemns. The glory of woman, according to his definition, lies "in her power of attraction, in her capacity for motherhood, and in her unswerving allegiance to the ethics which are special to her sex."

So our *Times*, of New York, in the editorial above referred to, modestly says: "One does not need to be a profound student of biology to know that some women, a very small minority, have a natural inclination to usurp the social and civic functions of men."

Simmer down this loosely gathered mass of opinion, and we find that it all resolves into the one assumption—that women have feminine functions and no others, and that social functions are masculine. Let us frankly examine these premises.

Without needing to be any more profound a student of biology than the editor of our *Times*, we must all admit that there are other functions besides the reproductive. As life spread wide upon the earth, each species developed its own means of locomotion, its means of self-defense, its means of getting a livelihood; all essential, all common to both sexes. Variations in size, in color, in intelligence, in agility, in courage, differentiate one animal from another; all essential, all common to both sexes.

Meanwhile, all creatures have some means of replenishing the earth after their kind, and we, as mammals, share in the methods of the higher orders, adding to the personal processes the vast advantage of our social processes; as in education, once wholly a maternal function, and now so largely civic and social. But while all kindred species share in the primal activities of reproduction, each is sharply distinguished from the others by its special activities in other lines.

As animals, we share in the universal distinction of sex; but as human beings, we alone possess a whole new range of faculties, vitally essential and common to both sexes.

It seems childish to insist upon so patent a fact, so simple and obvious a distinction which these one-ideaed upholders of the eternal masculine utterly fail to grasp. . . .

If we were to count up and contrast the number of characteristics of sex with the number of characteristics of species, we should find at once that race distinctions far exceed sex distinctions in number and importance. Take, for instance, a cow, a camel, and a whale. They all bring forth one living offspring and suckle it, the process being fairly identical. But a cow is easily distinguished from a camel and either from a whale.

Again, of two deer, the buck has a special secondary sex-distinction in his towering antlers; but his power of speed, his love of speed, is not a sex distinction but a race distinction, common to both sexes. When the doe wishes to run far and fast, she is not "unfeminine," she is not "making a buck of herself." She likes to run, not because she is a doe, but because she is a deer, just as much of a deer as he is.

This universal, glaring fact is what these sex-obsessed opponents of the normal progress of women cannot see. They see only the feminine characteristics of women, and fail to see the human ones. Yet with our species, beyond any other, the race-characteristics outnumber and outweigh all lesser distinctions.

Certain attributes we share with all matter, as weight, mass, extension; certain others with most animals, as digestion, circulation; others, again, including the reproductive processes, with the higher mammals alone; but the preponderant characteristics of humanity we share with no other creature. We, as a species, have far more conspicuous and important distinctions peculiar to ourselves than those we share with lower forms; and each and every one of these human distinctions belongs to both sexes.

Yet the male of our species, from the beginning of his power of conscious thought, has arrogated to himself as part of his sex the major attributes of humanity: religion, education, government, commerce—these were for him alone. In what he has termed "his female" he has seen, and for the most part still sees, only her femininity, never her humanity.

That she should concentrate all her human faculties upon the fulfil[l]ment of her feminine functions he has held quite right and proper; that she should at any time wish to use them, not as a female, but as a human being, is to him monstrous. So absolute has been this monopolization of human functions by one sex; so complete this obsession that has persisted in considering them as sex attributes, that even the range of industries originated by women, for ages practised wholly by women, have been gradually absorbed by men, and as rapidly as they were absorbed have become "masculine."

Mere extension in method has been similarly classified: as where a woman with distaff and spindle, or foot-run wheel, was considered feminine; but to run a woolen mill must be "man's work."

Let us look at our own race history. When we were all hunters, fishers, and root-gatherers, we were men and women, just as efficiently and completely as we are now. When we kept cattle we were not any the less, or more, men and women. When we developed agriculture, we were still men and women. When we specialized in industry, we remained men and women. Men were males and women females at any time in the whole long story.

But while remaining unchanged in these respects, we have changed enormously in our social features, our common human attributes.

Specialization has given us a thousand trades, arts, crafts, and professions. Organization has multiplied our power myriad-fold. Invention and discovery have enriched and enlightened the world. Religions have changed. Governments have changed. Society evolves from age to age. All these are human processes. They belong to our race. They are common to both male and female. They have no faintest connection with any sex distinction.

As to warfare, which our ultra males are so sure to fall back on in proof of their essential dominance: warfare is not a social process at all, but a social disease, freely admitted to be most characteristic of the male. It is the instinct of sex-combat, over-developed and misused.

The women of our age in most countries of the same degree of development are outgrowing the artificial restrictions so long placed upon them, and following natural lines of human advance. They are specializing, because they are human. They are organizing, because they are human. They are seeking economic and political independence, because they are human. They are demanding the vote, because they are human.

Against this swelling tide stands the mere mass of inert old-world ignorance, backed by the perverse misconception of modern minds, which even science fails to illuminate.

"Go back," says this mass. "You are women. You are nothing *but* women. You are females—nothing *but* females. All these things you want to do are male things. You cannot do them without being a male. You want to be males. It is abhorrent, outrageous, impossible!"

All these adjectives and horrors would be freely granted if women really could become males—or even if they wanted to! But what needs to be hammered into these male-ridden minds is that these things the women want to do and be and have are not in any sense masculine. They do not belong to men. They never did. They are departments of our social life, hitherto monopolized by men, but no more made masculine by that use than the wearing of trousers by Turkish women makes trousers feminine or the wearing of corsets by German officers makes corsets masculine. . . .

Whether in the accumulated literature of the necessarily unenlightened past, or the still accumulating literature of the wilfully unenlightened present, we find everywhere this same pervasive error, this naïve assumption, which would be so insolent if it were not so absurd, that only men are human creatures, able and entitled to perform the work of the world; while women are only female creatures, able to do nothing whatever but continue in the same round of duties to which they have been so long restricted.

They darkly threaten, do these ultra male opponents, that if women persist in doing human things they will lose the respect of man—yea, more, they will lose his pecuniary support.

They should study their biology a little more profoundly. The respect of the male for the female is based on the distinction of sex, not on political or economic disability. Men respect women because they are females, not because they are weak and ignorant and defenseless.

Women will never cease to be females, but they will cease to be weak and ignorant and defenseless. They are becoming wiser, stronger, better able to protect themselves, one another, and their children. Courage, power, achievement are always respected.

As women grow, losing nothing that is essential to womanhood, but adding steadily the later qualities of humanness, they will win and hold a far larger, deeper reverence than that hitherto vouchsafed them. As they so rise and broaden, filling their full place in the world as members of society, as well as their partial places as mothers of it, they will gradually rear a new race of men, men with minds large enough to see in human beings something besides males and females. . . .

Sylvia Kopald, Where Are the Female Geniuses? (1924)

Sylvia Kopald (1899———), born in Brooklyn, New York, received a Ph.D. from Columbia in 1924, the same year in which her book, *Rebellion in Labor Unions,* was published, and worked as a teacher for the International Ladies Garment Workers' Union, New York. The confidence displayed in the pre–1920 tracts is somewhat less apparent in later essays such as this, in which the writer contends that the more women work in the world, the more geniuses will appear among them. But she ventures no prediction as to when this will happen. ["Where Are the Female Geniuses?" in Freda Kirchwey, ed., *Our Changing Morality: A Symposium* (New York, 1924), pp. 107–26.]

Many years ago, Voltaire was initiated into the mysteries of Newton by Mme. du Châtelet. Finishing her translation and her rich commentary upon the *Principles,* in a glow he extended to her the greatest tribute which man has yet found for exceptional women. He said, "A woman who has translated and illuminated Newton is, in short, a very great man." Genius has long been a masculine characteristic, although some more generous authors admit its possession by certain "depraved" women. Only the courtesans of classical antiquity could be women and individuals at once, and, therefore, Jean Finot found it necessary to remind us emphatically even in 1913 that "women of genius and talent are not necessarily depraved." Not necessarily, mind you. No, the great woman may be, in short, a great man, but she is not necessarily depraved.

As the twentieth century progresses and women capture the outposts of individuality one after the other, the old questions lose much of their old malignancy. Women battle with the problem of how to combine a home and a career and men become less sure (especially in these days of high living costs) that woman's place is in the home. As women enter the trades and the arts and the professions, men begin to discover comrades where there were only girls and wives and mothers before. It is an exciting century, this women's century, and even though prejudices crumble slowly, they crumble. Yet one of the old questions remains, stalwart and unyielding as ever: Where are the female geniuses? . . . Women may have minds—every average man will now grant that. But (he will quickly ask) have they ever much more than average minds? Look at history, which this time really does prove what you want it to. Every high peak in the historic landscape is masculine. Point them out just as they occur to you: Shakespeare, Dante, Goethe, Virgil, Horace, Catullus, Plato, Socrates, Newton, Darwin, Pasteur, Watt, Edison, Steinmetz, Heine, Shelley, Keats, Beethoven, Wagner, Bach, Tolstoi. . . .

Where are the *female* geniuses?

It has really become much more than a question of feminist conversation. Science has attempted to put its seal of approval upon the implied answer to this rhetorical question. It has sought to put the notion that "a woman is only a woman, but a genius is a man," into impressively scientific lingo. The argument goes something like this: In regard to practically all anatomical, physiological, and psychic characteristics, the male exhibits a greater variability (i.e. a greater range of spreading down from and up above the average) than the female. The male is the agent of variation; the female is the agent of type conservation. This sex difference operates in the realm of mental ability as everywhere. In any comparable group of men and women, the distribution of intelligence will tend to follow the law of chances (Gaussian Curve). But female intelligence will cluster far more about its average than male. There will be more imbeciles and idiots among men, but there will also be more geniuses. . . .

According to Karl Pearson this "law of the greater variability of the male" was first stated by Darwin. Somewhat earlier, the anatomist Meckel had concluded that the female is more variable than the male. It is interesting to note in passing that he consequently judged "variation a sign of inferiority." By the time Burdach, Darwin, and others had declared the male more variable, however, variation had become an advantage and the basis and hope of all progress. To-day great social significance is attached to the comparative variability of the sexes, especially in its application to the questions of sex differences in mental achievement. Probably the outstanding English-speaking supporters of the theory in its modern form have been Havelock Ellis and Dr. G. Stanley Hall. But even so cautious a student as Dr. E. L. Thorndike has granted it his guarded support. And Dr. James McKeen Cattell has explained the results of his study of 1000 eminent characters of history by means of it. Indeed many others hold the theory in one form or another. . . . What is more important, of course, is that its supporters do not stop with the mere statement of the theory. They ascribe to it tremendous effects in the past and ask for it a large influence in the shaping of our policies in the present.

For Havelock Ellis, the greater variability of the male "has social and practical consequences of the widest significance. The whole of our human civilization would have been a different thing if in early zoölogical epochs the male had not acquired a greater variational tendency than the female." ("Man and Woman," p. 387.) Professor Hall builds up upon it a scheme of gushingly paradisaical (and properly boring) education for the adolescent girl, which "keeps the purely mental back" and develops the soul, the body, and the intuitions. ("The Psychology of Adolescence," Vol. II, Chap. 17.) Just because Professor Thorndike is so careful in his statements, his practical deductions from the theory are most interesting: "Thus the function of education for women, though not necessarily differentiated by the small differences in average capacity, is differentiated by the difference in range of ability. Not only the probability and desirability of marriage and the training of children as an essential feature of women's career but also the restriction of women to the mediocre grades of ability and achievement should be reckoned with by our educational systems. The education of women for such professions as administration, statesmanship, philosophy, or scientific research, where a few very gifted individuals are what society requires, is far less needed than education for such professions as nursing, teaching, medicine, or architecture, where the average level is essential. Elementary education is probably an even better investment for the community in the case of girls than in the case of boys; for almost all girls profit by it, whereas the extremely low grade boy may not be up to his school education in zeal or capacity and the extremely high grade boy may get on better without it. So also with high school education. On the other hand, post graduate instruction to which women are flocking in great numbers is, at least in its higher reaches, a far more remunerative social investment in the case of men." ("Sex in Education," *Bookman*, Vol. XXIII, April, 1906, p. 213.)

Before we begin the revision of our educational systems in accordance with this theory, we must make sure that it really explains away the "female geniuses." For although the theory is still widely held by biologists and psychologists, it requires only a short study to discover how tenuous is the evidence adduced in support of it—in all its phases, but especially in regard to mental traits. Darwin apparently gave no statistical evidence to support "the principle," as he called it, and those who have followed him have done little to fill the lack. Professor Hall offers evidence that is almost entirely empirical; Havelock Ellis has been attacked by Karl Pearson for doing much "to perpetuate some of the worst of the pseudo-scientific superstitions to which he [Ellis] refers, notably that of the greater variability of the male human being." Professor Thorndike, in spite of his conclusions, admits that it "is unfortunate that so little information is available for a study of sex differences in the variability of mental traits in the case of individuals over fifteen." And while the overwhelming majority of Professor Cattell's 1000 eminent characters are men, he merely states without proving his explanation that "woman departs less from the normal than man."

Wise feminists to-day are concentrating their forces upon this theory. Women have won the right to an acknowledged mind; they want now the right to draw for genius and high talents in the "curve of chance." And this is no merely academic question. For while genius may overcome the sternest physical barriers of environment, it is nourished and developed by tolerant expectancy. Men may accomplish anything, popular thought tells them, and so some men do. But if women are scientifically excluded from the popular expectation of big things, if their educations are toned down to preparation for "the average level," if motherhood remains the *only* respected career for *all* women, then the female geniuses will remain few and far between. And, more important still, all thinking women will continue restless over the problem of how to secure the chance to vary in interests and abilities from the average of their sex, and at the same time to be wives and mothers.

In this fight for a full chance to compete, woman may do one (or all) of three things. She may merely ignore the theory and go on "working and living," trusting that as environmental barriers fall one after the other, this final question, too, will lose its meaning. She can point out in support of this attitude that the past does contain its female geniuses, however few; and certainly if all the barriers that have been set up against woman's entry into the larger world have not entirely stifled female genius, we may at least look forward hopefully to a kinder future. Something of this attitude, of this demand for free experimentation, must make part of every woman's armor against the implications of this theory. But taken alone, it becomes more merely defensive than the status of the theory deserves. For it is really the theory that must defend itself. It must not only bring forward more affirmative evidence, but it must also meet the contrary findings of such investigation as has been made. It must, again, prove its title to *the cause* of the scarcity of female geniuses when so many other more eradicable causes may be at its bottom.

The actual evidence that has been gathered on this question is still uncertain and fragmentary. While it does not yet establish anything definitely, it points to rather surprising conclusions. In all cases investigated the discovered differences in variability have been very slight, and if they balance either way tend to prove a greater variability among women. Neither sex need have a monopoly of either imbeciles or geniuses, but women may yet be found to be slightly more favored with both!

The first painstaking investigation in this field was made by Dr. Karl Pearson who published his interesting results as one essay in his *Chances of Death and Other Studies in Evolution* in 1897. Under the heading "Variation in Man and Woman" (Vol. I, pp. 256–377), written as a polemical attack upon Havelock Ellis's stand in this theory, he set forth results of measurements upon men and women in seventeen anatomical characteristics. He obtained data from statistics already collected, from measurements of living men and women, and from post-mortem and archeological examinations. . . . [There follows a long passage containing additional data on both physical and mental variation, all casting doubt on the theory.—*Ed.*]

It seems hardly safe scientifically, therefore, to restrict women to the average levels in education and work and profession on the ground that eminence is beyond their range. But if the female geniuses have not been cut off by a comparatively narrowed range of mental ability, where are they? Certainly history does not reveal them in anything like satisfactory number. And it is now that women may bring forward their third weapon of attack. The female geniuses may have been missing not because of an inherent lack in the make-up of the sex, but because of the oppressive, restrictive cultural conditions under which women have been forced to live.

The important rôle played by cultural conditions in the cultural achievement of various nations and races has been noted with increasing emphasis by the newer schools of sociology and anthropology. No scholar can now defend unchallenged a thesis of "lower or higher races" by urging the achievements of any race as an index of its range of mental ability. Culture grows by its own laws and the high position of the white race may be as much a product of favorable circumstances as of exceptional innate capacities. Similarly the expression taken by the genius of various nations appears to vary strikingly. This is especially impressive in the realm of music. The Anglo-Saxon peoples are singularly lacking in great musical composers. Neither Britain nor America, nor indeed any of the northern countries have contributed one composer worthy of mention besides the Beethovens and Wagners and Chopins of their art. Indeed the great names in music are generally of German, Latin or Slavic origin. Yet no one thinks of urging this fact as evidence of an Anglo-Saxon failure of major creativeness. Instead we point to achievements in other fields or at most attempt to explain this peculiar lack by some external causation. Similarly all our impatience with the un-artistic approaches of the American people does not lead us to frame a theory of their lack of genius. There are many cultural factors to be considered first.

But as soon as we approach the problem of female genius, too many of us are apt to bring forward an entirely different kind of interpretation. We pass over the undoubted female geniuses lightly —granting Sappho and Bonheur and Brunn and Eliot and Brontë and Amster and Madame Curie and Caroline Herschel and perhaps even Chaminade and Clara Schumann and several others. We admit the undoubtedly significant parts women are playing in modern literature. But the question always remains.

Yet in no national or racial group have cultural influences exercised so restrictive an influence as among the entire female sex. Not only has the larger world been closed to them, not only has popular opinion assumed that "no woman has it in her," but the bearing and rearing of children has carried with it in the past the inescapable drudgery of housework. And this is "a field," as Dr. Hollingworth points out, "where eminence is not possible."

It was Proudhon who sneered in response to a similar argument that "women could not even invent their distaff." But we now know enough about the laws of invention to realize how unfair such sneering is. Professor Franz Boas and his school have long demonstrated that cultural achievement and mental ability are not necessarily correlated. For material culture, once it begins, tends to grow by accumulation and diffusion. Each generation adds to the existing stock of knowledge, and as the stock grows the harvests necessarily become greater. Modern man need have no greater mental ability than the men of the ice ages to explain why his improvements upon the myriad machines and tools that are his yield so much larger a harvest than the Paleolithic hunters' improvements upon their few flint weapons and industrial processes. For, as Professor Ogburn has well shown (in "Social Change," Part III) all invention contains two elements—a growing cultural base and inventive genius to work with the materials it furnishes. The number of new inventions necessarily grows with the cultural base. Even 50 times 100 make only 5000, but 2 times 1,000,000 make 2,000,000. Countless generations have added their share to the total material culture which is ours and which we shall hand down still more enriched to posterity.

It must be at once obvious that there has been no such cultural growth in housework. Housework has long remained an individualized, non-cumulative industry, where daughter learns from mother the old ways of doing things. The small improvements and ingenuities which most housewives devise seldom find their way into the whole stream of culture. Thus it is that the recent great inventions which are slowly revolutionizing this last stronghold of petty individualism have come from the man-made world. Workers in electricity could more easily devise the vacuum cleaner than the solitary housewife; the electric washer, parquet floors, the tin can, quantity production of stockings, wool, clothing, bread, butter, and all the other instruments that have really made possible women's emancipation have naturally come not from women's minds (any more than from men's) but from the growth of culture and the minds that utilize that growth for further expansion.

Consequently, as women participate in the work of the world and win the right to acquire the results of past achievement in science and technique and art, we may expect their contributions to the social advance to appear in ever greater numbers. Until we give them this full chance to contribute, we have no right to explain the paucity of their gifts to society by inherent lacks. And it seems reasonable to expect that such a chance will render the old quest for female geniuses properly old-fashioned. For they will be there—these women—the able and talented and geniuses— working side by side with men, not as "very great men" nor as necessarily "depraved" nor in any way unusual. They will be there as human beings and as women.

Emily Newell Blair, Discouraged Feminists (1931)

Emily Newell Blair (1877–1951), writer and lecturer, was a leader in the Missouri suffrage campaign in 1914 and a member and then vice-chairman of the Democratic National Committee in the 1920's. By the date of this article, the discouragement hinted at in the preceding article was frankly admitted, and Mrs. Blair here proposes a drastic economic solution to the problems that suffrage had not solved politically. ["Discouraged Feminists," *The Outlook*, July 8, 1931, pp. 302–3, 318–19.]

A few months before her death Dr. Anna Howard Shaw said to me that she did not envy women their after-suffrage endeavors.

"You younger women will have a harder task than ours," she said. "You will want equality in business and it will be even harder to get than the vote, for you will have to fight for it as individuals and that will not get you far. Women will not unite, since they will be competitors with each other. As soon as a woman has it for herself she will have entered the man's world and cease to fight as a woman for other women."

The other day a young woman said to me: "It isn't fair. John" —she mentioned a young man—"can start right away in his profession as a geologist with a good salary. I am just as smart as he. I have just as good an education, but every one tells me that I can only get a toe-hold in my profession by learning stenography and taking a position in the business as a secretary to some manager. Jim"—she mentioned another contemporary—"enters a staff position but I can only get into the same office by becoming a stenographer. If I am lucky I may get as good a position as his after five years' apprenticeship."

And I remembered Dr. Shaw's statement. Since she made it, women have entered the business world in large numbers but men still dominate this world. With rare exceptions, which stand out because they are exceptions, the women in it are still underlings. The positions that decide policies of any importance are still held by men. Women work only as assistants or secretaries. In the business world today most women play the part of servants, not equals.

We have only to note the membership of a Business and Professional Women's Club in the same town to realize this fact. The men who belong to the Chamber of Commerce are bankers, presidents of factories, owners and managers of stores, lawyers and doctors with offices of their own, and local executives for companies of national scope doing business in the town. They have annual incomes ranging from $5000 to $50,000. The women who join the Business and Professional Women's Club are, most of them, stenographers, clerks, teachers, with here or there a doctor or a lawyer, and an occasional owner of a small shop. Their incomes range from $720 a year to a very occasional $5000.

In Dr. Shaw's day women talked about this being a man-made world. They said that suffrage would help women to get into it and make it a partnership world in which men and women would coöperate in determining the way it would be organized. Some of them, and this was perhaps their first mistake, said that it has always been a man-made world. But that is not the way I read my history. In Harold Lamb's book, *The Crusaders,* he tells how women of the fifteenth century accompanied the armies even to the Holy Land; that some few led troops themselves, while the work at home was almost entirely carried on by women. The peasant women tilled the fields. The ladies of the manor administered their great estates.

As a matter of fact, in the feudal age women were not the quiescent creatures we sometimes think them, living entirely off men. While men fought and had to fight each other for mastery or self-defense, the women had to feed, clothe and house themselves, the children and even the men. Not only did they do the work, but they were in control of what they did. They decided what should be done and how it should be done. The house itself, sociologists have told us, was the invention, if it may be called that, of women. Methods of cooking, manners of furnishing, textiles and fashions were of women's designing. Customs they developed. Manners they evolved. While her husband was abroad to the wars the great lady ruled over a wide domain, and, since he was usually at the wars, she was master much of the time. She had hundreds of women working under her, spinning, weaving, embroidering, sewing, and also, be it noted, often hundreds of men ploughing, harvesting, forging and animal tending.

Surely it is not too much to say that women were partners in building the world of that day, nor was it built solely for men. Men dominated the political world, but women got the protection they needed in a day when might could take what it would. More, they got freedom to develop a civilized life inside their castles. If it is true that women instinctively think in terms of the race and men crave adventure, the world they built ever so slowly was the kind that women wanted rather than men.

Even the wife of the craftsman was a co-partner in his business, for she fed his apprentices, clothed and housed them. It must be remembered that in those days the providing of food and clothing meant the management of food and clothing factories. The kind of food men ate, the kind of clothes they wore, the way the workers were treated, therefore, was determined by these women managers. Thus their decisions and their work had a direct effect on customs, manners, and methods of manufacturing. So women were partners with men in building the world.

Suddenly, however, this partnership was dissolved on the wife. First, the clothing part of her job was taken from her by machines. Gradually food processes left the home. She kept on doing what was left her to do, not realizing that all these industries that were lightening her labors were being managed by men, and at last she woke up to find that instead of being a partner in making the world she was either a beneficiary or a mere cog in a great industrial organization. Man-controlled industry had determined what kind of clothes were manufactured, what kind of food was provided, how workers should be housed, and solved the labor questions. She should right then have gone after her work, mastered the mechanics of the age and taken part in its development, but the social taboos which had been the result of the old partnership held her back. Forgotten by that time were the feudal days when women shared the work of the world. Only the customs that had been built out of that partnership remained.

Feminism, in this country at least, expressed the desire of women once more to have a part in making the world. They were not asking for something they had never had before, but endeavoring to get back what they had lost. Queerly enough, in an age where politics counted less than before, they concentrated first on the effort to get political equality.

Of course the women who had worked for other women had followed their jobs into industry, exchanging a job under a woman in a home for a job under a man in a factory. But what these feminists wanted was not merely a chance to work for some man but a chance to rise to positions of authority so they could again be effective in determining the conditions under which they lived. What these women hoped for was a world in which men and women would work in competition with each other and the best individual win. The sex line was to be dropped and the world become the composite work of individuals of both sexes.

But it did not work out that way. The best man continued to win, and women, even the best, worked for and under him. Women were welcome to come in as workers but not as co-makers of the world. For all their numbers they seldom rose to positions of responsibility or power. The few who did fitted into the system as they found it. All standards, all methods, all values continued to be set by men, even those as regards food and clothes, once distinctly women's business.

It is plainly seen that women as individuals, forgetting their sex, have made little impress on this world. As individuals they have won little power. It continues to all effects and purposes a man's world. One can point to no great accomplishment and say: "That was a woman's work." Some one may retort: "But the same thing was true of the old partnership. You could not then point to any one great accomplishment of a woman." Perhaps not. But you could point to a part of the world's work and say: "That is women's accomplishment. That is what they contribute as women to the world. They are responsible for this and that institution."

They made their contribution as women. In that way women had a part in making the world. In today's world they have none. There is nothing that is done, except bearing children, that men cannot do and do not manage. There is no institution that bears the imprint of women. Is this, then, the end of the feminists' effort to find a place in this man's world? Not if I know women. When women cannot get what they want in one way they go after it in another. The habits of the mole are strong in them. However blind they may be, they are indefatigable and their patience is unlimited. But what other way, it may be asked, is there? Before we try to find the answer to that, let us remind ourselves of something that many of us seem to have forgotten in our struggle to compete with men.

Equality does not necessarily mean identity with men. It does not mean that women need do the same things as men in the same way as men. It means that what women do shall have the same quality, worth, power, effect, as what men do. Two men enter into an equal partnership. Each brings something to the business—one may contribute an idea, the other capital. The work is divided between them. In such a partnership equality is obtained by means of coöperation instead of through competition —by division of work instead of by identity of occupation.

Does this not offer a suggestion to women as to the way they may yet achieve a place in this man's world? Might it not be possible for women to take over some part of the world's business as their own and thus substitute coöperation between the sexes for competition? Practically the control by women of only one industry necessary to the world would force the man's world to reckon with them and thus bring about this coöperation. They should, obviously, choose industries in which the work from top to bottom could be done by women so that women would not have to compete in them with men but with each other and thus have an equal chance to rise in them.

But what kind of industries, it may be asked, could women thus take over? The business of providing food in cafeterias, tea rooms and restaurants is already to some extent in the hands of women. The wonder is that it is not more so, considering the long centuries that women have dealt with food. It is one of the few businesses in which women as individuals have become leaders, taking their places as economically equal to the men engaged in the same business. . . .

It should be possible for these and other women gradually to gain control of the food-serving industry of the country. If they did, they might in time run not only the restaurants but the hotels of the country. The hotel business is one for which women should have a special aptitude. They are entering it in great numbers, as clerks, housekeepers, stewards. Whether many of them rise to managership remains to be seen. But if this new movement assumed any proportions, it would not be too much to hope that women would invest in hotels and with the strangle-hold of capital insist that women have authoritative policy-making positions. . . .

. . . There are many things that women want and women make. Why should not an ambitious woman, instead of going into a department store where the chances are she will never rise to a vice-presidency, be she ever so able, look about her, see something that is needed in the home, or anywhere else for that matter, set women to making it and organize the business of selling it? I would not, however, limit the industries that should be controlled by women to those dealing with household needs or with women's traditional tasks. But they might serve for a beginning.

Such a division of labor would have to come about gradually, nor is it unthinkable that it should. Women have their share of ambition. They wish to rise. Naturally the wise ones will go into those businesses in which other women have seemed able to attain success. Still others will flock after them, and as the women enter these businesses or industries in increasing numbers, men will leave them to take the places left vacant in the businesses these women have left.

Of course, there will be objections raised to my contentions. Women who have succeeded as individuals, those who have been acclaimed in the public print as "the first this" and "the first that," will insist that there is opportunity here and now for women with ability to achieve equality. Those to whom the sweets of economic independence are far more important than participation in managership will hold tight to their jobs of working for some man instead of striving towards a policy-making position. And feminists of the old school will insist that to abandon identity with men is to sacrifice equality. They will see in such a movement a retreat to women's old position, for to them the only equality is that which gives them an equal chance to work at a job, hoping that some day, somewhere, their labors will bring equal rewards.

But the young women just out of college talk differently. They are not fooled by the appearance of equality. They look at what this man's world offers them and they are not satisfied. If they start out to enter it as individuals, they find they must start much further down the line than their brothers. They observe that most of the plums still go to men. They are, in short, realizing that suffrage and woman's opportunity to work at a job as an individual have not changed the fact that this is still a man's world and there is little opportunity for them to be effective in it.

This realization comes to them with a shock, for they have been taught that women had an equal part in it. And what they see does not spell for them equality. They are thus ripe for rebellion. Never having had experience with the period when woman was denied a chance to work as an individual in competition with men, the younger woman sees the inferiority of the positions open to her rather than the right to get into them. For what one has, one always values less than what one has not. Naturally she does not know what she owes those early feminists. She takes as a matter of course what they had to fight for. She does not realize that if they had not insisted on the rights of women to enter the man's world as individuals she would not now feel equal to a man. She does not realize that their fight cleared the ground of many prejudices against women entering business, removed many of her disabilities. So she enters the business world aware only that the "cards are stacked" against her and she is ready to call for a new deal.

But the next decade will see these younger women reaching for real equality. It will see women taking new means to obtain it. What they will be no one can foretell. They may seek the new division of work between men and women that I have outlined, or they may seek it by other means. But seek it they will. One has only to hear them talking to know that. When water is set upon a stove and a fire is built under it, sooner or later it will boil. It does not take a prophet's mind to know that. The next decade will set this question boiling.

Edith M. Stern, Women Are Household Slaves (1949)

Edith M. Stern (1901———), a New York City–born Barnard graduate, is a writer living in Washington, D. C. In this angry and witty attack on housewifery, Mrs. Stern makes it clear why a housewife with small children is likely to wither in mind and soul, but she makes no attempt to explain why most women choose this career willingly. ["Women Are Household Slaves," *American Mercury*, LXVIII (January 1949), 71–76.]

HELP WANTED: DOMESTIC: FEMALE. All cooking, cleaning, laundering, sewing, meal planning, shopping, weekday chauffering, social secretarial service, and complete care of three children. Salary at employer's option. Time off if possible.

No one in her right senses would apply for such a job. No one in his right senses, even a desperate widower, would place such an advertisement. Yet it correctly describes the average wife and mother's situation, in which most women remain for love, but many because they have no way out.

A nauseating amount of bilge is constantly being spilled all over the public press about the easy, pampered existence of the American woman. Actually, the run of the mill, not gainfully employed female who is blessed with a husband and from two to four children leads a kind of life that theoretically became passé with the Emancipation Proclamation. Its confinement makes her baby's play pen seem like the great open spaces. Its hours—at least fourteen a day, seven days a week—make the well known sunup to sundown toil of sharecroppers appear, in comparison, like a union standard. Beside the repetitious, heterogeneous mass of chores endlessly bedeviling the housewife, an executive's memorandum of unfinished business is a virgin sheet.

Housewifery is a complex of housekeeping, household management, housework and childcare. Some of its elements, such as budgeting, dietetics, and above all, the proper upbringing of children, involve the higher brain centers; indeed, home economics has quite as respectable an academic status as engineering, and its own laboratories, dissertations and hierarchy of degrees. Other of its facets, and those the most persistent and time-consuming, can be capably handled by an eight-year-old child. The rôle of the housewife is, therefore, analogous to that of the president of a corporation who would not only determine policies and make over-all plans but also spend the major part of his time and energy in such activities as sweeping the plant and oiling machines.

Industry, of course, is too thrifty of the capacities of its personnel to waste them in such fashion. Likewise, organized labor and government afford workers certain standardized legal or customary protections. But in terms of enlightened labor practice, the housewife stands out blackly as the Forgotten Worker.

II

She is covered by no minimum wage law; indeed, she gets no wages at all. Like the bondservant of another day, or the slave, she receives maintenance; but anything beyond that, whether in the form of a regular "allowance" or sporadic largesse, is ruggedly individualistic. Indeed, paradoxically, the more service she renders, the more hard labor she performs, the less munificent are her rewards! Which is the more likely to get a new fur coat: the housewife who does her own washing, lugs her groceries from the chain

store and makes all the children's clothes, or she who patronizes
a commercial laundry, markets by telephone and shops at Modes
for Moppets?

No state or county health and sanitation inspectors invade the
privacy of the home, as they do that of the factory; hence kitchens
and domestic dwellings may be ill-ventilated, unsanitary and
hazardous without penalty. That many more accidents occur in
homes than in industry is no coincidence. Furthermore, when a
disability is incurred, such as a bone broken in a fall off a ladder
or legs scalded by the overturning of a kettle of boiling water, no
beneficent legislation provides for the housewife's compensation.

Rest periods are irregular, about ten to fifteen minutes each, a
few times during the long day; night work is frequent and unpre-
dictably occasioned by a wide variety of factors such as the mending basket, the gang gathering for a party, a sick child, or even
more pressing, a sick husband. The right to a vacation, thoroughly
accepted in business and industry, is non-existent in the domestic
sphere. When families go to beach bungalows or shacks in the
woods Mom continues on almost the same old treadmill; there are
still little garments to be buttoned and unbuttoned, three meals
a day to prepare, beds to be made and dishes to be washed. Even
on jolly whole-family motor trips with the blessings of life in
tourist camps or hotels, she still has the job considered full time
by paid nurses and governesses.

Though progressive employers make some sort of provision for
advancement, the housewife's opportunities for advancement are
nil; the nature and scope of her job, the routines of keeping a
family fed, clothed and housed remain always the same. If the
male upon whom her scale of living depends prospers, about all to
which she can look forward is a larger house—and more work.
Once, under such circumstances, there would have been less,
thanks to servants. Currently, however, the jewel of a general
houseworker is virtually extinct and even the specialists who
smooth life for the wealthy are rarities.

Industry has a kind of tenderness toward its women workers that is totally lacking towards women workers in the home.
Let a plant employee be known to be pregnant, and management

and foremen, who want to experience no guilt feelings toward unborn innocents, hasten to prevent her doing any kind of work that might be a strain upon her. In the home, however, now as for centuries, a "normal" amount of housework is considered "healthy"—not to mention, since no man wants to do it, unavoidable. There may be a few proscriptions against undue stretching and heavy lifting, but otherwise, pregnant or not, the housewife carries on, turning mattresses, lugging the vacuum cleaner up and down stairs, carrying winter overcoats to the attic in summer and down from it in the fall, scrubbing kitchen and bathroom floors, washing woodwork if that is indicated by the season, and on her feet most of the time performing other such little chores beside which sitting at an assembly line or punching a typewriter are positively restful.

Despite all this, a good many arguments about the joys of housewifery have been advanced, largely by those who have never had to work at it. One much stressed point is that satisfaction every good woman feels in creating a home for her dear ones. Well, probably every good woman does feel it, perhaps because she has had it so drummed into her that if she does not, she is not a good woman; but that satisfaction has very little to do with housewifery and housework. It is derived from intangibles, such as the desirable wife-husband and mother-child relationships she manages to effect, the permeating general home atmosphere of joviality or hospitality or serenity or culture to which she is the key, or the warmth and security she gives to the home by way of her personality, not her broom, stove or dishpan. For a woman to get a rewarding sense of total creation by way of the multiple, monotonous chores that are her daily lot would be as irrational as for an assembly line worker to rejoice that he had created an automobile because he tightens a bolt. It is difficult to see how clearing up after meals three times a day and making out marketing lists (three lemons, two packages of soap powder, a can of soup), getting at the fuzz in the radiators with the hard rubber appliance of the vacuum cleaner, emptying wastebaskets and washing bathroom floors day after day, week after week, year after year, add up to a sum total of anything except minutiae that laid end to end reach nowhere.

III

According to another line of reasoning, the housewife has the advantage of being "her own boss" and unlike the gainfully employed worker can arrange her own schedules. This is pure balderdash, despite the fact that she may suit herself about such minor matters as whether she is going to make the beds in the morning or let them go until the afternoon, elect Thursday rather than Friday for closet cleaning. If there is anything more inexorable than children's needs, from an infant's yowls of hunger and Junior's shrieks that he has just fallen down the stairs to the subtler need of an adolescent for a good listener during one of his or her frequent emotional crises, it is only the pressure of Dad's demand for supper as soon as he gets home. "The show must go on" is not nearly so urgent as "the home must go on"; there is no understudy, and many a housewife drags through her performances in a state of semi-invalidism that would send any gainfully employed man or woman to bed on sick leave. What is more, not her own preferences as to hours, but those set by her husband's office or plant, by the schools, by pediatricians and dentists, and the children's homework establish when the housewife rises, when she goes forth, and when she cannot get to bed.

Something else makes a mockery of self-determined routines; interruptions from the outside world. Unprotected by butler or doorman, the housewife is at the mercy of peddlers, plain or fancy Fuller brush; odd-job seekers; gas and electric company men who come to read meters; the Salvation Army in quest of newspapers; school children hawking seeds or tickets or chances; and repair men suggesting that the roof is in a hazardous condition or household machinery needs overhauling. Unblessed with a secretary, she answers telephone calls from insurance and real estate agents who "didn't want to bother your husband at his office"; vendors of cemetery plots and portrait photographs. The doorbell invariably rings when she is two flights up cleaning the attic, or staunching a flow of blood from little Mabel's knee; the telephone, when she is snatching a hasty bath between changing the baby's diaper and putting on the pot roast. All such invasions have a common denominator: the assumption that the housewife's time, like that of all slave labor, has no value.

In addition to what housewifery has in common with slavery, there are factors making it even less enviable as a way of life. The jolly gatherings of darkies with their banjos in the Good Old Days Befoh de Wah may be as mythical as the joys of housewifery, but at any rate we can be sure that slaves were not deprived of social intercourse throughout their hours of toil; field hands worked in gangs, house servants in teams. The housewife, however, carries through each complex operation of cooking, cleaning, tidying and laundering solo; almost uniquely among workers since the Industrial Revolution, she does not benefit by division of labor. Lunch time, ordinarily a pleasant break in the working day, for her brings no pleasant sociability with the girls in the cafeteria, the hired men in the shade of the haystack, or even the rest of the household staff in the servants' dining room. From the time her husband departs for work until he returns, except for an occasional chat across the back fence or a trek to market with some other woman as childbound, housebound, and limited in horizons as herself, she lacks adult company; and even to the most passionately maternal, unbroken hours of childish prattle are no substitute for the conversation of one's peers, whether that be on a high philosophical plane or on the lower level of neighborhood gossip. The Woman's Club, happy hunting ground of matrons in their forties, is perhaps a reaction against this enforced solitude during earlier married life.

Something else enjoyed by slaves, but not by housewives, was work in some measure appropriate to their qualifications. The more intelligent were selected as house servants; the huskier as field hands. Such crude vocational placement has been highly refined in industry, with its battery of intelligence and aptitude tests, personnel directors and employment counselors. Nothing of the kind is even attempted for unpaid domestic workers. When a man marries and has children, it is assumed that he will do the best work along lines in which he has been trained or is at least interested. When a woman marries and has children, it is assumed that she will take to housewifery. But whether she takes to it or not, she does it.

IV

Such regimentation, for professional or potentially professional women, is costly both for the individual and society. For the individual, it brings about conflicts and frustrations. The practice of housewifery gives the lie to the theory of almost every objective of higher education. The educated individual should have a community, a national, a world viewpoint; but that is pretty difficult to get and hold when you are continually involved with cleaning toilets, ironing shirts, peeling potatoes, darning socks and minding children. The educated should read widely; but reading requires time and concentration and besides, the conscientious housewife has her own five-foot shelf of recipes and books on child psychology to occupy her. Most frustrating of all, education leads one to believe that a project attempted should be systematically carried through to completion. In housewifery there is inevitable hopping from one unrelated, unfinished task to another; start the dinner—get at the mending—collect the baby—take down the laundry—finish the dinner is about the maximum height of efficiency. This innate incoherence of housewifery is like a mental patient's flight of ideas; nothing leads quite logically from one thing to another; and the woman schooled like her husband to think generally and in sequence, has a bad time of it intellectually and emotionally as a result.

Perhaps even more deplorable is the loss to society when graduate nurses, trained teachers, lawyers, physicians, artists and other gifted women are unable to utilize their prolonged and expensive educations for the common good. Buried in the homemade cakes the family loves, lost among the stitches of patches, sunk in the suds of the week's wash, are incalculable skilled services.

But just as slaves were in the service of individual masters, not of the community or state or nation in general, so are housewives bound to the service of individual families. That it devolves upon a mother to tend her children during helpless infancy and childhood—or at any rate, to see that they are tended by someone—

is undeniable. But only a psychology of slavery can put women at the service of grown men. Ironically, the very gentlemen scrupulous about opening a door for a lady, carrying her packages, or helping her up onto a curb, take it for granted that at mealtime, all their lives long, ladies should carry their food to them and never sit through a meal while they never get up. A wife, when she picks up the soiled clothing her husband has strewn on the floor, lugs his garments to the tailor, makes his twin bed, or sews on his buttons, acts as an unpaid body-servant. If love is the justification for this rôle, so was love a justification for antebellum Mammies. Free individuals, in a democracy, perform personal services for themselves or, if they have the cash, pay other free individuals to wait on them. It is neither freedom nor democracy when such service is based on color or sex.

As long as the institution of housewifery in its present form persists, both ideologically and practically it blocks any true liberation of women. The vote, the opportunity for economic independence, and the right to smoke cigarettes are all equally superficial veneers over a deep-rooted, ages-old concept of keeping woman in her place. Unfortunately, however, housewives not only are unorganized, but also, doubtless because of the very nature of their brain-dribbling, spirit-stifling vocation, conservative. There is therefore little prospect of a Housewives' Rebellion. There is even less, in the light of men's comfortable setup under the present system, of a male-inspired movement for Abolition!

Mary I. Bunting, The Radcliffe Institute for Independent Study
(1961)

In the past decade educators have confronted the problem of finding a way to enable married women to pursue careers that satisfy their desire for creative activity outside the home and that enable society at large to benefit from a hitherto largely untapped intellectual resource. All the schemes proposed accept the traditional division of labor within the family and are in that sense conserva-

tive; the best known is the Radcliffe plan here outlined by Mary
I. Bunting. Mrs. Bunting, a biologist, was born in Brooklyn, New
York, in 1910, is a Phi Beta Kappa graduate of Vassar, and received her M.A. and Ph.D. from Wisconsin. After serving as dean
at Douglass College, she became president of Radcliffe in 1960.
["The Radcliffe Institute for Independent Study," *The Educational Record*, XLII (October 1961), 279–86.]

Events, circumstances, individuals, and a problem may sometimes combine spontaneously in a natural confluence that leads to
profound changes. Radcliffe College believes that such a confluence is in the making in the education of women in the United
States and that, imaginatively channeled, it can be made to produce powerfully beneficial results.

THE PREMISES

The explosion of knowledge now reverberating in every field
of human activity carries implications for the modern world that
become vividly apparent as one examines the dilemma facing educated women. Each person, and particularly the intellectually
able, must make a systematic effort to keep in touch with ever-
changing developments in his own field of interest or be left hopelessly behind. No longer can any man or woman expect to be
living and working twenty years from now as he or she is living
and working today. A comprehension of the inevitability of this
sort of change poses problems that, while not unique, are certainly
acute for educated women. Obviously, women who plan their lives
to include major responsibilities in the home during their early
adult years face special handicaps in keeping pace for which they
as individuals and society as a whole must make allowance. The
astonishing rate at which new knowledge is created and applied,
together with increasing longevity, makes it imperative then that
we plan higher education not as a preparation for, but as a continuing part of, adult life.

For almost a century women in America have been free to explore the myriad separate and interacting worlds that form the
realms of higher education. By and large, however, and with some

notable exceptions, there has been no clear, consistent, directed purpose in their educational patterns; only seldom is a brilliant record in student years sustained in serious intellectual productivity throughout a woman's life. This remains true, despite the fact that education at all levels has been extended to women so that no fields remain closed to them and there are virtually none in which some women have not excelled.

The simpler society which first offered formal collegiate education to women debated and decided the simpler questions: First, should a woman be well educated; second, where; and third, how. Yes, in any institution of higher learning, and following traditional curricula and methods for any profession that would accept her. Our more complex and more sophisticated society has only recently begun to realize that the most important questions have rarely been asked and never fully answered. Why should women be well educated? And perhaps even more basic: Where should that education lead beyond the vague assumption that an educated mother will be better able to cultivate intellectual values in her children?

Although once the woman who desired and obtained a college education was regarded with suspicion and even occasionally with distaste, this has not been the case for a very long time. No one now begrudges a woman either college or advanced degrees merely because she is a woman. Quite the contrary, as a glance at the college application figures for women demonstrates all too dramatically. But acceptance of the educated woman as a creatively functioning figure in our culture and in the economy of our society was extended reluctantly and slowly and is still limited. To some degree this attitude derived from the use the first women college graduates made of their advanced educations. Too often and understandably they became crusaders and reformers, passionate, fearless, articulate, but also, at times, loud. A stereotype of the educated woman grew up in the popular mind and, concurrently, a prejudice against both the stereotype and the education.

Today, several generations later, the bitter battles for women's rights are history. The cause has been won. The stereotype has disappeared and, with it, the hard prejudice. But not altogether. For there is still prevalent a form of anti-intellectualism which insists that whatever her aspirations, a woman must eventually choose between career and marriage, and that if she attempts to combine the two, both will suffer and the marriage probably the more keenly. Hence, the argument runs, society suffers.

Here, at least, there is some logic in the evolution of the attitude. A woman, educated or not, when she marries is dominated by her biological role of child-bearing and child rearing and by her psychological role in relation to her husband. She also has the traditional responsibility of homemaking but here, in an underlying contradiction that gives rise to additional complications, the modern woman frequently finds herself technologically only half-employed by an abundance of machines and gadgets. The domestic economy plays its part as well. The husband as the primary source of income must put the requirements of his own career before those of his wife. And even the most intellectually ambitious woman cannot quarrel with this if the preservation of her marriage is important to her.

A tacit recognition of these facts has led to a luxurious ambiguity in the present-day education of women: It has been assumed that while women are as educable as men, their intellectual development and performance need not continue beyond their middle twenties or whenever marriage claims them. Domestic responsibilities and preoccupations will draw them off, insulating and isolating them, and the loss to themselves and to society, the waste of trained brain power they represent must be accepted philosophically or, better perhaps, ignored.

Nor is this simply an outgrowth of male pride or prejudice. It is a belief commonly held, one in which the majority of women concur, some complacently, and some because they see no alternative. But it is also a belief that is wholly out of date in today's world of immeasurable intellectual, economic, and political demands and opportunities, and one that is essentially undemocratic. It is a negation of the promise that each individual shall have the opportunity to develop and use his or her potential abilities to the fullest. This belief denotes a pose of luxury we can no longer afford.

Furthermore, the effect of this waste on the intellectually gifted woman herself and on her family can be severely handicapping. Many years of her life may have been spent in the disciplined work and persistent effort that bring her to an insight and a proficiency in some field of knowledge. Then, when she marries and has children, she finds herself, as a rule, separated from her field and within a few years out of touch with everything new that has arisen in the interim. Thus, even if she chooses to return to her profession at some later date, she finds herself outdistanced and a drag, where once she would have been a significant asset. The opportunities once available to her no longer exist. An understanding of her isolation can be particularly disastrous for the woman with professional training or comparable attainments, and she restlessly seeks some substitute outlet for the mental energy that propelled her into advanced study originally. But there are usually few satisfactory substitutes for such women.

The same sense of stagnation strikes the woman with a bachelor's degree and no specialized training. In her case the lack of orientation may be still more poignant, as she is beset with ambitions without even theoretical goals. And this sense of stagnation can become a malignant factor in even the best of marriages when the gifted woman must spend her time inventing ways to employ herself mentally, and failing, or only half succeeding, may turn against the marriage itself in sheer frustration.

The implications inherent in our society's failure to value and use trained feminine talent are quickly communicated to the next generation. The mother whose education has led merely to personal frustration tends unwittingly to stifle the curiosity and ambition of the son as well as the daughter. It is, indeed, in the home that cultural values are transmitted. If, furthermore, the mother's sense of fulfillment centers simply around the provision for her children's creature comforts and does not also embrace dedication to broad human concerns and adventures, their vision and self-discipline will surely be limited. The drama of example is usually much more effective in instilling intellectual interests in the young than is the repetition of precept.

For once we seem to be faced with a major problem for which important remedial measures are both apparent and possible. The pattern of women's lives is different from men's during their early adult years. If they are to continue their education or to use it during this period, we must provide appropriately designed part-time opportunities. Hitherto we have been far more concerned, it would seem, with the package than with the product. That we have not made any respectable attempt to meet the special educational needs of women in the past is the clearest possible evidence of the fact that our educational objectives have been geared exclusively to the vocational patterns of men.

In changing that emphasis, however, our goal should not be to equip and encourage women to compete with men. The advancement of knowledge, the achievement of progress is not fundamentally a race between individuals or nations but a total of human enterprise. Women, because they are not generally the principal breadwinners, can perhaps be most useful as the trail breakers, working along the bypaths, doing the unusual job that men cannot afford to gamble on. There is always room on the fringes even when competition in the intellectual market places is keen. The unexplored is boundless.

To work in this way, a woman's motivation must spring from genuine curiosities and concerns. Unfortunately, since our society has not expected women to use their talents and training importantly in scholarship, medicine, research, politics, religion, or a host of other fields, it is not surprising that their motivation as a rule has been to win approval or, in some cases, to compete. In neither case is the woman led to discover the particular niche, to focus on the unrecognized possibility, to cultivate the unusual interest that could result in her greatest personal satisfaction and most valuable contribution.

As one studies the situation of the intellectual woman in modern society, the nature, scope, and significance of the problem are abundantly evident and the necessity for innovation leading to resolution clearly urgent. Radcliffe College, which from its founding has been concerned with the long view in the education of women, recognizes that the established routes must be widened. Radcliffe has for many years offered formal graduate training to women and supplemented this with an extensive schedule of advanced seminars in a great variety of subjects. These programs alone, however, are not adequate to overcome the present difficulty that comes with functional isolation from the growing edge of knowledge.

New measures are needed to help fulfill new expectations. Radcliffe believes that the time has come to embark on a wholly new exploratory venture beyond orthodox higher education. It sees this venture in relation to a basic question many thoughtful people have been pondering for years: Given the vast amount of leisure constantly being accumulated in an ever more efficient industrial society, how can that leisure best be used? The changing pace and shifting patterns of contemporary life bring to every educational institution the challenge to find ways of helping each individual lead a more creative life. In establishing its experimental program, the Institute for Independent Study, Radcliffe hopes to provide some small measure of response to that challenge for women. But the principles underlying its founding are equally applicable to men. It is the philosophy that no individual's talents should go unrealized for lack of opportunity to develop them and if the opportunities do not now exist, it is the business of educational institutions to bring them into being.

DESCRIPTION OF THE PROGRAM

Radcliffe College has established the Radcliffe Institute for Independent Study as an earnest of its belief that the educated woman has a potential of achievement that she should be allowed and enabled to fulfill. It hopes that in this exploration of more effective ways and means to help women put their talents and training to more productive and personally satisfying use, we shall recover a vital, but long-neglected, national resource and point the way to greater realization of our historic humanistic ideals. . . .

THE ASSOCIATE SCHOLARS. The associate scholar program has been designed for gifted women who wish to carry on independent scholarly or creative projects on a part-time basis. They will be appointed annually and need not, of course, be Radcliffe alumnae. The associate scholars generally will be women who hold an advanced degree or its equivalent in achievement and status, but the selection of scholars is not dependent on rigid academic requirements. They may be concerned with any reach of scholarship or creative art. Their particular fields of interest are not important; what is essential is that they be able to show evidence of past accomplishment and the promise of purposeful activity in a specific plan of work which they will be required to detail as a condition of their selection for the institute. It is recognized that the needs and qualifications of creative artists are distinctive and that they require special consideration.

The typical associate scholar may be a woman in her middle thirties who, as a graduate student, made an arresting, critical study of a little-known historical figure but who, in the intervening years, has been unable to pursue her subject to the point where she could make a significant contribution to knowledge. Her appointment as an associate scholar will give her the impetus, the freedom, and the means to do just this. Or, she may be a painter whose life has become so full she can produce only occasional paintings; or a writer with two published novels who has been unable to summon the sustained concentration to write a third; or a composer; or a sculptor. Her medium is irrelevant; what matters is her intent and ability. The institute's concern will be to enable her to free her time and her mind in order to develop and realize her talent. These, of course, are simply hypothetical examples. Women from every discipline and intellectual vocation will be eligible for institute consideration.

The institute offers to the associate scholar time that is free of personal pressures and obligations; a place to work; the facilities of a great university, from libraries to laboratories, from museums to computers; and the companionship and guidance of authorities in a hundred fields. It will provide the financial means for the qualified woman to take advantage of this opportunity on a part-time basis without abandoning her domestic responsibilities. It offers her a way to continue or to renew her commitment to her area of specialized knowledge and to make the contribution for which she has prepared. Hopefully, once she has been made visible professionally through her work at the institute, she will be claimed for further activity—in an academic institution, in government, in business, in industry, in the arts.

The program for associate scholars is directed primarily to the talented woman who, after marriage, finds it difficult, if not impossible, to continue to be intellectually creative without assistance. . . .

RESIDENT AND RESEARCH FELLOWS. Each year a small number of women who are already notable as scholars or creative artists or professional women who have been able to maintain continuous careers will be invited to come from all over the world to spend a year or more as resident fellows of the institute. They will be extended all the facilities available to associate scholars and given time to reflect, to initiate or consolidate research, to outline and execute new books—in short, to work for the future on projects for which their usual commitments may never leave time. Ordinarily, they will be granted stipends commensurate with their professional positions. . . .

THE INSTITUTE AND RADCLIFFE STUDENTS

While the associate scholars are continuing and renewing their own intellectual lives, they will, we hope, be acting as a positive and powerful force in the lives of the undergraduate and graduate students of Radcliffe. In addition to the enrichment that their scholarship will bring, it is thought that by their influence and example they may do much to strengthen the motive and clarify the direction of many an undergraduate's approach to her education. Those scholars who are married women with family responsibilities will demonstrate that waste and dispersal are not the inevitable end for the years of discipline that lead to a degree, from A.B. to Ph.D. Simply by their presence at the institute, they should serve to illustrate the unique personal satisfaction to be derived from the focused use of one's mind.

Further, the hope is that in the course of time there might emerge in the undergraduate a new psychology through which she would not necessarily look upon her married life as an automatic termination of her obligation to use her education extensively and meaningfully. Rather, as she senses the new expectations the world holds for her, she could come to think of the early years of marriage as offering new freedom and an unparalleled opportunity to experiment intellectually, to extend and deepen her understanding, and to explore as well as prepare for the interesting possibilities and choices available to her in the future.

All too frequently the undergraduate fails to take the long view of herself, her education, and, indeed, her life. To many a girl of eighteen or twenty, the age of forty is an impossible projection. And while most undergraduate men can see their years of preparation in relation to the stimulating and satisfying activities that will occupy their adult lives, many a woman undergraduate seeks only to reconcile herself to an acceptance of the unexpected. She lives from year to year, if not from day to day. But through her associations with the scholars of the institute, the undergraduate may be encouraged to look beyond her student years and to shape coherent plans toward exciting objectives for her future as a mature and intellectually responsible woman.

At a more modest level, it is believed that embedding an active center of research within Radcliffe, with the possibility of student participation in certain forms of the research and related seminars, will add additional dimensions to the depth and range of a Radcliffe education. Such contacts would help to give Radcliffe undergraduate and graduate students as well as the scholars themselves a measure of the challenge and interdisciplinary enrichment that are now provided for Harvard men through close and continuous association with the tutors in their houses.

THE RESPONSE

The response to the establishment of the Radcliffe institute has been dramatic—indeed almost overwhelming—and has given striking proof that the assumptions underlying its creation were soundly based in fact and not simply the product of wistful, wishful thinking. With no planned publicity beyond the formal announcement to the press, word of the institute spread with astonishing speed and thoroughness. A deluge of inquiries and informal applications has ensued from all parts of the United States and from various foreign countries. . . .

The range and variety of the applicants' fields of interest is an illuminating comment on women's potential for creativity and scholarship, for there is scarcely a discipline that is not represented. And within the disciplines, specialization extends over a wide arc from ancient numismatics to endocrine physiology, from Renaissance comedy to urban renewal. However different their interests, these women share one distinctive quality: an intense determination to make ever more effective use of their gifts and education. It is to help them succeed in this determination that the Radcliffe institute has been founded. . . .

National Organization for Women, Statement of Purpose (1966)

The following statement was adopted by an organizing conference of thirty-two men and women from twelve states and Washington, D.C. By July 1967 the National Organization for Women (NOW) had over a thousand members throughout the country. Its president is Betty Friedan, author of *The Feminine Mystique*.

STATEMENT OF PURPOSE

We, men and women who hereby constitute ourselves as the National Organization for Women, believe that the time has come for a new movement toward true equality for all women in America, and toward a fully equal partnership of the sexes, as part of the world-wide revolution of human rights now taking place within and beyond our national borders.

The purpose of NOW is to take action to bring women into full participation in the mainstream of American society now, exercising all the privileges and responsibilities thereof in truly equal partnership with men.

We believe the time has come to move beyond the abstract argument, discussion and symposia over the status and special nature of women which has raged in America in recent years; the time has come to confront, with concrete action, the conditions that now prevent women from enjoying the equality of opportunity and freedom of choice which is their right, as individual Americans, and as human beings.

NOW is dedicated to the proposition that women, first and foremost, are human beings, who, like all other people in our society, must have the chance to develop their fullest human potential. We believe that women can achieve such equality only by accepting to the full the challenges and responsibilities they share with all other people in our society, as part of the decision-making mainstream of American political, economic and social life.

We organize to initiate or support action, nationally, or in any part of this nation, by individuals or organizations, to break through the silken curtain of prejudice and discrimination against women in government, industry, the professions, the churches, the political parties, the judiciary, the labor unions, in education, science, medicine, law, religion and every other field of importance in American society.

Enormous changes taking place in our society make it both possible and urgently necessary to advance the unfinished revolution of women toward true equality, now. With a life span lengthened to nearly 75 years it is no longer either necessary or possible for women to devote the greater part of their lives to child-rearing; yet childbearing and rearing which continues to be a most important part of most women's lives—still is used to justify barring women from equal professional and economic participation and advance.

Today's technology has reduced most of the productive chores which women once performed in the home and in mass-production industries based upon routine unskilled labor. This same technology has virtually eliminated the quality of muscular strength as a criterion for filling most jobs, while intensifying American industry's need for creative intelligence. In view of this new industrial revolution created by automation in the mid-twentieth century, women can and must participate in old and new fields of society in full equality—or become permanent outsiders.

Despite all the talk about the status of American women in recent years, the actual position of women in the United States has declined, and is declining, to an alarming degree throughout the 1950's and '60's. Although 46.4% of all American women between the ages of 18 and 65 now work outside the home, the overwhelming majority—75%—are in routine clerical, sales or factory jobs, or they are household workers, cleaning women, hospital attendants. About two-thirds of Negro women workers are in the lowest paid service occupations. Working women are becoming increasingly—not less—concentrated on the bottom of the job ladder. As a consequence full-time women workers today earn on the average only 60% of what men earn, and that wage gap has been increasing over the past twenty-five years in every major industry group. In 1964, of all women with a yearly income, 89% earned under $5,000 a year; half of all full-time year round women workers earned less than $3,690; only 1.4% of full-time year round women workers had an annual income of $10,000 or more.

Further, with higher education increasingly essential in today's society, too few women are entering and finishing college or going on to graduate or professional school. Today, women earn only one in three of the B.A.'s and M.A.'s granted, and one in ten of the Ph.D.'s.

In all the professions considered of importance to society, and in the executive ranks of industry and government, women are losing ground. Where they are present it is only a token handful. Women comprise less than 1% of federal judges; less than 4% of all lawyers; 7% of doctors. Yet women represent 51% of the U.S. population. And, increasingly, men are replacing women in the top positions in secondary and elementary schools, in social work, and in libraries—once thought to be women's fields.

Official pronouncements of the advance in the status of women hide not only the reality of this dangerous decline, but the fact that nothing is being done to stop it. The excellent reports of the President's Commission on the Status of Women and of the State Commissions have not been fully implemented. Such Commissions have power only to advise. They have no power to enforce their recommendations; nor have they the freedom to organize

American women and men to press for action on them. The reports of these Commissions have, however, created a basis upon which it is now possible to build.

Discrimination in employment on the basis of sex is now prohibited by federal law, in Title VII of the Civil Rights Act of 1964. But although nearly one-third of the cases brought before the Equal Employment Opportunity Commission during the first year dealt with sex discrimination and the proportion is increasing dramatically, the Commission has not made clear its intention to enforce the law with the same seriousness on behalf of women as of other victims of discrimination. Many of these cases were Negro women, who are the victims of the double discrimination of race and sex. Until now, too few women's organizations and official spokesmen have been willing to speak out against these dangers facing women. Too many women have been restrained by the fear of being called "feminist."

There is no civil rights movement to speak for women, as there has been for Negroes and other victims of discrimination. The National Organization for Women must therefore begin to speak.

WE BELIEVE that the power of American law, and the protection guaranteed by the U.S. Constitution to the civil rights of all individuals, must be effectively applied and enforced to isolate and remove patterns of sex discrimination, to ensure equality of opportunity in employment and education, and equality of civil and political rights and responsibilities on behalf of women, as well as for Negroes and other deprived groups.

We realize that women's problems are linked to many broader questions of social justice; their solution will require concerted action by many groups. Therefore, convinced that human rights for all are indivisible, we expect to give active support to the common cause of equal rights for all those who suffer discrimination and deprivation, and we call upon other organizations committed to such goals to support our efforts toward equality for women.

WE DO NOT ACCEPT the token appointment of a few women to high-level positions in government and industry as a substitute for a serious continuing effort to recruit and advance women according to their individual abilities. To this end, we urge American government and industry to mobilize the same resources of ingenuity and command with which they have solved problems of far greater difficulty than those now impeding the progress of women.

WE BELIEVE that this nation has a capacity at least as great as other nations, to innovate new social institutions which will enable women to enjoy true equality of opportunity and responsibility in society, without conflict with their responsibilities as mothers and homemakers. In such innovations, America does not lead the Western world, but lags by decades behind many European countries. We do not accept the traditional assumption that a woman has to choose between marriage and motherhood, on the one hand, and serious participation in industry or the professions on the other. We question the present expectation that all normal women will retire from job or profession for 10 or 15 years, to devote their full time to raising children, only to reenter the job market at a relatively minor level. This, in itself, is a deterrent to the aspirations of women, to their acceptance into management or professional training courses, and to the very possibility of equality of opportunity or real choice, for all but a few women. Above all, we reject the assumption that these problems are the unique responsibility of each individual woman, rather than a basic social dilemma which society must solve. True equality of opportunity and freedom of choice for women requires such practical, and possible innovations as a nationwide network of child-care centers, which will make it unnecessary for women to retire completely from society until their children are grown, and national programs to provide retraining for women who have chosen to care for their own children full-time.

WE BELIEVE that it is as essential for every girl to be educated to her full potential of human ability as it is for every boy—with the knowledge that such education is the key to effective participation in today's economy and that, for a girl as for a boy, education can only be serious where there is expectation that it will be used in society. We believe that American educators are capable of devising means of imparting such expectations to girl students. Moreover, we consider the decline in the proportion of women receiving higher and professional education to be evidence of discrimination. This discrimination may take the form of quotas against the admission of women to colleges, and professional schools; lack of encouragement by parents, counsellors and educators; denial of loans or fellowships; or the traditional or arbitrary procedures in graduate and professional training geared in terms of men, which inadvertently discriminate against women. We believe that the same serious attention must be given to high school dropouts who are girls as to boys.

WE REJECT the current assumptions that a man must carry the sole burden of supporting himself, his wife, and family, and that a woman is automatically entitled to lifelong support by a man upon her marriage, or that marriage, home and family are primarily woman's world and responsibility—hers, to dominate—his to support. We believe that a true partnership between the sexes demands a different concept of marriage, an equitable sharing of the responsibilities of home and children and of the economic burdens of their support. We believe that proper recognition should be given to the economic and social value of homemaking and child-care. To these ends, we will seek to open a reexamination of laws and mores governing marriage and divorce, for we believe that the current state of "half-equality" between the sexes discriminates against both men and women, and is the cause of much unnecessary hostility between the sexes.

WE BELIEVE that women must now exercise their political rights and responsibilities as American citizens. They must refuse to be segregated on the basis of sex into separate-and-not-equal ladies' auxiliaries in the political parties, and they must demand representation according to their numbers in the regularly constituted party committees—at local, state, and national levels—and in the informal power structure, participating fully in the selection of candidates and political decision-making, and running for office themselves.

IN THE INTERESTS OF THE HUMAN DIGNITY OF WOMEN, we will protest, and endeavor to change, the false image of women now prevalent in the mass media, and in the texts, ceremonies, laws, and practices of our major social institutions. Such images perpetuate contempt for women by society and by women for them-selves. We are similarly opposed to all policies and practices—in church, state, college, factory, or office—which, in the guise of pro-tectiveness, not only deny opportunities but also foster in women self-denigration, dependence, and evasion of responsibility, under-mine their confidence in their own abilities and foster contempt for women.

NOW WILL HOLD ITSELF INDEPENDENT OF ANY POLITICAL PARTY in order to mobilize the political power of all women and men intent on our goals. We will strive to ensure that no party, candi-date, president, senator, governor, congressman, or any public offi-cial who betrays or ignores the principle of full equality between the sexes is elected or appointed to office. If it is necessary to mobilize the votes of men and women who believe in our cause, in order to win for women the final right to be fully free and equal human beings, we so commit ourselves.

WE BELIEVE THAT women will do most to create a new image of women by *acting* now, and by speaking out in behalf of their own equality, freedom, and human dignity—not in pleas for spe-cial privilege, nor in enmity toward men, who are also victims of the current, half-equality between the sexes—but in an active, self-respecting partnership with men. By so doing, women will develop confidence in their own ability to determine actively, in partnership with men, the conditions of their life, their choices, their future and their society.

Selected Bibliography

M. F. Ashley Montagu, *The Natural Superiority of Women*. New York, 1952.

Mary R. Beard, *Woman as Force in History*. New York, 1946.

Mary Benson, *Women in Eighteenth-Century America*. New York, 1935.

Harriot Stanton Blatch and Alma Lutz, *Challenging Years: The Memoirs of Harriot Stanton Blatch*. New York, 1940.

Arthur W. Calhoun, *A Social History of the American Family*. 3 vols., 1917–19. Reprinted in New York, 1960.

Otelia Cromwell, *Lucretia Mott*. Cambridge, Mass., 1958.

Carl N. Degler, "Charlotte Perkins Gilman on the Theory and Practice of Feminism," *American Quarterly*, VIII (Spring 1956), 21–39.

Sidney Ditzion, *Marriage, Morals, and Sex in America*. New York, 1953.

Mary Earhart, *Frances Willard: From Prayers to Politics*. Chicago, 1944.

Edith Finch, *Carey Thomas of Bryn Mawr*. New York, 1947.

Eleanor Flexner, *Century of Struggle: The Woman's Rights Movement in the United States*. Cambridge, Mass., 1959.

Betty Friedan, *The Feminine Mystique*. New York, 1963.

Josephine Goldmark, *Impatient Crusader: Florence Kelley's Life Story*. Urbana, Ill., 1953.

Elinor Rice Hays, *Morning Star: A Biography of Lucy Stone, 1818–1893*. New York, 1961.

Aileen S. Kraditor, *The Ideas of the Woman Suffrage Movement, 1890–1920*. New York, 1965.

Christopher Lasch, review of Andrew Sinclair, *The Better Half, Commentary*, XLI (April 1966), 100–6.

Gerda Lerner, *The Grimké Sisters from South Carolina: Rebels against Slavery*. Boston, 1967.

Max Lerner, *America as a Civilization*. (Chap. viii, "Life Cycle of the American," and chap. ix, "Character and Society.") New York, 1957.

Robert Jay Lifton, ed., *The Woman in America*. (Reprints of *Daedalus* articles.) Boston, 1967.

James W. Linn, *Jane Addams*. New York, 1935.

Alma Lutz, *Created Equal: Elizabeth Cady Stanton, 1815–1902*. New York, 1940.

———, *Susan B. Anthony: Rebel, Crusader, Humanitarian*. Boston, 1959.

James M. McPherson, "Abolitionists, Woman Suffrage, and the Negro, 1865–1869," *Mid-America*, XLVII (January 1965), 40–47.

Arthur Mann, *Yankee Reformers in the Urban Age: Social Reform in Boston, 1880–1900*, (Chap. ix, "The New and Newer Women as Reformers.") Cambridge, Mass., 1954.

Jacquelyn A. Mattfeld and Carol G. Van Aken, eds., *Women in the Scientific Professions: The M.I.T. Symposium on American Women in Science and Engineering*. Cambridge, Mass., 1965.

Edmund S. Morgan, *The Puritan Family*. (Chap. ii, "Husband and Wife.") New York, 1966.

Mary Gray Peck, *Carrie Chapman Catt*. New York, 1944.

Benjamin Quarles, "Frederick Douglass and the Woman's Rights Movement," *Journal of Negro History*, XXV (January 1940), 35–44.

Robert Riegel, *American Feminists*. Lawrence, Kans., 1963.

Anne Firor Scott, "The 'New Woman' in the New South," *South Atlantic Quarterly*, LXI (Autumn 1962), 473–83.

Andrew Sinclair, *The Emancipation of the American Woman*. (First published as *The Better Half*.) New York, 1965.

Robert W. Smuts, *Women and Work in America*. New York, 1959.

Bertha Monica Stearns, "Reform Periodicals and Female Reformers," *American Historical Review*, XXXVII (July 1932), 678–99.

Doris Stevens, *Jailed for Freedom*. New York, 1920.

Yuri Suhl, *Ernestine Rose and the Battle for Human Rights*. New York, 1959.

Eleanor Wolf Thompson, *Education for Ladies, 1830–1860: Ideas on Education in Magazines for Women*. New York, 1947.

Mason Wade, *Margaret Fuller*. New York, 1940.

Barbara Welter, "The Cult of True Womanhood, 1820–1860," *American Quarterly*, XVIII (Summer 1966, pt. 1), 151–74.

A Note on the Editor

Aileen S. Kraditor was born in Brooklyn, New York, and studied at Syracuse University, Brooklyn College, and Columbia University. Her major interests were art and philosophy before she turned to a study of American history, in which she received her Ph.D. from Columbia. Her dissertation won an Ansley Award and was published under the title *The Ideas of the Woman Suffrage Movement, 1890–1920*. She is also the author of *Means and Ends in American Abolitionism*, as well as articles and reviews in scholarly journals and magazines of opinion. Miss Kraditor has taught at Rhode Island College and now lives in Montreal, where she was Visiting Professor of History at Sir George Williams University in 1968–1969.